PRAISE FOR
WEB COPY THAT SELLS

"*Web Copy That Sells* is the only book on the market that can teach anyone how to write psychologically mesmerizing sales copy that gets readers salivating for your product or service. You simply won't know the value of this book until you read it and try out her incredible copywriting techniques for yourself. This book should be on every online marketer's desktop."

—Joel Christopher, Master List Builder, Publisher of *Access-2-Success* ezine

"*Web Copy That Sells* is a fabulous book! It takes a tremendous amount of sound marketing theory and shows you how to bring it to life into compelling, persuasive copy. It serves as a framework for thinking through what you want to get the customer to do, why he or she should do it, and how to explain it persuasively. Whether you are a beginner or a seasoned veteran, this book will get people to act on your words."

—George Silverman, Author of *The Secrets of Word-of-Mouth Marketing: How to Trigger Exponential Sales Through Runaway Word of Mouth*

"The Trifecta Neuro-Affective Principle that Maria Veloso teaches in this book is a compelling way to change prospects' minds in favor of your product or service, cause them to subconsciously 'feel right' about your offer, and cause them to look no further than your product or service to fulfill their needs. This formula alone is worth more than the book's weight in gold!"

—Elin Bullmann, www.TheWriteEffect.com, Bend, Oregon

"Maria, I'm very impressed with your book! You're the first one to really make a convincing argument and show concrete evidence why writing for the web (especially e-mail copy) is quite different from writing for the offline markets in several aspects. Thanks for your enlightening material."

—Kevin Wilke, founder of PureNetProfits.com and cofounder of NitroMarketing.com

"After spending thousands of dollars getting information from almost every Internet and marketing expert out there, I can say, without a doubt, *Web Copy That Sells* is the best investment that anyone wanting a profitable career on the Internet could make."

—Rick Miller, Certified Master of Web Copywriting, author of *Internet Mind Control*, and founder of ScientificInternetMarketing.com

"Without a doubt, Maria Veloso 'wrote the book' on how to turn a website into a selling machine. *Web Copy That Sells* is among the most important marketing books ever written. It should be required reading for all Internet marketers, webmasters, and copywriters. Maria has simplified the craft of writing direct-response web copy down to an easy, step-by-step blueprint that is so appealing even my wife has decided to become a copywriter!"

—Tim Russ, Editor, *Candle Light Magazine*

"Maria Veloso's Trifecta Neuro-Affective Principle is the most psychologically persuasive blueprint for writing copy I've ever come across, both online and offline."

—Diane Eble, Author of 11 books, professional book publishing coach/consultant, and copywriter, WordsToProfit.com

"*Web Copy That Sells* belongs on the desktop of any e-marketer who wants to make more sales and profits without spending a nickel more on advertising. Maria's web copy tips and techniques are like oxygen that'll breathe more life into your websites and e-mail campaigns. Chapter 5 alone is worth 100 times the price you'll pay for this copywriting book."

—Alex Mandossian, Web Traffic Conversion Strategist and CEO of Heritage House Publishing, Inc.

"When it comes to writing the words on your website that make people pull out their credit cards and buy whatever you're selling, Maria Veloso is an absolute genius. But what's truly amazing is her singular skill in simplifying the craft of writing web copy that sells into a discipline that's both learnable and infinitely easy."

—Thomas Myer, Freelance Technical Copywriter, www.myerman.com

"As a small business marketing expert, I constantly see small business owners struggle with the creation of effective copy. It is far more important than many people recognize. Maria Veloso offers many powerful, practical and highly effective recipes in her book *Web Copy That Sells*. I recommend this book to all my clients and all small business owners. It is essential!"

—Craig Jacobson, Small Business Marketing Expert, www.OpenSpacesMarketing.com

"I've only read 104 pages of *Web Copy That Sells* thus far and I have to say that it's even MORE POTENT than the book I previously regarded as the best book on writing killer copy, written by Murray Raphael over 18 years ago. Maria Veloso leaves nothing on the pitch when it comes to sharing massively rich content and strategies on how to create killer copy for the web. I can say categorically that anyone who has the discipline to follow Maria's methodologies can't help but succeed. I look forward greatly to promoting Maria's teachings with my Smácht clients to enable them to stand out in a frenetically crowded marketplace. Thank you, Maria, for creating unlimited possibility for those of us journeying the information highway."

—Pádraic Ó Máille, Creator of Smácht, Galway, Ireland

"I am just blown away by the way Maria Veloso takes complicated copywriting techniques, such as applying psychological tactics, and explains them so that I, a copywriting newbie, can easily understand them. And not only understand them conceptually, but understand how to use them and feel comfortable using them in my writing. Maria is nothing short of a copywriting genius, and *Web Copy That Sells* is the most outstanding book for learning how to sell on the web."

—Tim Warren, Dallas, Texas, CEO of GreatMarketingStuff.com

"I have a pretty thorough grounding in offline copywriting, but I've found the methods and techniques described in your book quite mind-boggling. They go beyond common practice and embrace a practicality that makes the whole discipline very comfortable. Much of what you've introduced is applicable to offline work as well. I thank you for expanding my vision of how this craft can be practiced and for opening my mind to developing a much broader array of tools to use."

—Bruce Midgett, Owner, MBP Custom Publishers, Missoula, Montana

"Maria, I cannot even begin to tell you how much I'm enjoying myself writing copy the way you've taught it in your book! I just love it—and whenever I write copy for anyone, they're always blown away by the results! And I've just barely gotten started. I actually look forward to getting out of bed every single day to write this way. I'm so grateful that I found your book! This has changed my life—and at a time when I was stagnating after doing non-stop traditional marketing for over 20 years. So glad I found your book—so glad, so glad . . ."

—Susan B. Loebl, Web Copywriting Specialist, www.webcopywriting.us

"Maria, you have definitely revolutionized the proper techniques for writing web copy that sells! Your book is absolutely the most astonishing and easy-to-follow guide for business owners who want to take their business 10 steps forward and start making a name for themselves in the online world. Thank you, Maria. You're absolutely amazing!"

—Carlos Garcia, Publisher, *Wealthy Secrets* newsletter, London, Ontario, Canada

"Maria Veloso's book, *Web Copy That Sells,* is a godsend. It is the best thing I have read regarding writing for the Web because it specifically discusses the unique culture, mind-set, and psychology of the Internet population, and presents an easy-to-follow five-step formula for getting people to buy what you're selling on your website. I have bought lots of books for my extensive copywriting library and none come close to Maria's book."

—Eugene Pepper, La Canada, California

"*Web Copy That Sells* changed the way I thought about my online business and gave me all the tools and the proper direction that I needed to write my own web copy. As a result, I now have a thriving online business, and I successfully sell my products and services on the Internet using the copywriting skills I learned."

—Connie Ragen Green, www.EbookWritingandMarketingSecrets.com

"Maria Veloso's copywriting book is simply incredible! I got a copy of *Web Copy That Sells* in the mail, and it's the most amazing book on copywriting I have ever seen. Maria breaks it down into a simple process so easy that anyone can follow it. I always thought of myself as a gifted writer, but by following the steps in her well-laid-out book, I was able to take my writing to the next level. I love the power of words; I feel like this book has helped me unleash a whole new palette to paint with. The words that resulted were simple, compelling, and powerful. I'm so thankful for this incredible book!"

—Kristie Tamsevicius, Work at Home Expert, www.KristieT.com

"Maria Veloso is a fantastic teacher! In her book, *Web Copy That Sells,* she presents ideas clearly and powerfully, and they pull the reader along painlessly—just like her web copy does! I initially took this attitude: 'Okay, let's see if Maria can really get me salivating for her book!' Sure enough, after only three paragraphs, I was ready to purchase! A person would have to be 'brain-dead' to not feel the power of the kind of copy she teaches."

—Lloyd Standish, www.AnemiaAnswer.com, Cornville, Arizona

"Maria Veloso's book, *Web Copy That Sells,* provides the unique skills and techniques that enable a copywriter or anyone who writes online copy to flat-out sell like never before. These techniques are so powerful and dynamic it's hard to believe. I've read all the books on online copywriting but *Web Copy That Sells* is, by far, the very best to date. I recommend this book to anyone who really wants to make their site sell or needs to understand how to write e-mail and get it through the spam filters as well as get it read. This book covers it all. Maria Veloso has done a great job and provided a valuable service. I highly recommend this powerful book to all copywriters and anyone who needs to write copy for the Web."

—Susanna K. Hutcheson, Executive Creative Director,
Power Communications LLC, www.powerwriting.com

"I've been in the direct marketing field for countless years and have made a lot of money at it. I've also done a massive amount of reading and research on the subject of copywriting, but Maria Veloso's book, *Web Copy That Sells,* stands out as one of the most memorable high points. It is superbly constructed—with zero fluff and puff. And it brings literally everything that's important about selling online together in one place. One standout worth its own mention is this: Never before has 'NLP for marketers' been introduced so well into a direct-response copy flow and made so accessible. As a Brit, I'm usually averse to obvious Yankisms—but this book really is 'awesome!' Well, well done."

—Chris Pay, United Kingdom

"This book is a must-have. I'm a good writer . . . but before I read this book, I didn't have a clue how to write web copy. I didn't really know how to get people to read my whole website and buy. I became so frustrated when I would look at my site stats. I noticed that people would go to my website, but they would only stay for a few seconds max. I did some research and I came across *Web Copy That Sells.* Since using the tips and suggestions that Maria talks about . . . I have seen a complete turnaround in how long people stay on my site. I am also able to close more sales for first-time visitors. This book is amazing!"

—Rachel Johnson, Website Owner and Copywriter, Miami, Florida

"I've read Hopkins, Caples, Collier, Sugarman, Schwab, Schwartz, Ogilvy, Bencivenga, Halbert, Carlton, Roy Williams, and many, many more—but Maria Veloso's book, *Web Copy That Sells,* is the best marketing book I've ever read."

—Chris Moreno, Kennebunkport, Maine

"*Web Copy That Sells* is far and away the best volume I've seen on writing for the Web. I'm already putting the techniques I learned from it into practice, and plan to read the book more than once."

—Peter Losh, Internet and E-Commerce Manager, FarStone Technology, Inc.

"Maria, I've just purchased your book, *Web Copy That Sells,* and started reading it. All I can say is . . . totally amazing! I have barely scratched the surface, yet I cannot believe the simplicity with which you break down the most important aspects of web copywriting! I am loving it . . . and must confess . . . you have lit the writer's fire in me once again! A while back, I enrolled in an expensive copywriting course offered by a prestigious writers' institute. Now that I have read your book, I can honestly say that course doesn't hold a candle to the advice you offer in *Web Copy That Sells.* Your unique 'mentoring' tone conveys an understanding of how human nature reacts, as a reader and writer of web copy. Your book is a refreshing change for the up-and-coming Internet entrepreneur who wants to master this make-or-break business tool. Thanks for giving me the advantage of making a connection with a 'true' voice in my education of web copywriting! *Web Copy That Sells* will enable my efforts at web copywriting . . . an attainable triumph!"

—Lourdes Torres, CEO and Founder, www.LatinoClicks.com, North Smithfield, Rhode Island

"I read Maria's book, not once, not twice—but three times over the past three months. That's because each time I would immerse myself in her proven web copywriting concepts and formulas, something inevitably would happen. My online sales increased! That's why her powerful book is extremely difficult to put down. Especially when you start considering what can happen when you apply her unique concepts to your promotional articles, free reports, newsletters, online ads, autoresponder e-mails, or website copy."

—Tony Ostian, Certified Master of Web Copywriting, The Web Copy Guy

"*Web Copy That Sells* has certainly helped to usher in a whole new era for copywriting. That's why it's not just copywriting anymore, it's web copywriting! The web copywriting process has been thoroughly tested and proven on the Internet. It works, and Maria shows you why and how! In her own convincing writing style she pours on an abundance of easy-to-understand concepts, strategies, and techniques and then supports all her claims. She literally walks you through the entire writing process effortlessly. Her knowledge is not only straightforward; her writing style is captivating, too. If you're looking for the "Sacred Book" on Web Copywriting. You've come to the right place!"

—Marshall A. Ronco, Web Copywriter, www.marcocopy.com

WEB COPY
THAT SELLS

THIRD EDITION

The Revolutionary Formula for
Creating Killer Copy That Grabs Their Attention
and Compels Them to Buy

Maria Veloso

AMACOM

AMERICAN MANAGEMENT ASSOCIATION

New York · Atlanta · Brussels · Chicago · Mexico City · San Francisco
Shanghai · Tokyo · Toronto · Washington, D.C.

Bulk discounts available. For details visit:
www.amacombooks.org/go/specialsales
Or contact special sales:
Phone: 800-250-5308
Email: specialsls@amanet.org
View all the AMACOM titles at: www.amacombooks.org
American Management Association: www.amanet.org

This publication is designed to provide accurate and authoritative information in regard to the subject matter covered. It is sold with the understanding that the publisher is not engaged in rendering legal, accounting, or other professional service. If legal advice or other expert assistance is required, the services of a competent professional person should be sought.

Library of Congress Cataloging-in-Publication Data
has been applied for and is on file at the Library of Congress.

About AMA

American Management Association (www.amanet.org) is a world leader in talent development, advancing the skills of individuals to drive business success. Our mission is to support the goals of individuals and organizations through a complete range of products and services, including classroom and virtual seminars, webcasts, webinars, podcasts, conferences, corporate and government solutions, business books, and research. AMA's approach to improving performance combines experiential learning—learning through doing—with opportunities for ongoing professional growth at every step of one's career journey.

PRINTING NUMBER

10 9 8 7 6 5 4 3 2

To laugh often and love much; to win the respect of intelligent persons and the affection of children; to earn the approbation of honest citizens and endure the betrayal of false friends; to appreciate beauty; to find the best in others; to give of one's self; to leave the world a bit better, whether by a healthy child, a garden patch or a redeemed social condition; to have played and laughed with enthusiasm and sung with exultation; to know even one life has breathed easier because you have lived—this is to have succeeded.

—RALPH WALDO EMERSON

CONTENTS

FOREWORD

On July 23, 2000, I received an e-mail with the following subject line:

> Subject: Mark, here are the Top 10 Reasons Why You Need to Have Me
> Working for You

I get hundreds of e-mails a day—but the subject line of this e-mail stopped me dead in my tracks. The e-mail was from a woman named Maria Veloso. Her e-mail began as follows:

> Dear Mark,
>
> Have you ever wished you could "clone" yourself so that all the ideas you have "in development" can materialize with lightning speed?

Then, the e-mail went on to give ten compelling reasons why Maria would be an asset to my company, Aesop Marketing Corporation.

I was sufficiently intrigued by her e-mail that I phoned her and told her that I might have a position for which she would qualify. However, I gave her this word of warning:

"It's the most miserable job you could possibly have in my company."

When I told her it was the job of a copywriter, she was puzzled. "Why do you think that's such a miserable job, Mark?" she asked.

"Because you'll be writing copy for me," I said. I told her I'd be extremely difficult to please because I had excruciatingly high standards. I also told her that because I had always done my own copywriting and never trusted anyone to write on my behalf, I'd constantly be cracking the whip on anyone who had the misfortune of becoming my copywriter.

Without skipping a beat, she said, "I'm up to the challenge, Mark."

I shook my head, feeling sorry that this woman didn't know what she was getting herself into. I agreed to interview her soon thereafter. She showed me her copywriting samples, and it was easy to tell that she was skilled in writing copy for the offline markets. But I wondered how well she could learn how to write web copy.

That's when she told me she's been a big fan of my unique approach to online copywriting for years—and that she had bought several products and services from my company over the years on the strength of the copy I wrote. She was eager to learn my style of copywriting and reiterated that she wanted to become my copywriting clone.

"Okay," I said. "You're hired!"

At the time, my company (Aesop) was already a multimillion-dollar enterprise and was enjoying international fame in Internet marketing circles because of the unconventional, nonconformist marketing campaigns we were running.

When I gave Maria her first copywriting assignment, I could tell she was eager to prove her skill as a copywriter. Three days later, when she handed me the copy she had written, I told her flat out that it wasn't the way I wanted copy at Aesop to be written. She definitely had great copywriting skills, but they were tailored for the offline world—not the web.

I thought my rebuff would discourage her, but she was undaunted. She was determined to learn the right way of writing web copy. Thus began my mentorship of Maria Veloso. I began to teach her the little-known mechanics and art of writing for the Internet buying public. She took copious notes and was a quick study. In as little as a few weeks' time, I saw her web copywriting begin to show promise.

In October 2000, two months after she started working for me, she handed me a six-page copy piece that pulled in *$18,000 in two days*. That was when I was convinced she was a *killer copywriter*. But that wasn't the end of her copywriting education. Not by a long shot.

Over the following months and years, I continued to conduct the most ambitious (and expensive) market testing ever attempted in Internet marketing. I hired an entire staff of programmers, statisticians, and analysts, whose only job was to test every conceivable element of the copy we produced at Aesop—from headlines to price points, offers, guarantees, formats, involvement devices, e-mail subject lines, lead-ins, and so on. You name it—I had my research staff test it, take the raw data, and convert it into usable form.

People called me "The Fanatic of Online Market Testing," but I rather enjoyed having that reputation. It was my attempt to identify those seemingly marginal elements of web copy and online marketing communications that made a significant difference in our sales figures. Because Aesop had amassed a database of millions of names, consisting of customers, subscribers, and prospects, we had the luxury of conducting huge marketing tests, wherein our test samples were as large as 20,000 names apiece—a number that was larger than most other companies' entire mailing lists. As a result, we produced the most scientifically validated—and conclusive—results ever obtained.

For 15 months, Maria had a ringside seat and witnessed the blow-by-blow action being churned out by my marketing statisticians and analysts. She was privy to some of the most priceless pieces of marketing intelligence ever assembled.

She saw, for instance, that many of the concepts that I had introduced to Internet marketing, such as the Zeigarnik effect, cognitive dissonance, the linear path, and so on (see Chapter 5), had a dramatic effect on click-through rates and sales conversions. She saw the full-scale findings of what has become known as my *Confidential Internet Intelligence Manuscript,* which my marketing staff had assembled at a cost of over $237,000—a manuscript that revealed e-mail marketing strategies that work (see Chapter 7), among other things.

Having had the benefit of all this, Maria's copywriting had nowhere to go but up. Being armed with as much web copywriting ammunition as any of the copywriting greats alive, she took the ball and ran with it. She's one of the very few copywriters in the world who "get" web copywriting. I am deeply gratified to have been instrumental in her becoming one of the top copywriting professionals in the industry today.

That said, it is also flattering to see that Maria has taken many of the concepts I pioneered and tested, and distilled them into the book you now have in your hands. If you're tempted to take the concepts she presents on these pages for granted, I'm here to tell you that you're walking past a gold mine. If the results of my extensive marketing research are any indication, I can say, without a doubt, that the information in this book is well-founded and accurate.

Some of the information in this book is indescribably powerful. I encourage you to use it ethically to take your online sales—or your copywriting career if you're a copywriter—to the highest level.

Mark Joyner
#1 Best-Selling Author of
MindControlMarketing.com,
The Irresistible Offer,
and others

ACKNOWLEDGMENT

This book would not have been possible if it weren't for the valuable lessons I learned from my mentor and friend, Mark Joyner. I owe a debt of gratitude to him for more things than I could possibly sum up here.

Mark was the first person I had ever seen use the editorial style of direct-response copywriting online. His approach to copywriting, where he wrapped his sales pitch in the cushions of an editorial piece, has become the copywriting model that I employ almost exclusively. It was Mark who taught me that writing sales copy for the web is distinctly different from writing sales copy for the offline (brick-and-mortar) world. Mark also taught me the significance of the prospect's frame of mind when it comes to selling (and it became the basis of my book *Frame-of-Mind Marketing: How to Convert Your Online Prospects into Customers*). Mark also introduced me to many of the psychological devices that I use in writing web copy, which have produced the signature model of web copywriting with which I'm identified today.

- *The Zeigarnik effect.* Although this principle has become widely used among marketers in recent years, Mark was the pioneer at successfully applying it to web copy and Internet marketing—along with the "linear path" methodology, which is part of his "Source of the Nile" theory.

- *Cognitive dissonance.* To my knowledge, this concept had never been mentioned in a marketing book prior to Mark's inclusion of it in his marketing course titled 1001 Killer Internet Marketing Tactics. Although other marketers may have previously used the cognitive dissonance technique, as well as the Zeigarnik effect, no one has ever identified the tandem concepts in relation to business and marketing or established their scientific validity the way Mark has.

Finally, the bulk of the e-mail strategies I discuss in Chapter 4 are owed in no small part to the research spearheaded by Mark at Aesop. For these reasons and more, I consider him the honorary coauthor of this book.

My goal is to bring what I've learned to you.

Maria Veloso
January 2013

INTRODUCTION TO THIRD EDITION

The Greek philosopher Socrates once said, "The only true wisdom is in knowing you know nothing." Very few stories convey the profound truth of his statement better than this story of Chinese Taoist origin:

> There was a farmer who lived in a poor country village. He was considered quite well-to-do because he owned a horse which he used for plowing and for transportation. One day his horse ran away. All his neighbors exclaimed how terrible this was, but the farmer simply said, "Maybe, maybe not."
>
> A few days later the horse returned and brought two wild horses with it. The neighbors all rejoiced and told the farmer how fortunate he was, but the farmer just said, "Maybe, maybe not."
>
> The next day the farmer's son tried to ride one of the wild horses; the horse threw him and as a result, his son broke his leg. The neighbors offered their sympathy and told the farmer what a terrible turn of events he had encountered, but the farmer said once again, "Maybe, maybe not."
>
> The next week draft officers came to the village to take all the able-bodied young men for the army. They rejected the farmer's son because of his broken leg. When the neighbors told him how lucky he was, the farmer replied, "Maybe, maybe not."

This story underscores what Socrates must have meant when he penned the words "The only true wisdom is in knowing you know nothing." Things of this world are in such a constant state of flux, that nothing remains the same for very long. Just when you think something is true, it ceases to be true—like Google's search algorithms. Therefore, true wisdom might be defined as freeing one's mind to be a blank canvas upon which the ebb and flow of the universe can paint a changing landscape.

Such is the outlook we must adopt when it comes to the rapidly changing world of the Internet and e-commerce. Instead of clinging to benchmark standards, methods, and techniques that have consistently shown superior results during the early days of the web, "best practice" must necessarily become *better* as improvements are discovered. Although we've all learned a few things since the dawn of the Internet, if we were to take the stance that we know a thing or two about Internet marketing or web copywriting, we may run the risk of "knowing just enough to be dangerous."

The operative word for our business behavior is therefore . . . *nimble*. Just as the Internet is nimble and ever-changing, so must the art of web copywriting be.

The first edition of this book (2004) presented web copywriting principles that catered to the prevailing business climate at a time when Yahoo! reigned supreme as the brightest star among web directories, Google was still in its infancy, and Facebook and Twitter had not made their entrance yet. By the time the second edition was released in 2009, Google had become a verb in our vocabulary (due to the popularity and dominance of the eponymous search engine), and the YouTube revolution had come to dominate the hearts and minds of Internet surfers. I introduced advanced online communications in that second edition that were tailored to the then-emerging age of Web 2.0. Within a few short years thereafter, the Internet had metamorphosed into the next-generation version of itself and has yet again altered the way we communicate to our prospects, customers, and the general public online.

It is this next generation of the Internet (Web 3.0, if you will) that the third edition of *Web Copy That Sells* addresses. In order to stay a step ahead of the trends that dominate the web, you must also change your online communications at the speed of change, while still embracing fundamental principles that are the undercurrent of all marketing and copywriting.

There is another reason why the aforementioned tale of the farmer is one of my favorite stories of all time. It illustrates one of the psychological devices that I present in this book, called *reframing* (see Chapter 5, "Using Psychology to Motivate Prospects to Become Purchasers"). Reframing, simply put, suggests that the meaning of any event depends upon the "frame" in which we perceive it. When we change the frame, we change the meaning. When the farmer gains two wild horses, for example, that event might be perceived as a good thing until it is seen in the context of the farmer's son's broken leg. The broken leg appears to be an unfortunate event in the context of peaceful village life, but in the context of the draft, it suddenly becomes fortunate. Reframing is one of the most powerful web copywriting devices, which I discuss in greater length in this third edition.

The Trifecta Neuro-Affective Principle™ (Chapter 6) is another powerful device that is designed to change your prospects' minds in favor of your product or service and accelerates their decision to buy what you're selling. This device, which can be utilized in any selling situation either on or off the web, has exceedingly more applications within the current Internet trends. This comes at such an opportune time because the current landscape of the web tends to favor short, succinct, digestible bites of copy, for which I coined the term *cyber bite*. Cyber bites have the power not only to create a sales-advancing impact on people but also potentially to become *memes* (a term coined by Richard Dawkins in 1976, derived from the words *mime* and *mimic,* representing cultural ideas that are passed from one individual to another in a manner analogous to the propagation of biological genes) that get transmitted verbally and virally, thereby creating significant buzz for any product or service.

The expanded material in the third edition makes this book useful not just for online marketers and copywriters but for anyone who sells anything—either on or off the web.

Web copy refers to the words on a website, in an e-mail, or in other online marketing communications that cause prospects to do what you want them to do—pick up the phone, register, subscribe, or buy your product or service.

The World Wide Web is forging ahead, and the age of Web 3.0 is already upon us, yet I find that most people who do business on the Internet are still in the dark as far as selling on the web is concerned. The fact is, most companies, business enterprises, and entrepreneurs who are selling products and services on the Internet are still conducting marketing and sales operations online the way they do business in the brick-and-mortar world. They're still taking marketing principles that work well in the offline world and trying to force them to work on the web. And they still don't realize that many principles that are effective in print, on the radio, on billboards, in direct mail, and via other types of offline advertising simply do not translate well on the web. In fact, they can even kill sales.

Most of all, they still make the common mistake that most website owners, Internet entrepreneurs, and online companies make: They drive traffic to their website before making sure they have web copy that sells.

Words are the true currency of the web. The single most important ingredient in a commercial website is web copy. Words make the sale, and no amount of cool graphics, interactive bells and whistles, cutting-edge design, or sophisticated e-commerce infrastructure could ever compare to the selling ability of compelling web copy.

Because selling on the web is text driven, nothing happens until someone writes the words that get people to click, sign up, read, register, order, subscribe, or buy whatever you're selling. According to a four-year study, conducted by Stanford University and the Poynter Institute for Media Studies and published in 2000, of the habits of Internet news readers on normally scrolling screens, "the first thing people look at on a webpage tends to be text." The Poynter Institute's EyeTrack '07 study conducted in July 2007, which had 600 participants from 18 to 60 years old, corroborates the same.

I've sold everything from books to software to stock-picking services, franchises, self-improvement programs, career development products, handcrafted gifts and art pieces, consumable products, membership clubs, weight loss products, tax-saving programs, seminars, consulting services, and more on the web, and in the process I've learned that both the five-step blueprint and the other principles and devices revealed in this book can help any website owner take a casual website visitor and turn that surfer into a prospect and, subsequently, into a customer—all through the sheer power of words.

Jakob Nielsen, one of the top usability engineers for the web and author of *Designing Web Usability* (Peachpit Press, 1999) and other books, wrote:

Words are usually the main moneymakers on a website. Better writing is probably the single most important improvement you can make to your site.

For this reason, if you have a website (or plan to create one) that sells a product or service, you need to hire a web copywriter—or learn the craft of web copywriting yourself. This brings me to the reason for this book. When I wrote the first edition in 2004, I was motivated by the fact that every time I surfed the Internet I came across countless websites that were so poorly written that I couldn't imagine them generating a single sale. Some of those websites offered excellent products and services, but they utilized weak web copy that didn't do justice to the products and services. Several years have passed since the publication of the first and second editions, and I'm dumbfounded that most companies and individuals doing business on the web still haven't discovered how to use the power of words to sell effectively via their websites. It's a shame, because the web provides an incredible channel for marketing virtually anything to anybody in any part of the world.

Adding to the challenge facing website owners and Internet entrepreneurs is the fact that there is a scarcity of web copywriting specialists equipped to take on the unique challenge of web communication and online selling. This situation is unlikely to change in the foreseeable future because even with the increasing numbers of professional writers transitioning into web copywriting, the numbers of e-commerce websites that need professional web copywriting are increasing at an even faster pace. Consequently, even if you're a website owner, Internet entrepreneur, or online company that could find good web copywriters and could afford to pay their standard rates of $125 to $235 per hour—or $3,000 to $12,000 or more for a sales page—chances are that the good ones would be too busy to take on your project.

My solution—and my reason for writing this book—is to teach you the principles of web copywriting so you can write web copy yourself. Whether you are a businessperson writing your own copy or a writer entering the business or transitioning from other kinds of advertising copywriting, my goal is to teach you how to take your writing skills and apply them to web writing. Writing web copy that converts prospects into customers is a discipline all its own. It's a highly specialized genre of writing that combines marketing wherewithal with a deep understanding of the Internet's unique culture, mindset, psychology, and language.

Additionally, this revised edition redefines web copy in the context of the continually evolving commercial landscape of the Internet and establishes updated rules for communicating successfully in the age of Web 3.0—the third generation of web-based communities and applications, including but not limited to the following forms of online communications:

* Audio
* Video (such as YouTube, DailyMotion, and Vimeo)
* Social networks (such as Facebook, Google+, and LinkedIn)
* Blogs (including microblogging services such as Twitter)
* Viral communications (including social news websites, such as Digg, and social bookmarking sites, such as StumbleUpon, Reddit, and Delicious)

Furthermore, this new edition includes copywriting principles not only for direct-response types of websites but also for corporations, advertising agencies, catalog-style businesses, and newbies who want to grow their online businesses with killer web copy. With Internet advertising revenues exceeding $31.7 billion in 2011, a 22 percent increase over 2010 (source: Internet Advertising Bureau), due emphasis has also been given to strategies for writing short-form ads.

What most online businesspeople and some professional copywriters don't realize is that web copywriting is distinctly different from any other kind of advertising copywriting and offline marketing communications. It is also quite different from writing content for the web. Of course, it also bears some similarities to all of these. Additionally, web copy encompasses more than just words in cyberspace. It's a way of communicating on the web that takes into account the ever-changing lifestyles and preferences of the Internet buying population. Sometimes that includes the use of graphic depictions of words to better communicate ideas and change people's minds in favor of your product or service (see Chapter 6). The trends that are in a constant state of flux necessitate continuing education on how people are willing to consume marketing messages, as will be shown in the discussion of the YouTube revolution in Chapter 9.

In this third edition, it is also my objective to provide the newest strategies, techniques, devices, and tools for writing copy in a market that has become immune and unresponsive to the marketing strategies that were effective three or more years ago. Most of the general web copywriting rules that I presented in the first and second editions have remained the same, but the *delivery* and *execution* have changed with the times.

Who needs this book? You do, if you are

- An Internet marketer, entrepreneur, or website owner who sells (or plans to sell) a product or service online via your own e-commerce website
- A marketing professional who is in charge of your company's online sales operations (an advertising, marketing, or brand manager)
- An advertising professional who plans, approves, or executes Internet marketing campaigns or writes advertising copy on behalf of clients
- A writer who is tired of being underpaid and barely earning a living—and who wants to transition to the lucrative specialty of web copywriting
- A webmaster who wants to learn the skill of web copywriting in order to expand the services you provide your clients
- An aspiring online entrepreneur who is seeking the most cost-efficient way to start a successful online business using a simple web copywriting formula
- Someone with moderate-to-good writing skills who wants to become a highly paid professional writer in one of the hottest, most in-demand fields in today's marketplace

Whether or not you aspire to become a professional web copywriter, you can apply the principles presented in this book to any website, incorporate them into your marketing communications (e-mail, online advertising, newsletters, online video, audio, etc.), and generate measurably increased sales and profits.

Although the web copywriting principles I present herein are largely derived from direct-response types of web copy, they can be adapted to virtually all copywriting applications on the web. Whether your goal is to write web copy for branding purposes or to generate leads, build a mailing list, generate more sales, obtain repeat customers, ensure customer satisfaction, or improve customer retention, you will benefit from the principles revealed in this book because they will sharpen the edges of your marketing messages, making them more effective.

I've been writing advertising copy since 1977 and specializing in web copywriting since 1996, and this gives me a broader perspective of the craft than most people have. Yet I "stand on the shoulders of giants," learning from those who came before me—masters of influence like Robert Cialdini and marketing legends like Rosser Reeves, Victor Schwab, Robert Collier, and Eugene Schwartz—whose powerful concepts I've battle-tested and fine-tuned for the web.

WHAT THIS BOOK WILL DO FOR YOU

When I encountered the World Wide Web in 1996, I already had 19 years of copywriting experience under my belt, but I soon discovered that writing copy for the web was a highly specialized craft. There was a multitude of things to learn—and unlearn. It's my goal to teach you the things I've learned and help you avoid some of the errors I made.

As you go through the book, here are some of the lessons and tools you'll find:

- Chapter 1 introduces you to the three fundamental rules for writing web copy that appeals to the unique predisposition of the Internet population and reveals a technique that will give you the mindset of a killer web copywriter in five hours or less.
- Chapter 2 discusses the five simple questions (about your product or service) that, when answered, make your web copy practically write itself.
- Chapter 3 reveals the formula for measuring the selling quotient of your copy, showing you how to evaluate your copy's selling ability and how to get an immediate boost in your response rate.
- In Chapter 4 you'll discover the amazing power of e-mail marketing, how to write attention-grabbing e-mail copy, and new ways of rising above the overcrowded e-mail jungle.
- The most powerful psychological principles underlying web copy that sells are explored in Chapter 5, which offers devices, strategies, tactics, and tips that can make any website sizzle with sales activity.

- Chapter 6 reveals the Trifecta Neuro-Affective Principle, which features the three principal triggers that you need to employ to change your prospects' minds in favor of your product or service and to accelerate their decision to buy.
- The most important involvement devices that dramatically increase the "stickiness" of your website—and make website visitors more likely to buy what you're selling—are discussed in Chapter 7.
- In Chapter 8, I show you how to write compelling online ads, newsletters (or e-zines), autoresponder messages, and other marketing communications that can propel your online business to uncharted heights.
- Chapter 9 provides the essential guidelines for creating short online videos that get high Google rankings and generate sales; crafting effective marketing messages and gaining visibility, sales, and even fame via the social dynamics of Web 3.0; and bridging online marketing with the underutilized (but powerful) offline advertising channel that most marketers on the web often ignore.
- After you've learned the craft of web copywriting, Chapter 10 reveals the four-step foolproof secret to success in all your copywriting endeavors and introduces "the perfect customer life cycle," which, when mastered alongside the web copywriting principles in this book, radically transforms your online business's sales and profits.
- Finally, Chapter 11 shows how you can parlay the web copywriting knowledge you'll learn from this book into a lucrative career, including how to find an unlimited number of web copywriting clients, an irresistible prospecting e-mail you can use to persuade clients to hire you; and how to license your intellectual property (your web copy) and structure joint-venture deals with online enterprises to generate a six-figure income.

You simply can't model successful websites and expect to succeed on the web. You need to model the process through which the success is attained, not the outcome of that process. For this reason, we examine the steps, the psychology, and the philosophies that are considered in writing successful web copy rather than modeling the web copy itself and trying to adapt it where it isn't appropriate. Instead of simply presenting blueprints or power words and phrases,

I'll demonstrate how to acquire the mindset with which to view websites, e-mail, and all other marketing communications so that you, too, can write web copy that sells.

In my experience, selling on the web is quite different from selling via any other marketing channels in the brick-and-mortar world. Online selling is about achieving a click and a sale as swiftly and efficiently as possible. In order to illustrate how this is accomplished, I use examples throughout the book consisting of web copy pieces I've written for clients as well as websites that I manage or own. I invite you to regard these in the context of the lessons being presented in this book, regardless of your interest in the products being sold.

Very few people truly understand the complexities of communicating on the Internet. However, by the time you finish reading this book, you'll know more about web copywriting than 99 percent of the population. More important, you will be able to parlay that specialized knowledge into a six-figure income in the field of web copywriting or dramatically increase the sales of your website.

WEB COPY THAT SELLS

CHAPTER 1

GETTING STARTED

The Dynamics of Web Selling

Don't worry that you'll take a shot and you'll miss. The fact is, you'll miss every shot you don't take.

—ANONYMOUS

In the advertising world, the words employed to communicate a sales message in an advertisement or commercial are called *advertising copy*, and the people who write these words are known as *copywriters*. (This term should not be confused with *copyright,* which is a legal mechanism that protects your ownership of what you write.)

Similarly, *web copy* refers to the words employed to communicate a sales message on the web, and the people who write these words are *web copywriters*. Although distinctly different in tone from advertising copy, web copy has the same objectives—that is, to generate leads, customers, sales, and, consequently, profits for a website. (Web copy also should not be confused with web content, which consists of words written for the web for the purpose of informing, communicating, entertaining, or edifying the reader, not necessarily communicating a sales or marketing message.)

Web copywriting is one of the most exciting crafts and professions I know of. I often equate it with alchemy, but whereas alchemy is the science that turns base metals into gold, web copywriting turns words into money seemingly out of thin air. Think about it. The Internet is the only place where anyone can truly market every day for little or no money and have the chance at making a fortune. Personally, I have seen many companies and entrepreneurs do it—even on a shoestring budget.

Whatever your writing skills are, don't worry! Practically anyone with moderate to good writing skills can learn how to write web copy. One of the best copywriters in the offline world, Joe Sugarman, almost flunked English in high school. One of his copywriting students, a grapefruit farmer who had never written sales copy, made millions of dollars over the years using sales copy he wrote to sell grapefruit by mail.

Before any discussion of web copywriting is attempted, it is necessary to consider a few facts and figures about the web in order to have a clear concept of the online marketing environment in which one needs to operate.

- As of May 2012, there were approximately 662.9 million (662,959,946) websites (according to a Netcraft Web Server Survey)! That's a 378 percent increase over the 175.4 million websites that existed in 2008.
- The average Internet surfer who uses a search engine visits 25 websites among the displayed search results in three to four minutes. Therefore, the average duration of stay on each website is approximately eight seconds, including the click and load time.
- An estimated 107 trillion pieces of e-mail were sent out in 2010 (approximately 294 billion e-mails a day—and growing). An estimated 89 percent of these are automated spam mails.

Why would the staggering number of websites and e-mails be of any concern to you when doing business on the web—especially since all those other websites are not necessarily your competitors? Here's why: On the Internet, you're competing for a piece of the Internet surfers' online time, and you're also competing for mind share. In a cyberuniverse characterized by information overwhelm, every company, individual, or entity that has any kind of Internet presence competes for your prospects' online time and mind share and is therefore your competitor, for all intents and purposes.

With the aforementioned facts in mind, we can now lay the foundation for communicating successfully on the web.

THREE FUNDAMENTAL RULES FOR WRITING WEB COPY THAT SELLS

It amuses me that whenever I run a successful campaign with great web copy, I find a few dozen copycats mimicking certain parts of my work. Invariably, however, they merely copy the words but fail to duplicate the *strategy* or *tactic* behind the words, which is what really makes the copy effective. The writing strategy I employ in every web copy piece that I write is founded on three relatively simple rules.

Rule 1: Don't Make Your Website Look Like an Ad

Depending on which source you believe, the average person is exposed to anywhere between 1,500 (*Media Literacy Report* published by UNICEF) and 5,000 (Charles Pappas, Yahoo! *Internet Life* columnist) advertising messages per day from TV, billboards, radio, the Internet, and practically everywhere we turn. That's an average of 3,250 advertisements per day.

"It's a non-stop blitz of advertising messages," Jay Walker-Smith, president of the marketing firm Yankelovich, told *CBS News* recently. He estimates that we've gone from being exposed to about 500 ads a day back in the 1970s to as many as 5,000 a day today.

Therefore, the last thing we want to see when we land on a website is yet another ad. Additionally, since most of us have been inundated with ads for most of our lives, we have developed instinctive mechanisms to tune out commercial messages.

Yet many online businesses seem to go out of their way to make their websites look like ads, billboards, or other commercial media. Don't fall into this trap, because if you do, you'll turn away potential customers. Always remember that consumers don't hate advertising—it's *bad* advertising that they detest. It stands to reason, then, that your website should engage your prospects, it should provide the solid information that they are looking for, and whenever possible it should have an editorial feel to it. Above all, it should be free of hype. Why? Because people usually go online to find information. Few people log on saying, "I can't wait to see ads, and I can't wait to buy stuff!" No, that usually doesn't happen.

People go online to find information. That's why they call it the information superhighway. Even if they are shopping for something—say, a DVD player or an antiaging skin care product—they are generally seeking information, not advertising, about those products. There is a myth that the Internet is an advertising medium or one big shopping channel. It's *not*.

Here's the first distinction between offline advertising copy and effective web copy. Web copy needs to provide good information that appeals to the target audience; that is, ideally, it must not look or feel like a sales pitch.

Editorial-Style Web Headlines

Don't Buy a DVD Player Unless It Meets These 5 Criteria

**How a Simple Formula Has Been Scientifically Proven to Cure Cancer
and Virtually All Diseases**
[Courtesy of 1MinuteCure.com]

**How to Sell Your Home Fast at Top Dollar—Even in a
Soft Real Estate Market**

**"Topical Botox": The New Way to Erase the Look of Wrinkles and Lines
from Your Skin—Without Injections**
[Courtesy of TransformationAntiAgingCream.com]

**Can Streaming Audio Really Double Your Website Sales?
A recent Internet research study says you can.**

**What You Don't Know About Foreclosure Could
Cost You Much More Than Just Your Home**
[Courtesy of SurviveYourForeclosure.com]

**11 New Breakthrough Cures That Transform Your
Health and Well-Being—and Add Years to Your Life**

Not All Miracle Cures Are Created Equal
**How to Tell if a So-Called "Miracle Cure" is Scientifically
Proven—or Utter Falsehood
Now You Can Separate Healing Facts from Myths**

**An Amazing Little-Known FDA-Approved Therapy for Pain Relief,
Smoking Cessation, Weight Loss and the Healing of 350 Diseases**
[Courtesy of ScienceOfAuriculotherapy.com]

**The World's Richest Source of Cash—and How You Can Tap Into It
to Start or Grow Your Business**

**Melt Away Cancer From Your Body
Using Nothing More Than Your Fingertips?**

Where does the selling come in? It comes from expertly crafted copy that tilts the website visitor's favor toward your product or service. In other words, avoid blatant sales pitches; instead, provide irresistible information that slides smoothly into a sales pitch for your product.

Why? Because people online do not want to be sold to. A study conducted by web usability experts John Morkes and Jakob Nielsen (reported in a paper titled *Concise, Scannable and Objective: How to Write for the Web*) showed that web users "detest anything that seems like marketing fluff or overly hyped language ('marketese') and prefer factual information." If web visitors ever do get sold on something, they want to be engaged and finessed, not bombarded by blatant advertising.

The operative principle here is *engagement*. Just as a high engagement level—not just the number of likes—is an important indicator of a healthy Facebook page, so too must a website have a high engagement score.

It bears repeating that your sales pitch should not sound like an ad, but rather it should read like an editorial, testimonial, advice, case study, or endorsement. If you want an example of this kind of writing in the brick-and-mortar world, think advertorial (editorial-style ads) or press release. In the offline world, editorial-style ads boost readership significantly over standard-looking ads. David Ogilvy, legendary advertising man, wrote in his book *Ogilvy on Advertising* (John Wiley & Sons, 1983), "There is no law which says that advertisements have to look like advertisements. If you make them *look* like *editorial pages,* you will attract more readers. *Roughly six times* as many people read the average article as the average advertisement [emphasis mine]. Very few advertisements are read by more than one reader in twenty." In fact, in a split-run test conducted in *Reader's Digest,* an editorial-style ad boosted response by 80 percent over the standard ad layout.

Naturally, not every website can employ the editorial-style approach to web copywriting. It may not be feasible for catalog-style websites, for instance, to use editorial articles for each one of their products, especially if they carry hundreds of products. However, the informational guideline can still be adapted when crafting headlines and catalog descriptions. Here are a few examples:

**A year of exposure to the sun is like a week
at the beach without sunscreen.**

(This editorial-style headline was used by a skin care company to advertise a product that provides sun protection.)

**Replacing Sour Cream and Mayonnaise in Your Creamy
Dressing and Dip Recipes Cuts Down as Much as 1800
Calories. But You Can't Do That With Just Any Yogurt.**

(This editorial-style headline was used by a yogurt company.)

**Losing One Pound of Weight Takes 4 Pounds
of Pressure Off Your Knees.**

(This headline was used by the makers of a pain relief medicine.)

Notice that in each of the preceding examples the headline provides information that is not only interesting but also speaks to the needs of the product's target audience. An interesting phenomenon happens when you give information that is useful to your prospects. They are likely to feel, at the subconscious level, that in order to get the benefit alluded to in the headline (i.e., protection from the sun, weight loss, or pain relief), only your product will do the job. The yogurt company brought that idea home with the line "But You Can't Do That With Just Any Yogurt"; however, the other two conveyed the same idea.

When I worked as the director of creative web writing at Aesop Marketing Corporation, Mark Joyner commissioned extensive in-house marketing research to test the effectiveness of every imaginable element of our web copy and other online marketing communications. To give you an idea of the magnitude of the research, Aesop's database consisted of millions of Internet entrepreneurs, and we frequently tested copy elements on samples of 20,000 names for each testing variable. The sales results I witnessed at Aesop made clear to me the effectiveness of the editorial style of copywriting. In the tests in which I've been involved, editorial-style web copy outpulled sales letter–style web copy every single time. Remember, people generally tune out ads, but they tune in to editorial information. (See Figure 1.1.)

Rule 2: Stop Readers Dead in Their Tracks

Online business owners spend a lot of time and money trying to get traffic to their websites. Building web traffic is very important, but it won't mean a thing unless you do one thing first. That is, create compelling web copy that will stop them dead in their tracks and get them to do what you want them to do when they get there.

Back in April 2004, when the first edition of this book went to press, Google had 36 million webpages indexed, and as of July 2008, just four years later, that number had multiplied by a factor of almost five, to 175.4 million webpages. At the time of this writing, now for the third edition, in May 2012, Google had 56.5 billion webpages—yes, that's *billion*, not million—all clamoring for attention! It's no wonder, then, that in order for words to wield their magical power on the web, they have to be tailored specifically for the information-flooded Internet public, among whom attention span is a rare commodity.

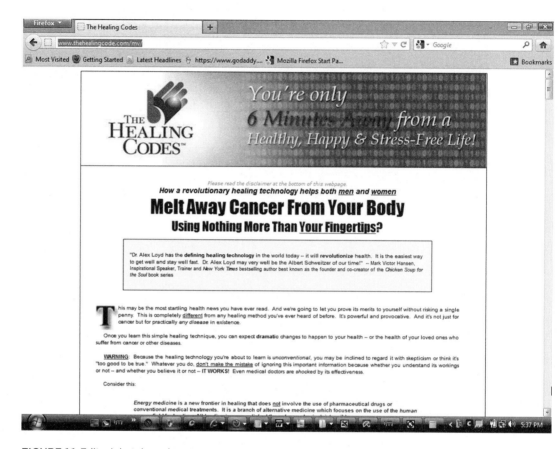

FIGURE 1.1 Editorial-style web copy.

FACT: If your website is little more than an online brochure, it's not only a very weak selling tool, but it has very little chance of selling anything in the crowded Internet marketplace. (See Figure 1.2.)

The home page of 1MinuteCure.com is a good example of a website that stops visitors dead in their tracks. The headline incites curiosity ("How a Simple Formula Has Been Scientifically Proven to Cure Cancer and Virtually All Diseases"), and the subheadline ("Why this one-minute therapy is being suppressed in the U.S. while more than 15,000 European doctors have been using it to heal

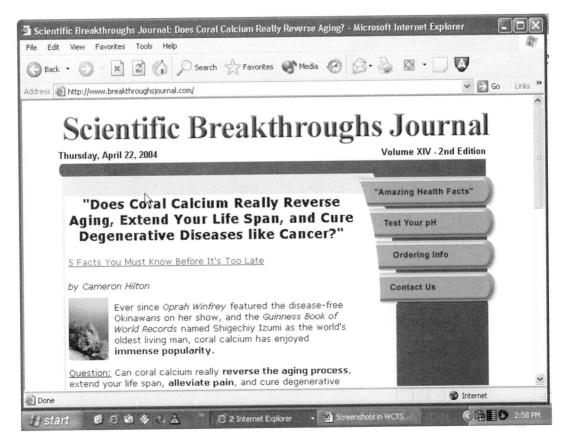

FIGURE 1.2 Attention-grabbing website.

millions of patients") injects emotion, drama, and credibility. Its copy, written in the editorial style, follows through by giving readers a sense that they're reading a news item, not an advertisement.

Rule 3: Capture E-Mail Addresses

For a website to succeed, it must have effective direct-response web copy that induces action from a single exposure. Just think: What's the point in getting someone to come to your website if the site visit doesn't generate a response such as picking up the phone and calling your business, subscribing to your newsletter, signing up for your mailing list, or buying your product or service?

Generating a response means more than impressing web visitors with cool graphics or technology or getting them to bookmark your site. What's the point in having cutting-edge web design, eye-popping graphics, and a sophisticated e-commerce infrastructure if you are unable to entice your visitors long enough for them to do what you want them to do?

If you are selling something on your website, chances are that less than 5 percent of your site's visitors will ever buy your product. Conversion rates vary with each industry, but the typical healthy rate for online stores is 0.5 percent (.005) to 1.5 percent (.015), according to the *Bock Newsletter* on Yahoo! Store (issue 32). "Conversion rates of 2 percent to 5 percent are fairly typical today," according to a report entitled *Getting Clicks with Casual Customers* at CNET News. Even the best marketers with the most successful websites seldom convert more than 5 percent of their web visitors into customers.

What happens to the 95 percent of your web visitors who came and went? For most websites, nothing. Those prospects are gone for good, never to return. That's why it is absolutely essential for your website to have an opt-in mechanism. The chances are slim that people will buy from you the first time they visit your website. After all, they don't even know you. Rather than lose them, ask for something that is easier and less intimidating than pulling out a credit card—ask them to give you their e-mail address. It's a simple, nonthreatening way to initiate a relationship.

Trust, as we all know, is an important issue in e-commerce, and finding ways to build trust in an online environment is a continuing challenge for Internet businesses. On the web, people buy from people they like and trust. They like people who provide them with information they need, who are not overly aggressive in trying to market their products, and who are easy to do business with. They trust people who deliver on the promises they make, who take time to develop a relationship with them, who provide good customer service, and who have an articulated privacy policy to which they strictly adhere. Capturing contact information is the first step in developing rapport with prospective customers and in building a relationship that fosters online sales—now and in the future. (See Figure 1.3.)

An opt-in offer, such as "How to Pay Less . . . ," is one way to capture a visitor's e-mail address. (See Chapter 3 for a complete discussion of opt-in mecha-

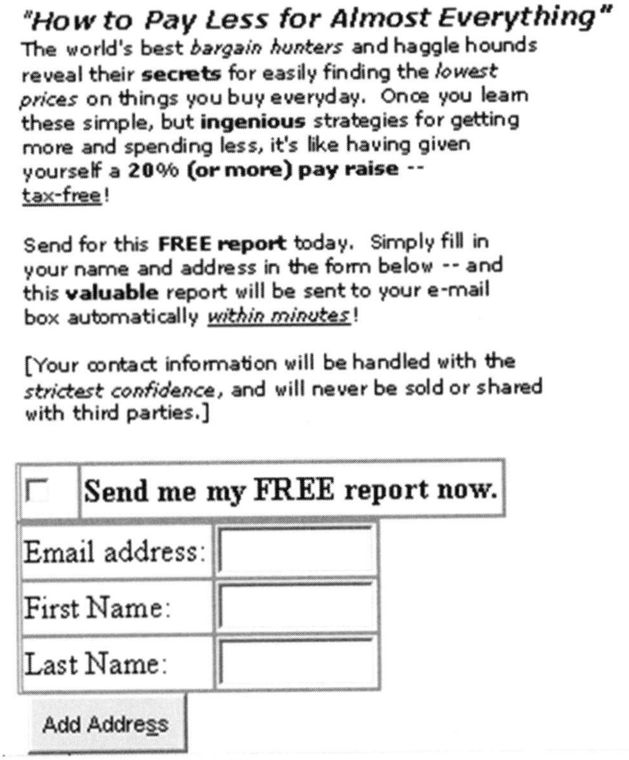

"How to Pay Less for Almost Everything"
The world's best *bargain hunters* and haggle hounds
reveal their **secrets** for easily finding the *lowest
prices* on things you buy everyday. Once you learn
these simple, but **ingenious** strategies for getting
more and spending less, it's like having given
yourself a **20% (or more) pay raise** --
tax-free!

Send for this **FREE report** today. Simply fill in
your name and address in the form below -- and
this **valuable** report will be sent to your e-mail
box automatically *within minutes*!

[Your contact information will be handled with the
strictest confidence, and will never be sold or shared
with third parties.]

☐	**Send me my FREE report now.**
Email address:	
First Name:	
Last Name:	

Add Address

FIGURE 1.3 Exit pop-up opt-in offer.

nisms, and Chapter 10 for crafting online campaigns that send your opt-ins
through the perfect customer life cycle.)

THE FIRST LOOK

What is the most important element of a website? The first screen (or the first
eyeful) is the prime selling space of your website, and what you put in it makes
or breaks its success. Do not confuse the first screen with the first page, which
is often referred to as the home page or the landing page of a website. The first
screen is only part of the page that appears on the screen when you land on a
website; it's the screen you see before you scroll down or sideways. In a print
newspaper, its counterpart is the information above the fold, which draws maximum readership.

Often, the first screen is the first, last, and only thing people see on a website before they click away. For this reason, don't make the mistake many companies do of putting a large logo or your company name in gigantic letters on that screen. Some companies do this for branding purposes, but in most cases the company name and logo don't have to take up half of the first screen. Your logo doesn't need to be large—it's not a selling feature. While it may stroke your ego, it won't increase your sales. An oversized logo wastes valuable space, which you could use to engage your prospects or put them in a frame of mind that makes them ready to purchase from you.

A headline *must* be included in the first screen. It is the most important component of a webpage. Consider how pointless it would be for a newspaper to have no headline. A website without a headline is just as pointless, yet it's remarkable how many websites fail to put a headline in this prime selling space.

In my years of surfing the web, I've observed that the majority of commercial websites that do have headlines have weak, uninteresting ones, and, as a result, they are missing a critical opportunity to attract and retain website visitors.

When I wrote the copy for 1MinuteCure.com, I used the headline "How a Simple Formula Has Been Scientifically Proven to Cure Cancer and Virtually All Diseases," followed by the subheadline "Why this one-minute therapy is being suppressed in the U.S. while more than 15,000 European doctors have been using it to heal millions of patients." (See Figure 1.4.) This headline calls out to a target audience: those who are interested in discovering a cure for cancer. A headline that calls out to a specific target audience—and utilizes a specific angle—is one way to capture the attention of the web visitor effectively. Contrariwise, when you call out to everyone—or use an angle that is too broad—you often call out to no one.

Case in point: It is interesting to note that the original headline that I wrote for the product in question was as follows: "How a Simple Formula Has Been Scientifically Proven to Cure Virtually All Diseases." Notice that the headline calls out to a wide audience and does not specifically name cancer as one of the diseases that can be cured. That original headline generated only lukewarm interest. It was only when I utilized specificity and employed the cancer angle that the headline riveted the most attention. In fact, just by inserting three words ("Cure Cancer and"), the revised headline outpulled the original one by a factor of seven.

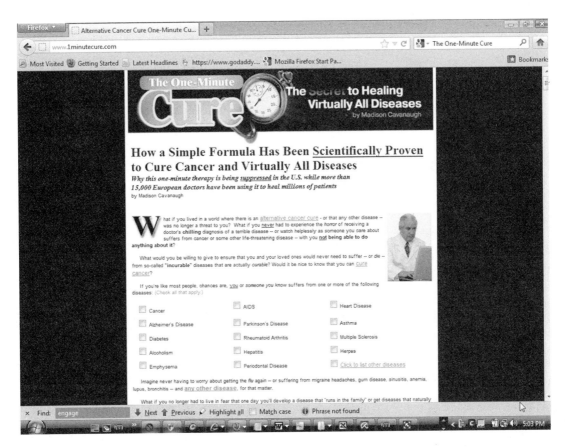

FIGURE 1.4 Targeted headline captures attention.

With regard to the body copy, I began with a series of questions:

What if you lived in a world where cancer—or any other disease—was no longer a threat to you?

What if you never had to experience the horror of receiving a doctor's chilling diagnosis of a terrible disease—or watch helplessly as someone you care about suffers from cancer or some other life-threatening disease—with you not being able to do anything about it?

Questions are a powerful way to engage your prospects or readers. That's because whenever you ask a question, the brain is compelled to answer it. Readers are more likely to believe an idea that their brain seems to have come up with on its own than an idea that is presented from outside.

Never underestimate the power of your reader's imagination. Compare the impact of the following two examples (one a question and one a statement) that I tested on my website, WebCopywritingUniversity.com:

1. What if there was a way you could convert 15 percent, 25 percent—even 50 percent or more—of your website visitors into customers; how much more money would you earn as a result?
2. Your business can convert 15 percent, 25 percent—even 50 percent or more—of your website visitors into customers and earn a lot of money.

Notice that the statement makes a claim that a reader may or may not believe. Contrast that with the question, which introduces the possibility of an ideal scenario and allows the brain to draw its own conclusions and paint its own pictures.

I like to use "What if . . ." questions or "Imagine what would happen if . . ." or "Think back . . ." That way, you let your readers envision the scene for themselves. According to Robert Collier, publisher and author of several books, most notable of which is *The Robert Collier Letter Book* (Robert Collier Publications, 2000), which many consider the bible for writing sales letters, "The reader colors that mental picture with his own imagination, which is more potent than all the brushes of all the world's artists." The things that people imagine about your product or service often exceed the reality.

WEB COPY DOs AND DON'Ts

Do strive to write in a conversational style. The more friendly and approachable, the better.

Do use contractions. When people talk, they frequently use contractions. It's intimate, and it increases readership. Use "I've" instead of "I have," "it's" instead of "it is," "we'll" instead of "we will."

Do use common colloquialisms. When you use colloquialisms, you draw your reader closer because you appear more familiar, more friendly, more up close and personal instead of distant and at arm's length.

Use colloquialisms that are understandable to most people who have a reasonable familiarity with the English language. Some colloquialisms that have found their way into mainstream online communications include:

dough	money
slam dunk	a sure thing
laid-back	calm, relaxed
make waves	cause trouble
bent out of shape	become upset
broke	having little or no money
come up for air	take a break
cool	great
twenty grand	$20,000 (fifty grand for $50,000, a hundred grand for $100,000, etc.)
keep your cool	remain calm
blown away	greatly impressed, amazed, surprised
megabucks	a lot of money
blow a fuse	lose your temper
bummed	depressed
con	deceive
has deep pockets	has a good source of money
glitzy	fancy
honcho	boss
get a kick out of	enjoy

Avoid using colloquialisms that might cause misunderstandings. Because the Internet is international, some colloquialisms such as "table a proposal" (postpone the discussion) or "the presentation bombed" (the presentation was a complete failure), which are generally understood by most Americans, may mean something completely different to non-Americans. You should also avoid using regional or locally based colloquialisms and slang, as they frequently are misunderstood by Americans from other parts of the country as well as non-Americans.

Don't use corporate jargon (also called corporatespeak), as it may communicate very little to anyone outside a particular industry.

Consider the following two examples written for a fictitious online business called My Web Store:

1. My Web Store is an e-commerce solutions provider committed to helping people leverage the power of technology to create value-added, win-win cyberspaces that impact global retail markets.
2. My Web Store is a first-of-its-kind form of e-commerce that enables anyone to open a 24/7 online store in as little as five minutes—for just $1 a day.

Which statement are web visitors more likely to understand? The second, of course. The first employs highfalutin jargon instead of clear, straightforward words and phrases that people can understand. Even if you read it several times, you'd still be wondering what it's trying to say. Corporatespeak such as this constitutes a blatant failure to communicate effectively. Contrast that with example 2, which immediately communicates a clear benefit, singularity, ease, and economy—everything a prospective customer wants to know.

In direct-response marketing, if no one understands what you're saying, no one will buy what you're selling. Therefore, avoid corporatespeak and opt for clear, uncomplicated language.

Do use strategically placed testimonials. Testimonials are a powerful sales tool, whether you're selling online or offline. To apply testimonials successfully when selling online, they need to be positioned strategically throughout the website. An ideal place to position a powerful testimonial is very early on the webpage, preferably in the first or second screen. In that position, the testimonial puts a blanket of credibility on the rest of the copy. (See Figure 1.5.)

Ringing Cedars, a publishing company offering a series of books that has sold over 10 million copies without the benefit of advertising, uses dynamically generated testimonials on its website, displaying a different testimonial every time any webpage on the website is refreshed or reloaded. Web visitors are therefore presented with ever-changing testimonials every time they visit the website or click through to other webpages within the website.

It's also important to sprinkle testimonials strategically throughout your

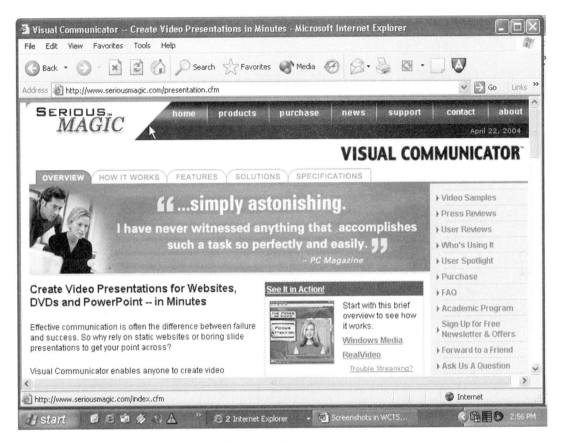

FIGURE 1.5 Powerful testimonial from *PC Magazine* in the first screen.

web copy, especially in areas where they reinforce your selling arguments. Testimonials are also particularly useful in your order form, right before you ask for the order (before your call to action), and in your order confirmation e-mail (to reinforce the sale).

Don't try to impress your readers with your fancy vocabulary. Effective copywriting isn't about making grandiose claims. It is about communicating in a way that people can easily understand.

Don't be pompous. Let the testimonials make you look good. People online don't like marketese or bragging, boastful language.

READING ON THE WEB

How do people read on the web? According to Jakob Nielsen, author of *Homepage Usability: 50 Websites Deconstructed* (Pearson, 2001) and holder of 71 patents relating to making the Internet easier to use, "They don't."

Yes, you read that correctly. People don't read online. They scan.

Nielsen, together with John Morkes, director of the Human-Computer Interaction Group at Trilogy Software and, like Nielsen, a usability expert, conducted several scientific studies about reading and writing on the web. They discovered that people read webpages very differently than printed pages. In 1997, they reported that the majority (79 percent) skim webpages quickly (stopping only when something interesting catches their eye); only 16 percent read everything word for word. This corroborates the more recent tests conducted by the Poynter Institute for Media Studies in July 2007; using eye-tracking equipment on 600 participants from 18 to 60 years old, these tests found that most readers are indeed scanners.

This is very important to those of us who write web copy or sell on the web. It indicates that writing successful web copy means writing scannable web copy.

Five Ways to Write Scannable Copy

1. Use bulleted lists to summarize content.
2. Highlight (by using **bold** or *italic* fonts or by <u>underlining</u>) selected keywords to help scanners move through your web copy.
3. Write meaningful subheads.
4. Present one idea per paragraph.
5. Use the inverted pyramid style of writing; that is, present key points and conclusions first, followed by less important information and background material.

Exercise: Using your scroll bar, scan through a website. Is the copy inviting to read? Does it incorporate elements that make it scannable and engaging—or does it have huge blocks of text that discourage you from reading further? How many times does something in your copy catch your eye and cause you to read something of interest? Make your copy more scannable by applying the five suggested techniques.

Bonus idea: Use text boxes to feature interesting anecdotes, stories, testimonials, and case histories and to further break up your web copy into readable, bite-size chunks.

Think about how you read a sales letter that comes in the mail. It's three-dimensional, and it exists in a spatial realm, whereas a webpage is two-dimensional—it's in a flat realm. Whether you realize it or not, you write in a manner suitable for the printed page, not the web, because that's the medium you are accustomed to. There are big differences.

Imagine you have a multiple-page sales letter in your hands. You can view an entire page in one glance; you can shuffle through or skim through the pages quickly; you can go straight to the order form or the last page to read the P.S. (the P.S. is the second-most-read part of a sales letter because people can get to it in a second). Now look at a webpage—you see only one screen, which is just a fraction of a page, at a time. You don't have the luxury of shuffling through the pages. The best you can do is use the scroll bar or a mouse click to go from page to page.

Do you see why you can't simply take offline copywriting principles and apply them to the web?

WORDS TELL, EMOTION SELLS

People's emotions are the primary motivating factors for buying. People buy on emotion and justify their purchases with logic. Both on and off the web, a strong copy platform is built on proven emotional drivers such as anger, exclusivity, fear, greed, guilt, and salvation, to name a few.

Take a look at the first screen of the 24 Techniques for Closing the Sale website (Figure 1.6). Notice that good web copy starts with a dramatic promise.

Headline: These Ain't Your Granddaddy's Closing Techniques, Boy!

Subheadline: These are 24 of the most ruthless tactics—kept under wraps for years—that can turn even your most hard-nosed prospects into cash-generating customers.

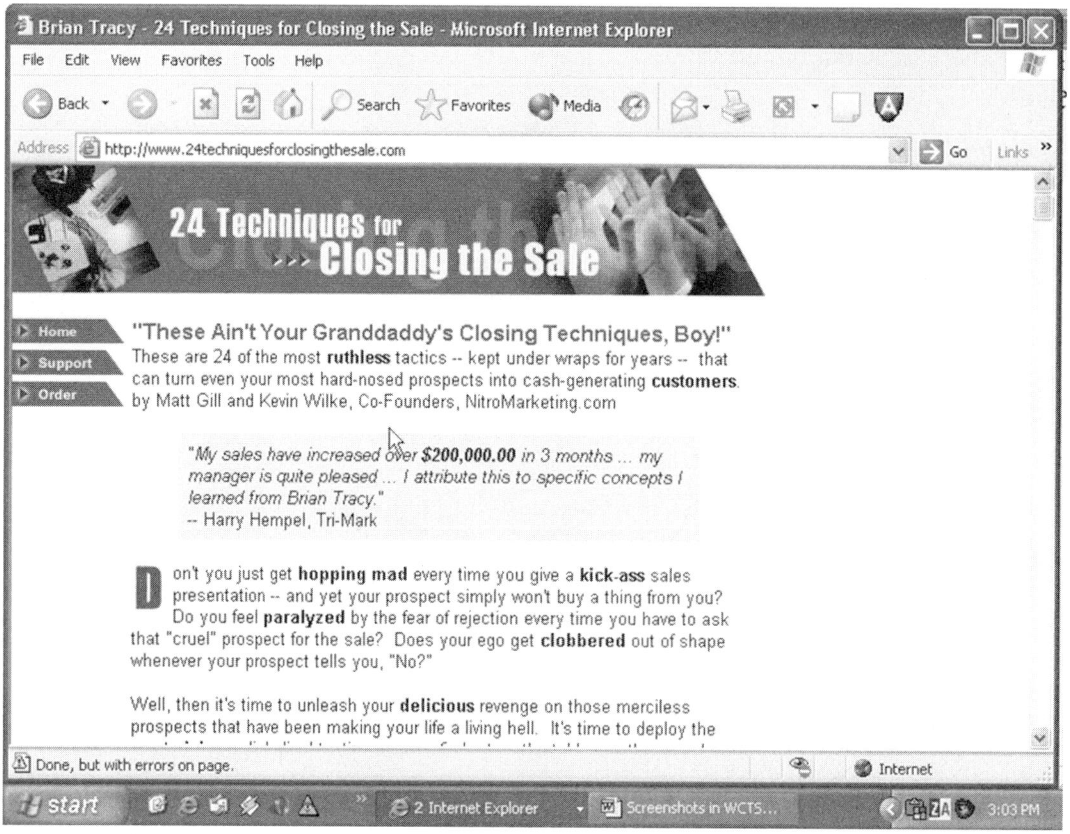

FIGURE 1.6 Screen shot of the 24 Techniques for Closing the Sale website.

The purpose of the headline—and, to a certain extent, the subheadline—is to offer compelling information, solve a problem, take away pain, help someone achieve a goal, and fulfill a desire. Conversational language that sounds the way people do helps crank up the emotional volume.

The language used on this website carries the emotional intensity of the headline through to its opening paragraph:

Don't you just get **hopping mad** every time you give a **kick-ass** sales presentation—and yet your prospect simply won't buy a thing from you? Do you feel **paralyzed** by the fear of rejection every time you have to ask that "cruel" prospect for the sale? Does your ego get **clobbered** out of shape whenever your prospect tells you, "No"?

The copy leads the target audience (salespeople) through the excruciating agony of the traditional sales process, a process with which they are all too familiar. It builds the selling proposition on the reader's emotions so that the reader feels the pain and begins to beg for the benefits promised in the headline and subheadline.

Consider the following headlines that I recently found on websites:

How to Stop Your Divorce
Even When Your Spouse Wants Out of Your Marriage

What Will You Do When Creditors Try to Seize Your Assets
to Collect on Debts You Owe Them?
Is Your Personal Property at Risk?

Both headlines appeal to the reader's fear of loss—one of the greatest motivators. The fact is, people generally go to greater lengths to keep from losing what they have than to gain something of the same (or greater) value. The old sales adage "Fear of loss is greater than the desire for gain" is as true online as it is in offline selling situations.

I recently saw a pop-up ad that shocked the living daylights out of me. The pop-up looked like an Instant Message box and had a shadowy image of a man as the inset picture, with the caption "Mr. Hacker." Underneath the picture were these words:

I read your e-mails. I pay with your credit card number. I transfer money from your account to mine.

I felt the blood drain from my face and my body went cold all over as I read and reread the words. The shock finally wore off when I realized that it was an advertisement for an antispyware program—and I would have bought the program if I hadn't already had one on my computer. That's an excellent, albeit extreme, use of the fear-of-loss motivator.

HOW TO BECOME A GREAT WEB COPYWRITER IN FIVE HOURS OR LESS

Perhaps you've heard of the concept of modeling success. If you want to achieve success at anything, the fastest way to do it is by modeling the strategies of those who are already successful at it. That way, you take something complex and synthesize it into its essence so you can use it immediately.

You've probably heard of real estate agents going into selling mode by constantly repeating to themselves, "I'm going to sell this house." Annette Bening did this so well in her portrayal of a Realtor in the movie *American Beauty*. Successful real estate agents start off with the mindset that the sale is already made. Model the strategy that successful people use to be successful.

In web copywriting, the best way to model success is to select a website that you admire greatly and that you know has produced tons of sales for its owner. Start copying it by hand. *Write the entire sales letter out in your own handwriting*. Write it out two or three times over the next week. Depending on how fast you write, this will take roughly five hours—less if you write quickly or if the sales letter you choose is short.

This takes a lot of discipline, not to mention time, but I assure you, it is worth the effort. You will not know the value of this until you do it. It's positively eye-opening. I learned this technique from Ted Nicholas, a renowned direct marketer, copywriter, and author of several books, including *Magic Words That Bring You Riche$* (Nicholas Direct, 1998).

Once you write this sales letter over and over again, you will start internalizing the wording, the phraseology, the rhythm, even the mindset of the person who wrote the copy. Your brain assimilates it, and you practically step into the mind of the writer. This is by far the best modeling exercise I've found for accelerating web copywriting skills.

Next time you sit down to write web copy, the wording, the phrasing, and even part of the writer's thought process will have become a part of you, and you will find that it becomes much easier to sit down and begin flowing right into a winning sales piece.

CHAPTER 2

A SIMPLE BLUEPRINT FOR WRITING KILLER WEB COPY

Internalize the Golden Rule of sales that says, "All things being equal, people will do business with, and refer business to, those people they know, like, and trust."

—BOB BURG

Before you write one word of copy, you must first

- Know your *objective.*
- Know your *target audience.*
- Know the *product or service.*

Your objective: What are you trying to accomplish? What response are you trying to obtain? Your objective might not be to make a sale but, rather, to get your reader to send for free information or to get your reader to sign up for your mailing list. Or your objective might be to sell your product or service.

Your target audience: The more you know about your target audience, the easier it is to convince them that they need your product or service. The

FIGURE 2.1 This targeted headline calls out to a specific audience.

more specific your knowledge of your target audience is, the better. Let's say you are selling a book on weight loss. Your target audience is overweight people, but you might fine-tune that to target overweight people whose jobs revolve around computer work and who have no time to work out, let alone go to the gym. This is the target audience of a website that sells a book titled *Megabolic Weight Loss*. (See Figure 2.1.)

Your product or service: After identifying the audience to whom you are writing, it's essential to know the product or service about which you're writing. Immerse yourself in it. The five Ws of journalism are a handy tool to use for this: What? Why? Where? When? Who? and the bonus How? Before you begin writing, ask yourself:

What is the product or service? What is it made of?
Why was it invented or developed?

Where did it originate?

When was it discovered?

Who invented or discovered it?

How is it made?

Learn everything you can about your product or service. Uncover the benefits of owning your product or using your service. Only after you identify your objective, familiarize yourself with your target audience, and know your product or service thoroughly is it time to start writing.

CREATING THE BLUEPRINT: FIVE SIMPLE QUESTIONS YOU MUST ASK

I've distilled the entire web copywriting process into five easy steps that make the task of writing web copy as easy as pie—and as enjoyable. Each step in the blueprint takes the form of a question. Once you answer each of the five questions about any product or service, you'll have the blueprint, a miniversion of your web copy. Note: As you are answering these five questions, *don't get creative.* Just answer factually. We'll get creative later.

Question 1: What Is the Problem?

Most sales, both online and offline, are based primarily on solving a problem. Having identified your target audience, your job now is to identify the problem that your target audience has that can be solved by your product or service. In copywriting terms these are known as the *three Ps*—pain, problem, or predicament.

This is where you play doctor. You diagnose the problem. The people in your target audience may not even know they have a problem, so it is your job to make them recognize it. Many web copywriters and marketers shove the solution down their viewers' throats before their readers recognize that there is a problem. That's like a doctor prescribing medicine before you feel sick.

There's another aspect to it as well. Once your audience understands that they have a problem, you have to let them know that you understand their problem. There's an old saying that goes something like this: "People don't care how much you know until they know how much you care."

Step 1: Write down your target audience's problem. A few sentences will do. Your reader must be able to say, "Hey, she really understands my problem," or "He reads me like a book," or "She knows me so well it's as though she's been eavesdropping on my conversations or reading my mail." That's why I keep emphasizing that before you write a word of copy, you have to know your audience.

Question 2: Why Hasn't the Problem Been Solved?

Extending the doctor metaphor, this is where you further identify the history of the problem, predicament, or pain and look into the previous remedies or solutions that have been attempted but failed. As you progress through all five steps of this blueprint, you'll begin to see how the answer(s) to this question serves to build your audience's anticipation about a new solution you're about to reveal.

Step 2: Write down the reason(s) why the problem continues, persists, or lingers. How is it that they haven't solved their problem, and why are they still stuck in the rut? Again, a few factual sentences will do.

Question 3: What Is Possible?

In coaching, this is called *possibility thinking.* This is where you set the stage for what life could be like and what could happen when your audience's problem, pain, or predicament is eliminated. You must go beyond stating the obvious. "The pain in your lower back will disappear" is not enough. You must draw a picture of what is possible now that the pain is gone. "You will be able to engage in activities [*specify activities*] you were unable to engage in because of your back pain," or "You can accomplish all your goals and dreams because the pain is no longer there to stop you." This is the dramatic promise.

Step 3: Write down what's possible. Paint a picture of the way things will be when your prospect's problems are solved. Again, a few sentences will do.

Question 4: What Is Different Now?

How will things change for your prospects? This is where you explain who you are and how your product or service can help them, as well as what's different about your product or service that will eliminate their problem. This is where your *unique selling proposition* (USP) comes in. A USP is something that sets you, your product or service, or your business apart from every other competitor in a favorable way. It's the competitive advantage that you proclaim to your prospects, customers, or clients.

> *Step 4: Write a few sentences about what differentiates your product/service.* Present just the substance—not the details.

Question 5: What Should You Do Now?

If you answered the first four questions and established your objective, you know what the answer to this question is. You simply tell your viewers to do what you started out wanting them to do—that is, to sign up, pick up the phone, register, opt in, or buy the product or service you're selling.

> *Step 5: State clearly what you want your prospect to do.* This is the call to action.

There you have it. Once you have answered the five questions, you have the blueprint for building your web copy. You now have the structure; all you have to do is decorate it. The fact is, with this blueprint alone, you can make some sales.

The Anatomy of the Blueprint

Recently, I had the opportunity to observe a business acquaintance named Ralph, a personal development coach, generate leads for his services during a Chamber of Commerce networking event. I noticed how successfully he was able to interest several people in his coaching services in such a small amount of time, so I took a closer look at how he could accomplish this with just a few words to each prospect. It didn't take long to realize that his sales pitch was nothing more than skillfully weaving the five steps of the blueprint into casual conversation. His conversations went something like this:

PROSPECT: What kind of work do you do, Ralph?

RALPH: I'm a personal development coach.

PROSPECT: Hmmm . . . what exactly is that?

RALPH: Let me ask you a question: Are there three things you'd like to accomplish in your life right now that for some reason or other you haven't been able to accomplish yet?

PROSPECT: Sure. I think I can think of more than three things.

RALPH: Why do you think you haven't been able to accomplish them?

PROSPECT: [*Answers vary from person to person. They range from "I haven't focused enough attention on accomplishing them" to "I have an unsupportive boss/spouse/family" to "I can't seem to find the time or energy to devote to them" to "I'm stuck in a rut and I'm still trying to figure my way out of it," and so on.*]

RALPH: What if you were able to eliminate [*here, Ralph reiterates the challenge the prospect mentioned for not accomplishing his or her goals*]; how would your life change?

PROSPECT: [*Again, answers to this question vary from person to person. "Why, I'd be able to spend more time with my family, and that would make me happy," or "I'd be able to work less and earn more," or "I'd have the money to buy a house/send my kids to college/go on more vacations," etc.*]

RALPH: What if I told you I have a unique approach to help you take care of [*again, Ralph names the prospect's problem*], which will help get you from where you are now to where you want to be—not in a few years, but within the next 60 to 90 days? Would you be interested in a 15-minute free consultation to find out how I can do that for you?

PROSPECT: Sure, why not?

At this point, Ralph takes his business card out of his pocket and asks what day and time would suit the prospect for the free consultation. When the prospect answers, Ralph writes the appointment on the card and hands the card to the prospect, telling the prospect to call him at the appointed date and time. He then turns the card over and points to a diagram on the back.

RALPH: Right before you call me, I'd like you to do something fun. I'd like you to do this quick exercise here, tell me what your answer is when you call me, and I'll explain what your answer means.

PROSPECT [*looking at the card*]: Okay, you got it. I'll call you then.

Do you see what Ralph did? He managed to get a prospect interested in his services in a matter of one or two minutes, and he generated a lead that might eventually turn into a client, which, of course, was his objective.

Let's examine the conversation more closely to see how it relates to our blueprint. When prospects ask Ralph about his work, Ralph uses it as an opportunity to identify their problems (step 1). Instead of making an educated guess about what their problem(s) might be, he makes the prospects identify their problems by asking them to think of the top three things they have yet to accomplish. Then he asks why they haven't been able to accomplish them (step 2), and the prospects give specific reasons. Ralph next asks the "What if . . ." question; that is, he makes prospects imagine how life would be different if the problem(s) were eliminated (step 3). After his prospects answer the question, Ralph mentions his unique approach to helping them take care of the problem(s) so they can get from where they are in life to where they want to be in the next 60 to 90 days (step 4). This is followed up with an offer of a free 15-minute phone consultation at an appointed date and time (step 5). The fun exercise on the back of the card is a device Ralph employs to make sure prospects call him and to minimize no-shows.

Ralph's networking sales pitch is one small example of just how powerful the blueprint is. When you are able to successfully identify your prospect's problem and explain why the problem hasn't been solved, what's possible, what's different now, and what the prospect should do now, you have the basis of a successful sales pitch in a nutshell. Although the blueprint works exceedingly well on the Internet, where web buyers' attention is difficult to capture, it can be applied to almost any situation that requires a direct response, both online or offline—from an "elevator speech" to a full-scale sales presentation.

Are you beginning to see how powerful the blueprint is? Do you think you can answer these five questions for any product or service you want to sell? If you answered yes, you're already a web copywriter.

Outstanding web copy starts with the five-step blueprint. Now let's examine how a website started out as a blueprint, was fleshed out into six pages of web copy that sold several hundred thousand dollars' worth of a product in a few months, and continues to sell to this day. The product is a $27 e-book that shows Internet entrepreneurs how to get free money from the government to start, grow, or expand their Internet businesses. The author is Matthew Lesko, who has written more than 100 books (including two *New York Times* bestsellers) showing everyday people how to get grants and free money from U.S. government sources. Before we look at the web copy, we'll take a look at the five-step blueprint upon which the copy was built:

Step 1. What's the problem? Internet entrepreneurs like you need money to start, grow, or expand your business.

Step 2. Why hasn't the problem been solved? Loans and financing for Internet businesses are hard to come by or qualify for. Free money programs, such as government grants, are neither advertised nor generally publicized—therefore, very few people know about them. The few who are aware of them lack the specialized knowledge of how to successfully obtain the free money.

Step 3. What's possible? Now you can get as much money as you need for your Internet business—and you don't have to pay it back.

Step 4. What's different now? The real trick is in knowing how to ask for the money. Matthew Lesko has developed a completely legal and ingenious secret formula that works every time. He discovered the secret formula because for the past 30 years he has specialized in uncovering obscure government programs that most ordinary citizens know nothing about.

Step 5. What should you do now? Get the e-book that shows you step-by-step how to get the free money to which you're entitled.

That's it! End of blueprint.

Now take a look at the website at www.FreeStuffForEntrepreneursOnThe Internet.com, shown in Figure 2.2., to see how the blueprint was fleshed out into a compelling six-page web copy piece that sells.

Every piece of web copy that I've written follows the same sequence and development set forth in the blueprint. Years of copywriting have made me instinctively structure my sales copy in that logical sequence. It wasn't always that way. When I first started writing copy, I would force-feed my brain with all manner of clever, innovative ways to craft my sales proposition—and usually ended up with volumes of words, research, and web copy that I later had to spend hours (sometimes days) chiseling down to a lean, mean selling machine. In other words, I was doing everything backward.

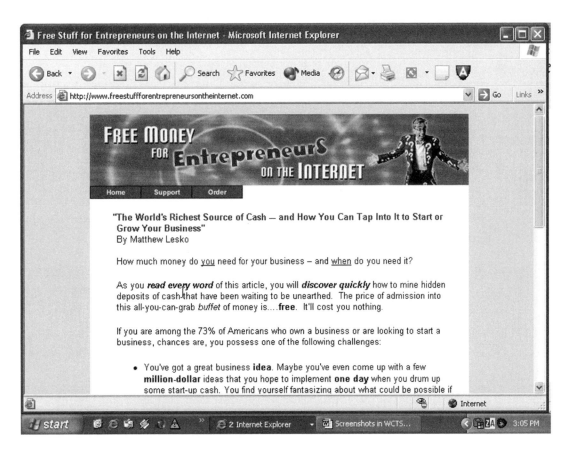

FIGURE 2.2 A fleshed-out version of the blueprint.

Then I devised this blueprint that made web copywriting a breeze. It is a loose adaptation of an executive summary template developed by my colleague and friend Alex Mandossian, a marketing consultant, copywriter, and CEO of Heritage House Publishing, Inc. I realized that if I started with this blueprint and fleshed it out only as necessary, I came up with the same quality of web copy that I'd been producing for years, but, using the blueprint, I slashed as much as 80 percent off the time it took to write copy.

When you model success, you need to model the strategy, not the result (meaning you don't mimic someone else's writing style; you simply use the technique). The blueprint is one of the most important strategies that I can teach you. In my opinion, if you follow it, it's almost impossible to experience writer's block—and you won't have to put on the "writer's hat," so to speak. You won't struggle to be creative or clever or amusing or profound. You just write down the facts. Later, during the fleshing-out phase, you make those facts come alive.

This five-step blueprint is the "formula" that facilitates the process of writing web copy. The Trifecta Neuro-Affective Principle (see Chapter 6) works in tandem with this blueprint and often makes this blueprint write itself. If you prefer to write short copy as opposed to the long copy often associated with direct-response types of websites, go directly to Chapter 6 now. But if you prefer to write long, fully fleshed-out copy, read on.

PUTTING THE BLUEPRINT TO WORK: FIVE EASY STEPS TO MAKING YOUR WEB COPY SELL

Let's suppose you've written down the five steps of the blueprint: You've identified the problem, you've described what's possible, you've established why the problem hasn't been solved, you've established what's changed, and you've suggested what action should be taken. What have you got? Is this your web copy? Obviously not, but it is the heart and soul—the framework—for writing web copy.

Some people will buy simply based on your answers to those five questions, but to get *most* people to buy, you must flesh out the blueprint until it becomes a virtual salesperson who sells for you day and night, 24/7, weekends and holidays, 365 days a year, without a vacation or sick leave.

You have created your blueprint. How do you build your house? As with the blueprint, there are five steps you need to take to flesh it out and make readers respond.

Step 1: Inject Emotion

I don't care how wonderful your vocabulary or how excellent your grammar is, if your words lack emotion, you won't sell a thing unless you can appeal to an emotion. Remember, people *buy on emotion and justify with logic.*

There are many ways to inject emotion. Here are a few examples:

- Does it frustrate you that your business is making only a small fraction of its profit potential?
- Don't you just get hopping mad every time you give a kick-ass sales presentation and your prospect *still* won't buy a thing from you?
- Do you suffer from feelings of isolation or of being left behind—and worry that you're doomed to a lonely, unmarried life?
- Does your impending foreclosure make you feel like a failure, like the world is closing in on you—and so overwhelmed and depressed that you wish you were dead?
- How outraged would you be to realize that 539,835 people die of cancer every year—including some of your friends and relatives—when there's a safe, natural, yet virtually unknown alternative that could have saved the lives of 95 percent of them?

Injecting Emotion into What's Possible

- Can you imagine what your life would be like if all your debts were paid and you had triple-A credit?
- How would you like it if your business earned a five-figure income every month—even while the economy is on a downswing?
- What would it mean if you were the featured guest of popular radio and TV shows? Imagine thousands—potentially millions—of people hearing your story.

It's seven o'clock Monday morning. You're not really looking forward to another **grueling** week of selling, so you turn on your computer. While you **sip your morning coffee,** you watch Brian Tracy on RealVideo giving you 24 Techniques for Closing the Sale in 63 minutes flat.

It's now 8:03 A.M., and you're feeling **unstoppable** and positively **empowered** because Brian Tracy has just given you a personal coaching session that got you **charged up** with everything you need **to get those sales.**

The next moment, you're out the door. You talk to your first prospect, and moments later you make your first sale with the **greatest of ease.** Feeling **high** on your victory, you go on to your next prospect, and, again within moments, you've got another sale in your pocket. No sweat! This goes on all day long, and you **surprisingly** find yourself smiling all the time. Gone are the stress and fear that you used to have—and in their place is a deep-seated confidence that you can **win over** any prospect you speak to. It's never been this easy!

Then, toward the end of the day, you pick up the phone to set up your future appointments. Every single prospect you call says yes, they'd be happy to see you or talk to you this week.

You think to yourself, "If only every day could be like this . . . why, I might just earn a **six-figure income** this year."

Could this really happen to you? Don't be surprised if it does.

FIGURE 2.3

Figure 2.3 illustrates a device I call the *emotional scenario*. It paints a vivid picture of what it would be like for the reader to experience your product or service.

An emotional scenario such as this one accomplishes several things:

- It connects your reader to your product or service on an *emotional* level. Emotion sells.
- It assumes that the sale is already made.

- It allows the reader to take ownership of the product and have a *virtual experience* of it with excellent results.

Oftentimes, what you're really selling is the *emotional experience,* sometimes even more so than the product or service itself. This is explained in more detail in the section titled "The Cyrano Effect" (see Chapter 5).

Step 2: Add Bullet Points, Bonuses, Guarantee, and Close

The formula for writing bullets is first to state the benefit and then follow up by painting a picture of how your viewer's life will change when he or she gets that benefit—or by elevating the desirability of that benefit by injecting emotion, drama, or intrigue. Bullets need to be powerful and tight.

Mouthwatering Bullets
Here are examples of great bullets (the first is an example of injecting emotion, drama, or intrigue; the second paints a picture):

- Our revolutionary tutoring technology improves your child's math skills at least two grade levels higher than his or her present grade level. Imagine how confident your child will be when he finally realizes that math is easy—and how proud it will make you!
- How a self-made millionaire invented this irresistible tactic. It virtually eliminates the need to close the sale because the sale will close itself for you—like a ripe apple dropping out of a tree into your hand.

I learned how to write bullets by studying and writing out by hand the bullets of great copywriters. You can do the same.

Bonuses
It is a widely accepted belief in direct marketing that significantly more sales are generated by an offer that includes a free bonus or gift. Although there aren't scientific studies that support this belief, it stands to reason that receiving attractive incentives creates a significantly greater desire to purchase the core product.

It is not uncommon for people to buy a product primarily because of the freebies they get by buying it. "Gifts with purchase" have become a staple at cosmetics counters everywhere because they significantly encourage impulse buying. Obviously, the bonus or gift must be desirable to the target audience and must relate in some way to the product or service being offered. If it has a dollar value worth noting, you should also mention that.

Free bonuses or gifts are particularly powerful when attached to a deadline for ordering, because the deadline injects urgency. You need to set a deadline to compel the reader to respond immediately instead of putting off the buying decision. That's where a dynamic date script is helpful. This is a small script that advances the deadline date displayed on your webpage every day. When people read your web copy, it looks something like this:

> When you order the Memory Foam mattress pad by Friday, December 28, 2012, you will also receive two (2) Memory Foam pillows absolutely free. These pillows are sold separately for $89.00 apiece, but they're yours *free* when you purchase a Memory Foam mattress now.

The day and date advance by one every day, automatically updating your deadline. Dynamic date scripts are widely available for free from various script sources on the web. You simply decide how many days into the future you'd like your prospect to act on your offer, and any web developer or programmer (or anyone who's familiar with html) can simply insert that into the script and install the code into your webpage.

Guarantees

Often, the sale is made with the promise of a money-back guarantee. This is where you eliminate the risk to the buyer and remove any remaining obstacles to making a sale.

The Close

Just because you have presented your offer doesn't mean your prospect will buy what you've offered. You have to close the sale. It's no different from visiting a store and looking at a product you are interested in buying; even after all your questions have been answered, until a salesperson closes the sale with a question like "How would you like to pay for that?" the sale isn't made unless you happen to be a highly motivated buyer, determined to buy that item then and there.

Before you ever ask for that order, it's essential that the prospect be primed for the close. The sequence of presenting copy elements (and hot buttons) is crucial. Unlike a store, where the price is out there for the buyer to see, in your web copy you must wait until the end to reveal the price and ordering instructions. This puts your reader in the proper frame of mind to buy, because by the time you present the price, you have laid out all the benefits and information your prospect needs. This is another way to keep the editorial feel of your web copy and not reveal your sales pitch too soon.

This is one of the reasons I generally do not put an Order button on the left navigation bar of websites over which I have total control. If I've gone to a lot of trouble to make my web copy look like an editorial, I don't want to ruin that by putting an Order button on the first screen, thereby removing all doubt that the editorial is actually an ad in disguise.

Another reason is that many web visitors click on the Order button even before reading the web copy because they want to know what they are getting themselves into and whether or not they want what you're offering. If they click before they read, the order page then determines whether visitors read your web copy or not. It defeats the purpose of your copy, which is to use its power to get readers happily involved with your product or service.

In addition, an Order button allows people to make a judgment about the price before knowing the details of your offer. If I had an Order button on my Web Copywriting University website, for instance, and you clicked on it and found that my audio course costs $297, would you read my web copy? The bottom line is, few people are predisposed to spend that much money until they understand the value of what they are getting for that investment.

One of the major mistakes website owners make is that they fail to close the sale. They go to great lengths to get people to visit their websites, and they do everything possible to make a compelling selling argument about their product or service, but at the last moment, when the prospect is just about ready to buy, they drop the ball and fail to ask for the order. Internet marketers who are reluctant to ask for the order are usually among the unsuccessful ones. For any offer to be successful, you must be clear and explicit when you ask for the order. Include every detail, even those that seem obvious to you. Make it easy for the prospect to buy.

What Does It Take to Close a Sale?

Online or offline, simply asking for the order does not close the sale. "Click here to order" or a similar phrase does not constitute a close. As a rule, web visitors click on the Order button only after you have done the necessary steps to close the sale. If you haven't given enough information, you haven't closed the sale. Period.

Closing the sale starts on the home page or sales landing page—usually as early as the first or second screen. Those of you who have sold offline know that clinching the sale often takes several trial closes leading up to the final close. Just like a real-life salesperson, your website should contain trial closes. If you look at the website shown in Figure 2.4, you'll see that I used eight closes to sell the *Sculptor 3* software program.

You must always remember that people's *buying decision times vary*. Some people are ready to buy after they have found a benefit or two, and some aren't ready to buy until they've read every word on the website. For this reason, you have to catch them at every point at which they're likely to buy.

Step 3: Add Credibility-Building Elements

If you've immersed yourself in your product or service, you have probably un-covered testimonials, interesting stories or case studies, significant facts, quotes, or statistics related to your product or service. If for some reason you haven't, you can do speedy research on the web to fill in the gaps.

Again, for examples of these all you have to do is take a look at my web copywriting samples—particularly the ones enclosed in text boxes. See the stories that pull people in, the testimonials that support and strengthen the selling proposition, the interesting stories that both inform and whet my readers' appetites for what I have to offer, and so on. For specific examples, go to www.real medicalhelp.com, www.TheHealingCode.com/mv, www.PsychologicalTriggers .com, www.1MinuteCure.com, www.FreeStuffForEntrepreneursOnTheInternet .com, and www.Top10CancerCures.com.

8 Trial Closes (and 1 Final Close) Were Used to Sell *Sculptor 3*
Note: Underlined words are text links that lead to the order page.

1) I've shown you how *Sculptor 3* uses computerization to literally immerse you in 7 of the top manifesting technologies simultaneously—and materialize your desires faster than you ever thought possible. Now, it's time for you to <u>act on this</u>.

2) Well, the good news is that you can own *Sculptor 3* for less than $100! Yes, that's right. Valuable as it is, *Sculptor 3* can be yours for a one-time investment of just $97 (USD). If you're in a hurry and can't wait to get started, click here to <u>experience *Sculptor 3* now</u>.

3) <u>Get started</u> creating your ideal life now.

4) So you have nothing to lose when you <u>give it a try</u> today. Within minutes, you will get download instructions, and you can start enjoying the benefits of *Sculptor 3* immediately.

5) To give you an even better value on your *Sculptor 3* investment, you'll also get 7 FREE gifts valued at $127 when you order <u>right now</u>.

6) Remember, I can't guarantee that you'll receive the 7 FREE gifts above unless you order *Sculptor 3* right now.

7) With *Sculptor 3*, you don't have to learn anything. Instead, it can do all the work for you—making it easy to apply manifesting principles to your life and helping you get what you want the easy and effective way. <u>Get started now</u>.

8) Imagine ... in as little as a few days or weeks, you could be manifesting the life you've always dreamed of. Imagine being totally debt-free, enjoying improved health ... happy and loving relationships ... your dream house ... all because you decided to say "YES" today.

9) Final Close:

[Click to ORDER Via Our SECURE SERVER!]

FIGURE 2.4 Several attempts to close the sale are necessary for successful web selling (www.affirmware.com.au).

Step 4: Add Psychological Devices and Involvement Devices

These are such important and complex topics that I devote all of Chapters 5, 6, and 7 to them. Among the topics we examine are the following:

- Persuasion devices that get people to commit to the sale such as using your readers' desire to appear consistent to themselves and others, testimonials from satisfied customers, or even your readers' emotional satisfaction, investment, and involvement in your service or product
- Psychological devices such as cliffhangers to excite your readers' sense of anticipation to get them to read every word of your copy
- Hypnotic commands that bypass your readers' conscious minds and overcome resistance, and how to embed them into your copy

- Specific words that make your web copy much more believable to your readers

Step 5: Replace Rational Words with Emotional Words

You probably have heard the concept of right-brain and left-brain functions: The left hemisphere of the brain is the rational, logical, organized, analytic, linear, critical side; the right hemisphere is the creative, emotional, intuitive side, the realm of the imagination. Since people buy on emotion, the more you appeal to the right side of the brain, the more you'll sell. You do this by using emotional words, not intellectual, rational, bland, and boring words. Here are a few examples:

Use the phrase *find out* instead of the word *learn*.
Instead of saying *accolade* use *applause*.
Use *rich* instead of *wealthy*.
Say *worried* instead of *concerned*.
Instead of saying *The following are . . .* , say *Here are . . .*

Try this: Take a look at the list of left-brain and right-brain words in Figure 2.5. Next, look at the web copy you've written, identify any left-brain (or rational) words, and replace those left-brain words with the right-brain (or emotional) words. How can I make it simpler than that?

Paul Galloway, an Internet programmer, created a neat little Common Gateway Interface (CGI) script to automatically replace all instances of left-brain (rational) words on any website with right-brain (emotional) words. A CGI script is a small program that takes data from a web server and does something with it; in this case, it replaces certain words from one database (rational words) with corresponding words from another database (emotional words).

If you go to http://www.paulgalloway.com/utilities/emotional_words.cgi and type in the URL of your website, it shows your website with all the rational words displayed in red, followed by the suggested emotional words you might want to replace them with.

Left-Brain (Rational) Words/Phrases	Right-Brain (Emotional) Words/Phrases	Left-Brain (Rational) Words/Phrases	Right-Brain (Emotional) Words/Phrases
accelerate	speed up	inform	tell
accolade	applause	intelligent	bright
additionally	here's more/there's more	I regret	I'm sorry
aid	help	jesting	joking
allow	let	large	big
anticipate	expect	learn	find out
astute	smart	manufacture	make
at an end	over	notion	idea
attractive	good looking	nude	naked
avid	eager	observed	seen
beneficial	good for	obstinate	stubborn
challenge	dare	omit	leave out
circular	round	perceive	see
combat	fight	perhaps	maybe
completed	finished	peril	danger
concerned	worried	perspiration	sweat
concerning	about	pleased	happy
construct	build	preserve	save
courageous	brave	prevent	stop
demise	death	purchase	buy
difficult	tough/hard	propitious	favorable
diminutive	small	receive	get
disclose	reveal/explain	requested	ask for
donate	give	reply	answer
elderly	old	select	pick/choose
facilitate	ease	soiled	dirty
famished	hungry	stomach	belly
fatigued	tired	strike	hit
fearful	afraid	subsequent to	since
following is/are	here's/here are	sufficient	enough
for	because	superior	better
fortunate	lucky	tardy	late
futile	hopeless	terminate	end
gratification	enjoyment	tidings	news
hasten	hurry	utilize	use
huge	giant	wealthy	rich
humorous	funny	youthful	young
ill	sick		
immediately	right now		

FIGURE 2.5 Left-brain versus right-brain expressions.

Take a look, too, at Figure 2.6, which gives a list of web words and phrases that sell.

Tip: Replace the word *if* with *when* whenever you are describing what people will get from you. This is part of assuming that the sale is made.

---

acclaimed, amazingly simple, announcing, appetizing, astonishing, automatically
booming, breakthrough
cash in, critical
discover, does the trick
easy-to-follow, enhanced, electrifying, exciting, exclusive, exponential
fantastic, fascinating, first, free
generous, good-as-gold, guaranteed
how-to
improved, incredible, initial, introducing
limited offer, love
handy, high-voltage, honest-to-goodness
immaculate, in-depth, ingenious, innovative, instantly, intensity, invaluable,
    irresistible
legendary
megawatt, mouthwatering
never been easier, new, no-holds-barred
one-stop shopping, outstanding, overwhelming
phenomenal, pioneer, powerful, proven techniques
rack up profits, rejuvenating, renewed, renowned, reproducible, revealed,
    revolutionary
satisfying, secrets, serene, shocking, skilled, special, spectacular, startling,
    step-by-step, successful, super
tactic, tempting, time-sensitive, trailblazing, trick
ultimate, unbeatable, unforgettable, uninhibited, unique, unlimited, urgent
within minutes, wonderful
you

FIGURE 2.6 Web words and phrases that sell.

REINFORCING THE FRAMEWORK: A SUMMARY

First, *identify* your objective and your target audience; then get to know your product or service thoroughly.

Second, *create* your blueprint by answering the following five questions:

1. What's the problem?
2. Why hasn't the problem been solved?
3. What's possible?
4. What's different now?
5. What should you do now?

Third, *flesh out* your web copy by taking the blueprint and

1. Injecting emotion into it
2. Adding bullet points, bonuses, the guarantee, and the close
3. Adding credibility-building elements such as testimonials, interesting stories or case studies, significant facts, quotes, or statistics
4. Adding psychological and involvement devices
5. Replacing all rational words with emotional words

CHAPTER 3

CRAFTING YOUR COPY

You can have everything in life you want if you will just help enough other people get what they want.

—ZIG ZIGLAR

Now that you know how to create a blueprint for writing web copy and understand how to use the five simple steps for fleshing out the body copy, it's time to put your copy together and add some important touches—the keys to making your web copy sell.

CONSTRUCTING YOUR WEB COPY

The purpose of web copy—and it can't be said too often—is to generate leads, customers, sales, and, consequently, profits for a website. Its objective is to compel the online prospect to respond in some way or take action of some kind. It tells the audience to do something specific during or at the end of the presentation of the marketing message.

The AIDA Principle

The four fundamentals of writing good copy are summed up in the time-honored AIDA principle:

A   Capture the audience's *a*ttention.
I   Get the audience's *i*nterest.
D   Build *d*esire for your offer.
A   Induce *a*ction.

Benefits and Features

Features are the attributes, properties, or characteristics of your product or service. Benefits, on the other hand, are what you can do, what you can have, or what you can be because of those features. Consumers buy benefits—and not features. This is one of the most important lessons you can learn in writing copy. For example, people don't buy a power drill for its impressive specs; rather, they buy the holes that the power drill makes.

When writing copy that sells, therefore, keep your eye firmly on the benefits. The best way to distinguish benefits from features is with the following exercise: Begin by stating the feature. Then follow it up with the sentence "What that means to you is . . ." or the phrase ". . . which means that you can . . ."

Feature: Your *Windows Mobile* phone gives you the mobile version of Microsoft Office . . .

Benefit: . . . which means that even when you're on the road, you can open and edit Word and Excel documents and view PowerPoint documents.

Feature: Your *Windows Mobile* phone comes with Outlook Mobile.

Benefit: What that means to you is that while you're on the move, you can catch up on your e-mail, manage your calendar, and update your contacts with the familiar Outlook features you know from your PC.

The Unique Selling Proposition

One of the cornerstones of writing sales-pulling copy is the unique selling proposition (USP), the thing that sets you, your product/service, or your business apart from every other competitor in a favorable way. It's the competitive advantage that you proclaim to your prospects, customers, or clients.

The late Rosser Reeves (1910–1984), an American advertising executive, pioneer of television advertising, and author of the advertising classic *Reality in Advertising* (Knopf, 1961), is credited with having introduced the USP concept to the world of advertising. To Reeves, a USP is the *one reason* a customer needs to buy a specific product or service, or why it is better than its competitors.

Some of the best-known and most recognizable USPs are these:

Avis: *"We're number two. We try harder."*
FedEx: *"When it absolutely, positively has to be there overnight."*
Domino's Pizza: *"Fresh, hot pizza in 30 minutes or less."*
Apple iPhone: *"Twice the speed, half the price."*
Secret® deodorant: *"Strong enough for a man. But made for a woman."*
Altoids: *"Curiously strong mints."*
M&M's: *"The milk chocolate that melts in your mouth, not in your hand."*
Wonder Bread: *"Wonder Bread Helps Build Strong Bodies 12 Ways."*

More than just slogans, these USPs convey the idea that no other company, product, or service compares with theirs.

Amazon.com proclaims itself "Earth's Biggest Bookstore," a claim that has been accepted without question by the media, both online and offline. Its USP implies that it has the best selection of books—in essence, "if you can't find it here, you can't find it anywhere"—thereby distinguishing Amazon from all other bookstores. Although Amazon.com is indeed the largest online-only bookstore in the world, Barnes & Noble has held on to its reputation as "the world's largest bookseller" through 2010, with $300 million in online and in-store book sales annually. Over the years, Amazon.com had managed to blur the distinction between "Earth's Biggest Bookstore" and "world's largest bookseller" by achieving top-of-mind positioning with its USP. As of 2011, Amazon overtook

Barnes & Noble and became the biggest book retailer, both in North America and overseas.

A USP positions your offering as being different from, and consequently more valuable than, your competitors' offerings. It distinguishes your product or service from everyone else's, and in a world that's flooded with products and services of every kind, creating a strong USP is absolutely imperative. Not only does a strong USP give your reader a specific and compelling reason to buy from you instead of your competitors, it establishes the direction of copywriting and is the undercurrent of all marketing efforts as well.

There are online companies whose USPs are clearly conveyed by their domain names. Lowestfare.com (which claims to provide the lowest airfares in the air travel industry) and SurviveYourForeclosure.com (which claims to help people confront their foreclosures head-on and win) are examples of these. So are FreeCreditReport.com and OneMinuteCureForAllDiseases.com, whose names say it all.

One way to develop a USP is by starting with the words "Unlike most of its competitors . . . ," then filling in the blanks about what differentiates you or your product offering from those of others. For example:

> Unlike most other fat-burning products, ABC Product makes you lose up to 5 pounds of pure body fat per week—without the use of stimulants that may be harmful to your health.

Another way to develop a USP is to highlight a feature or benefit that only your product or service contains or features.

Serious Magic, a software company, sells a product called Visual Communicator. Its USP is that it enables people with no technical experience to create with ease—in minutes and without any video editing—video presentations for websites, DVDs, and PowerPoint that have the professional look of a TV newscast. The specificity of the USP ("people with no technical experience," "professional look of a TV newscast in minutes," and "without any video editing") is compelling and serves to differentiate the product from other programs offering video creation capabilities.

The possibilities for crafting a USP are endless. The key is to adopt a USP that fills a void in the marketplace that you or your product can genuinely fill. Remember, too, that a USP can even be used as a headline or as an underlying theme or branding mechanism for all copywriting.

MAKING AN IMPRESSION: THE FIRST PARAGRAPH

The first paragraph is crucial because it is where readers are likely to stop reading if you don't provide them with sufficient reason to continue. Ideally, it should immediately demonstrate that there are desirable rewards for reading on.

There's no need to be lengthy or elaborate. Often, short, punchy, easy-to-read sentences suffice as long as they hold the viewer's attention. One device that leading copywriters, as well as I, use is to ask a question that will grip the readers' interest and compel them to continue reading.

THE OFFER YOU CAN'T REFUSE

The offer is the very heart of your copy. It is the reason the copy is being written. When writing copy for offline consumption, once you have captured the attention of your readers you need to present your offer as soon as possible to let them know what you are selling and what kind of deal you'll be making. When writing web copy for direct-response offers, that's not necessarily the case. Particularly when writing editorial-style web copy, you must be careful not to uncover your hidden selling point too soon. If you do, you will remove all doubt that your editorial is actually an ad in disguise.

Whether you are writing copy for on- or offline use, your offer needs to be clear, concise, and, above all, *irresistible*. For example:

> Own this deluxe set of knives that never need sharpening for just $19.95—and you'll never buy another set of knives again. It comes with a lifetime replacement guarantee. In the unlikely event that any of these knives should break—we will replace any or all of them free of charge—forever.

Your offer must align with your target audience's desires and needs, and, as you know, it must appeal to their emotions.

What motivates people to buy? In his book *Who Am I? The 16 Basic Desires That Motivate Our Actions and Define Our Personalities* (Tarcher/Putnam, 2000), Steven Reiss, a professor of psychology and psychiatry at Ohio State University, describes his theory of human motivation. Reiss, who spent five years conducting studies involving 6,000 people, discovered that 16 desires—power, independence, curiosity, acceptance, order, saving, honor, idealism, social contact, family, status, vengeance, romance, eating, physical exercise, and tranquility—motivate all human behavior. Other studies add the desire to belong, security, integrity, consistency, ownership, exclusivity, safety, admiration, and acknowledgment. All of these complex human desires can be grouped into two basic human needs: the desire to gain pleasure and the desire to avoid pain.

Since copywriting ultimately is about fulfilling human desires and needs, the more successful you are at representing your product or service in a way that plays to those desires and needs, the more successful your sales copy will be. When articulating the offer, your primary viewpoint should always be that of your readers. In other words, you need to focus entirely on your readers. One of the best ways to pull your readers into your copy is by weaving the words *you*, *your*, and *yourself* throughout. This gets your readers involved in what you are saying and makes them feel as though you are writing to them.

Your offer must summarize the key benefits and advantages of the product or service you're selling. This is effectively done through bullet points—to make the copy more readable and inviting. The following are examples of bullet points for a software program aimed at novel writers:

- Walks you, step-by-step, through the process of writing your story—it's like having a personal writing mentor and tutor interactively showing you how to write a great novel.
- Simplifies the process of developing a solidly constructed plot and outline for your novel—the plot generator gives you instant access to thousands of suggested plots from virtually all kinds of stories.
- Enables you to create rich, dynamic characters with the easy-to-use character developer.
- Allows you to instantly find answers to specific questions and get targeted advice for resolving problems while you write.

- Provides suggestions for overcoming 100 stumbling blocks that frequently face beginning novelists.
- Includes a troubleshooter function that takes you from your writing problem to its remedy with a click of the mouse.

TESTIMONIALS: EFFORTLESS SELLING

Testimonials add *credibility* because they are the actual words of real people, not actors or spokespeople. They can be quite disarming because your readers are able to identify with other people's experiences with your product or service.

No one knew the power of testimonials as well as W. Clement Stone, the late philanthropist and author, who founded the Combined Insurance Company of America in 1919 and was one of the richest men in America during his lifetime. In 1930, Stone had over 1,000 agents selling insurance for him all over the United States. He was known to have a simple way of training his agents. He instructed them to go into people's homes but discouraged them from making any sales pitch. Stone told them they didn't need to go through the song-and-dance routine that other insurance agents went through of trying to appeal to people's fear of dying and leaving their loved ones behind without any money. Instead, Stone sent each agent out in the field with a three-ring binder filled with about 200 pages of testimonials from satisfied insurance clients. The agent was instructed to flip through the binder, showing his prospective client a few pages of testimonials. Afterward, he would try to close the sale, and if the prospect wasn't ready to sign with his service yet, he would flip through a few more pages of testimonials, try to close the sale again, and repeat the process. Invariably, by the time the agent got to page 25 (or sooner), the prospect was sold. With this simple sales technique, agents were able to close new insurance policy sales like clockwork, and, as a result, Combined Insurance Company of America grew into a billion-dollar company.

Everyone knows that life insurance is a hard sell because you're selling an intangible concept. So why did the testimonials work so well in closing insurance sales? Because of what Robert Cialdini, author of *Influence: The Psychology of Persuasion* (Collins Business, 2006), calls *social proof,* a psychological phenomenon that occurs in social situations when people are uncertain how to behave and therefore assume that other people possess more knowledge about the situation than they do. They deem the behavior of others appropriate or better informed and, consequently, do what those others have done. Insurance prospects, being unsure of which decision to take, defer to the perceived wisdom of the people who bought the insurance policies before them and, consequently, buy the insurance policy themselves.

If testimonials work so well in effortlessly advancing the sale of life insurance, doesn't it stand to reason that they would effortlessly advance online sales as well? We don't have to look too far to know that the answer to this question is yes. Just take a look at all the blogs, forums, and social networking sites where people congregate to obtain other people's opinions about products or services they're considering buying. When you feature testimonials on your website, you save prospects the trouble of having to ask for other people's opinions of your product or service elsewhere. The majority of people base their buying decision on the strength of testimonials alone.

I can cite several instances when testimonials have caused me to buy without as much as a second thought, but the one that is most illustrative of the power of social proof is an e-mail newsletter I received recently. The newsletter sender reported that he was a member of a mastermind group consisting of 45 seasoned Internet marketers. Each month, they had a teleconference during which each member was given five minutes to share any tips, tactics, techniques, or strategies that made the biggest financial impact on their business with the least amount of effort. In that month's call, he reported that one particular tactic was named the fastest cash generator by 21 of the members. He also mentioned that at one point in the teleconference, five members talked about it consecutively. Essentially, the tactic they were talking about was a piece of software that deploys a virtual chat screen whenever a visitor leaves your website without buying your product or service. That chat screen turns nonbuying website visitors into customers in a matter of minutes—and has the potential of increasing a website's sales by up to 40 percent. A link to the software website was provided, and within minutes I had clicked the Order button and paid $197 to get my hands on it.

I had decided I was going to buy the software, sight unseen, even before I arrived at the software website. In fact, it took me less than ten seconds to make a buying decision. It wasn't the promise of a 40 percent increase in website sales that enticed me. I'm quite immune to exaggerated promises made by advertisers, and I'm not one who gets sold very easily. When I analyzed the reason I bought, it could only have been because I figured that if 21 seasoned Internet marketers were impressed by the results they got from this piece of software—enough to report it at the mastermind teleconference—there must be something about the software that's of high value. That's social proof at its best.

There's a software developer I met who created a piece of software that automated the process of gathering the keywords and ad descriptions of the most frequently clicked Google AdWords ads. During the beta test phase of software development, he gave away the software for free to his intended audience just so they could try it out and give him feedback on it. He received dozens of enthusiastic comments about the software from the beta testers. A month before the software was available for sale, before he even had web copy written for his website, he posted all the comments of the beta testers on his website's home page to replace the standard "Site Under Construction" page that was there. There wasn't even a form that captured the contact information of website visitors. All he offered at the bottom of the webpage was his e-mail address for those who wanted more information. By the time he actually launched the product, he had received 351 advance orders from people who didn't even bother asking how much the software cost! This software developer had implemented a variation of the W. Clement Stone method of selling—without even knowing it.

Another website that successfully employs the W. Clement Stone approach is one that sells a dog book titled *Your Dog's Love Letter* (see http://www .DogsLoveLetter.com). The web copy consists of only one short paragraph, the slogan "It's not just a book—it's an emotional experience!" followed by a litany of testimonials from people who support the slogan's claim.

The power of testimonials cannot be overemphasized, and yet many companies that do business online regard them as an afterthought. In spite of the fact that testimonials have become so commonplace and you see them overused or misused in some instances, their power for advancing sales, particularly online, where trust is a big issue, is undeniable. In my experience, a website that has one powerful testimonial positioned strategically in the web copy or even the headline can single-handedly sell ten times more than an identical website without that testimonial.

You can obtain testimonials by simply asking customers for them when you fulfill orders or by calling or e-mailing customers and asking for their comments. What was their experience with your product or service: Did they enjoy it? Are they glad they purchased it? When you get positive comments, ask permission to use them in your ad, and don't forget to get a signed release.

The best testimonials are the ones that are specific and, preferably, *quantifiable*.

> With the ABC weight loss program, I lost 10 pounds in 9 days without dieting.
>
> I earned 5 times my salary in my spare time by following the ABC trading system.

If your product or service is new, or you don't yet have enough customers who can provide you with testimonials, give away your product or service for free to members of your target audience in exchange for their feedback. Another way to inject the power of social proof into your web copy when you haven't obtained testimonials yet is to use case studies whenever they are available or appropriate for the product or service you're selling.

I have a client, a therapist by profession, who wrote a relationship book that helps women get their ex-boyfriends back. When he came to me to have his web copy written, he had countless stories to tell about women whom he had helped rekindle their relationships. However, due to the sensitive nature of relationship issues, very few of those who had success stories to tell wanted to go on record with a public testimonial that the whole world could see. I asked my client to provide me with case studies based on the success stories his readers told him. Here is a sample case study that I included in the web copy:

The Break-Up That Led to a Happily-Ever-After

This is an actual case study. Names have been changed for privacy reasons.

A client named Charlene came to consult with me last year. She had been dating a man named Martin for six months. Charlene was 43 and had four children. The relationship was going beautifully for a few months, when, out of the blue, Martin told her that he wasn't ready to get married—so he stopped seeing her.

She felt devastated, and when she came to my office for counseling, she broke into tears often as she told me her story. I showed her the **proven game plan** for getting Martin back that I describe in *How Do I Get Him Back*—and she began to implement it. At first, nothing happened and she thought the plan wasn't working—but she stuck to the plan anyway. Seven months later, Martin proposed to her—and three months thereafter they were married.

If you were to ask Martin what caused his change of heart, he would never be able to tell. But Charlene and I know that "the plan" had everything to do with it!

A case study such as the one presented here can be as powerful as, if not more powerful than, a testimonial. That's because, unlike testimonials that usually just state the end results, case studies tell a story. A good story captures your prospects' attention and helps to create a bond between your prospects and you. Case studies also present another opportunity to engage the emotions of your readers and cause them to identify with your subject's pain, problem, or predicament—and vicariously experience triumph in the solution you offer. With a case study, you can also elevate the perceived value of your product in your own words, as compared to a testimonial, where you're limited to using the actual words of your customer, whether those sentiments are well articulated or not. Furthermore, a case study tends to appear more factual and objective than a testimonial, as there is a general sense of objectivity conveyed.

TALKING ABOUT MONEY: HOW TO INTRODUCE THE PRICE

First and most important, you must never introduce the price until you've stated the offer. If you do, the majority of your readers might click away before ever learning the more salient points of your offer. The only exception to this rule is if you happen to be selling a product or service that has a price point your target audience already knows, and you're clearly offering a good price on it. Example: "Samsonite 3-Piece Spinner Luggage Set at an Unbeatable Price of $89!"

Second, when you do introduce the price, equate it with a ridiculously minor purchase or reduce it to a daily cost.

The Minor-Purchase Technique

Here's how the minor-purchase technique was used to introduce the price of a book about how to write news releases:

> Bottom line is, for a few bucks more than the price of a movie for two with popcorn, you can get your hands on the secrets that would mean truckloads of hot leads, sales that would make your head spin, a surge of cash flowing into your business, and first-rate recognition for you and your product that money just can't buy.

Here's how the same technique was used to equate the price of a health book to a minor purchase:

> Your investment in *The One-Minute Cure: The Secret to Healing Virtually All Diseases* is less than the price you'd pay for a single flu shot at a doctor's office (which costs $35 to $45 these days)—but the priceless knowledge you'll gain from it can protect you and your family not just from the flu, but from virtually all diseases!

The Daily-Cost Technique

Here's how the price was introduced for a shopping cart service that costs $29 per month:

> For just $1 a day, you can now automate your . . .
> * order processing
> * e-mail marketing
> * ad tracking
> * credit card processing
> * recurring billing

- affiliate program
- digital delivery of your electronic products
  . . . and all other e-commerce activities your website requires.

This tactic, known as *equating,* can also be used when you are conveying a time frame in your web copy. For example, "In the time it takes you to brew a cup of coffee, you're done with your marketing for the day."

KEEP ON SELLING: WRITING THE ORDER FORM

When I worked as director for creative web writing at Aesop Marketing Corporation, Mark Joyner designed an order form that increased orders by more than 30 percent. Ever since Mark revealed this information in his report *Confidential Internet Intelligence Manuscript,* it's been used successfully by online marketers all over the world. I often use the proven format shown in Figure 3.1.

> ☐ **Yes!** I want the *Promotional Products Distributorship Program* delivered to me immediately, and to learn how to grab my share of the $18 billion promotional products industry in as little as 1 week. I understand that I will also receive the following **bonuses** Worth $1300!
>
> - A **$100 discount** off the regular $995 price of the Distributorship Program. (Therefore, my price is <u>only $895</u>.)
> - A 15-minute telephone consultation with Joe McVoy personally (an **$87.50 value**) – absolutely FREE – to help me get off to a great start in the industry
> - **Unlimited e-mail consultation** for 2 full months (60 days). (**$350 value**)
> - **Annual directory updates** – FREE promotional product manufacturer directories (**$770 value**)
> - A FREE copy of *Promotional Marketing* Magazine, a valuable resource of product information for distributors. Plus information on how to get this magazine sent to you automatically every month at absolutely no charge.
>
> I understand that my order is absolutely **risk-free**. If, after one year, I have not earned <u>at least</u> **5 times my investment** – that is, **$4,475** – by implementing any of the powerful money-making tactics found in the Distributor Program, I can return it for a 100% refund.
>
> I authorize Promotional Products Consulting, LLC to charge my credit card the amount of $895.00 (+ applicable shipping charges; UPS Ground is only $47.25, UPS 2nd Day is $127.00, Alaska/Hawaii 2nd Day is $139.50).

Here's what Joe Ferraro of Universal Showdown Marketing says: "I've had a screenprinting business for 10 years. I added a promotional products profit center to my business by simply following exactly what Joe McVoy taught me to do in his Distributor Program – which had all the factory sources I needed. In only 7 months, I've started earning a 6-figure income. I've decided to close down my screenprinting business to concentrate on my lucrative promotional products business full-time."

Click here to proceed to the <u>secure order form</u>.

FIGURE 3.1 Order form that increases orders and minimizes shopping cart abondonment.

The order form features the following components:

- Check box—an involvement device that compels prospects to agree to the sale the moment they click on the check box
- Summary of offer, bonuses, and guarantee
- Price
- Assurance of secure ordering (and, whenever applicable, mentioning the level of security the order transaction will undergo—for example, "This site is protected by Secure Sockets Layer (SSL), which offers the highest level of encryption security possible for your order.")
- How the product or service will be delivered—and when
- Testimonial as reinforcement of purchase

THE MONEY-BACK GUARANTEE: A DEAL MAKER

Frequently, the sale is clinched on the promise of a money-back guarantee. This is where you eliminate the buyer risk, thus removing any remaining obstacles standing in the way of the sale.

Simply stating "Money-back guarantee" is an ineffective use of a guarantee, however. You have to craft the guarantee as compellingly as possible so as not to waste this prime opportunity for closing the sale. A common template for creating a guarantee is as follows:

Do this [*whatever you're asking them to do*], and if you don't [*achieve the result you're claiming they'll get*], then simply give us a call, and we will cheerfully refund your entire purchase price.

For example:

Take the ABC system for a test drive. If you don't triple your sales in 60 days, then return it for a full refund.

By removing the risk, you make it easier for the prospect to say yes. It is a well-documented fact in direct marketing that the number of people who take you up on a compelling offer significantly outnumber those who ask for a refund.

> **Try the Memory Foam mattress pad** *now,* **risk-free.** If it doesn't give you the most restful sleep you've ever had, or if, for any reason, you're not completely satisfied with it, just let us know within 30 days and we will issue a no-hassle refund, and even send you a Merchandise Return Label so that you can send the mattress pad back to us at no cost to you—we'll pay for the shipping. In the unlikely event that you would be less than **thrilled** with your new Memory Foam mattress pad, should you decide to request a refund, the 2 Memory Foam pillows are yours to keep and enjoy as our gift just for taking us up on this offer.

A strong guarantee conveys conviction, which has the power to persuade your prospect. It is sometimes possible to construct a guarantee that is so compelling that it could be the reason someone chooses your product or service over your competitors'. In fact, your guarantee could be so powerful that you might also consider using it as your headline:

**Drive This New Pontiac for 30 Days—and If It's Not the
Greatest Car You've Ever Had, We'll Buy It Back**

Drop 5 Strokes on Your Golf Game Today—Guaranteed

THE CLOSE: SIGNING ON THE DOTTED LINE

Legendary marketer and copywriter Vic Schwab, who authored the classic *How to Write a Good Advertisement: A Short Course in Copywriting* (Wilshire, 1985), said, "Delay is the enemy of a sale." In writing web copy, your close needs to remove all obstacles that stand in the way of the reader taking action on the offer. The way to do it is by first making the offer and then injecting a sense of urgency in taking action on the offer.

Injecting urgency simply means giving the reader a reason to act now. You can employ one or more of the following:

- A free gift/bonus or a discount or reduced price if the reader responds on or before a certain date in the near future. Sweeten the deal, and whet the appetite. Sometimes the bonus can be so compelling that, like the guarantee, it can even be the headline.
- A time limit on an offer.
- A limited supply.
- A notification that prices are going up soon.

The close should also emphasize what the reader gains by responding quickly or loses by delaying action.

The Call to Action

The *call to action* (CTA) is part of the close. Here, you must tell your readers *exactly* what to do. Some marketers miss this important step. Even if it's obvious to you what readers ought to do next, you must direct them to do it. Always use action verbs in the CTA:

Click on the Download button to start your 30-day free trial.
Check the box to select your preference, and then click on the secure online form to proceed with your order.
Simply type your name and e-mail address in the form below, and the free report will be in your e-mail in-box within minutes.
Click on the link below to start generating eBay profits now.
Type in your e-mail address, then click on Go to lock in your position.

GET A CALLING CARD: THE OPT-IN MECHANISM

We all know that most visitors to websites don't become buyers on their first visit—maybe not even on the first several visits. What you need to do is find out how to reach them again.

The best way to do this is with an opt-in mechanism (a tool to get a reader to agree to accept your e-mailed information and correspondence). Remember, the odds are against people buying something the first time they visit your website. After all, they don't even know you. Therefore, you must develop an irresistible—and easy—way for your visitors, at minimum, to give you their e-mail addresses before they go.

In my opinion, crafting your opt-in offer is infinitely more important than crafting the offer for the product itself. That's because you can get as much as 90 percent of your business from those with whom you build e-mail relationships. This is the usual objective, but I advise you not to be shortsighted and focus only on selling but also on building relationships. In Chapter 8, I'll go into detail on how to parlay your e-mail relationships into "monetizable" content.

Another version of the opt-in offer is the *name squeeze page,* also known as the *squeeze page.* A squeeze page is a landing page that offers access to content, a free report, secret passwords, or other information in exchange for the website visitor's e-mail address and sometimes additional information. It is also called a *lead capture* or *registration page.*

By whatever name, many people frown on this marketing practice because, in most cases, it requires website visitors to give up their contact information before being given access to the website's main pages. With the amount of spam circulating, people are wary about giving their e-mail addresses away, especially to some unfamiliar marketer who will most likely bombard them with a series of unwanted e-mails. What ends up happening, in many cases, is that in order to get access to the information being offered, website visitors resort to giving false names and e-mail addresses. Easily, a double-digit percentage of people give false information just to get past the registration form and get access to the information.

Although, in essence, a name squeeze page does the same thing an opt-in offer on a website does, it's the timing of the offer that differs. An opt-in offer is usually delivered after website visitors have had access to the information on the website's main page and they have some kind of indication of what the website is about or who's behind it. Therefore, the opt-in offer doesn't come across as overly intrusive. The name squeeze page, on the other hand, is often a landing page that provides no information and yet asks website visitors for their contact information before they're willing to give it. This is no different from a man walking up to a woman he's never met and asking for her name and phone number, with the promise that he'll deliver some goodies at her doorstep.

Even Google tends to frown on websites that have little else on the site but the squeeze page and offers the following guideline: "Try to provide information without requiring users to register. Or, provide a preview of what users will get by registering." (See Figure 3.2.)

Having stated the drawbacks, the advantage of a name squeeze page is that, from a marketer's point of view, it may be the best way to capture the contact information of as many of their prospects as possible.

To reduce the number of false opt-ins, you can seek the assistance of a programmer to install a script that is set up to work with your registration form. Such scripts enable you to enforce the completeness and accuracy with which website visitors fill out the form. While they type, the registration form checks for e-mail validity, password strength, and other essential information.

An infinitely more engaging, irresistible, and minimally intrusive way to present a squeeze page is through the use of an interactive webpage (see Figure 3.3) that any good programmer can create. When using interactivity such as that shown in Figure 3.3, your squeeze page would still offer the requisite free information, but in addition it would present an offer of a customized blueprint that you prewrote for your particular audience. Your programmer can help you configure the webpage for a wide variety of applications. The interactive website in Figure 3.3, which was created by Mohit Saxena (Innovators Web.com) at a price of only $70, was designed for an entrepreneur who sells a relationship book for men. Go to the website http://www.webcopythatsells .com/InteractiveSqueezePage.htm and fill out the multiple-choice form to see it in action.

When website visitors fill out the form and submit the information, a sales page appears, giving customized information based on the information the website visitors supplied. This provides instant gratification to the website visitors, and they begin to feel that their needs are understood, that it's as though someone read their minds. Therefore, they'll be likely to click on the link at the bottom of the page that will take them to the sales page in the proper frame of mind. This mechanism combines the functions of both a name squeeze page and an involvement device, and it goes a long way toward building the rapport and trust that pave the way to the sale.

FIGURE 3.2 This registration page provides content in the form of a short video. The video provides a preview of what users will get once they register.

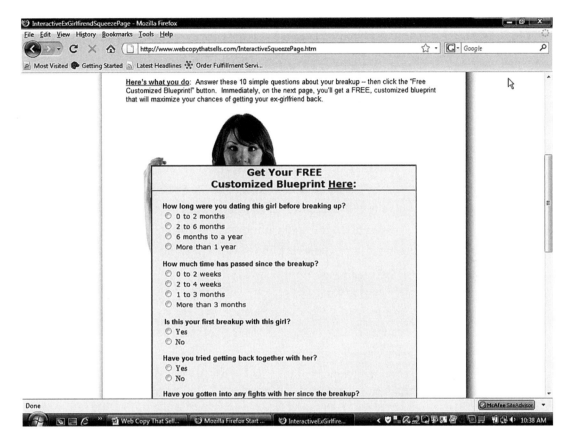

FIGURE 3.3 Registration page with customization.

HOW TO CONSTRUCT A RIVETING HEADLINE

According to David Ogilvy, founder of the Ogilvy & Mather advertising agency and author of *Confessions of an Advertising Man* (rev. ed., Atheneum, 1988) and *Ogilvy on Advertising* (John Wiley & Sons, 1983), "On the average, five times as many people read the headlines as read the body copy. It follows that, unless your headline sells your product, you have wasted 90 percent of your money."

Here's a plan for crafting never-fail headlines:

Step 1. Write 30 to 50 headlines before you decide on the one you're going to use.

Step 2. Step back from the headline for a day and read it again with a fresh perspective.

Step 3. Ask yourself, "How can this headline be better?" "Is this the best possible headline for my objective, my target audience, and my product or service?"

Most important, don't take shortcuts when crafting the headline. If you write a weak one, you will have failed, because no matter how good the rest of the piece is, no one will ever read it, and, consequently, no one will buy what you're selling. Remember, the most important element of a website is the first screen, and the most important element of the first screen is the headline. Therefore, you must give it the attention it deserves.

The headline is the most important component of any direct-response ad, whether it's a printed sales letter or an advertorial on your website. If you don't stop readers dead in their tracks with your headline, you don't stand a chance of making a sale.

The sales-producing ability of your website is directly proportional to the number of people who read what's on it. That is, the more people who read your web copy, the more sales it will generate. Therefore, the headline must grab the reader's attention, since its primary purpose is to induce people to start reading the copy.

John Caples, the advertising industry's advocate for rigorously tested, measured, and verifiable advertising effectiveness, said in his book *Tested Advertising Methods* (Prentice Hall, 1998), "In a print ad, 75 percent of the buying decisions are made at the headline alone." I'm speculating that online that percentage might be a bit less—perhaps 60 to 65 percent. After factoring in the attention deficit, information overwhelm, and general skepticism so prevalent on the web, 60 to 65 percent is still significant enough that you should take the subject of headlines more seriously than any other aspect of web copy.

What's in a Headline?

Your headline should convey a benefit of interest to your target audience. It must answer the reader's unspoken question, "What's in it for me?" As we've learned, there are two basic approaches to answering that question, and each stems from one of two basic human needs: (1) to gain pleasure or (2) to avoid pain.

You can appeal to the human need to gain pleasure by pointing out how the readers can attain or accomplish something by using your product or service. More particularly, your headline can demonstrate how your product or service will meet your readers' needs or solve their problems. Here are some classic examples of headlines with appeals based on pleasure:

The Secret to Making People Like You

Make Over Your Body Exactly the Way You Want in Just 6 Weeks

Make Anyone Do Anything You Mentally Command—With Your Mind Alone!

How to Win Friends and Influence People

Why Some Consultants Earn $100,000 to $250,000 per Year While Most Struggle Just to Get By

Play Guitar in Seven Days or Your Money Back

Alternatively, you can appeal to the human need to avoid pain by showing how readers can reduce or eliminate undesirable things such as discomfort, embarrassment, loss, illness, mistakes, poverty, and boredom, to name a few. Here are a few famous ones that play on that need:

Do You Make These Mistakes in English?

Are You Ever Tongue-Tied at a Party?

You Can Laugh at Money Worries—If You Follow This Simple Plan

When Doctors Feel "Rotten," This Is What They Do

Do You Have These Symptoms of Nerve Exhaustion?

Do You Do Any of These 10 Embarrassing Things?

All of these successful headlines are compelling. Not only do they capture the attention of prospective buyers, they also make an immediate connection with them. They give readers a good reason to read on.

The Building Blocks of Winning Web Headlines

Headlines are the starting point of successful web copy. If your headline fails to capture the attention of readers, it doesn't matter how good your body copy is because your readers won't ever get there. According to master direct marketer and author Ted Nicholas, who reportedly has sold $500 million worth of products in 49 industries, a good headline can be as much as 17 times more effective than a so-so headline. Simply changing one word or one figure in a headline can dramatically improve the response.

A successful headline engages or involves the reader by

- Offering a strong, compelling promise
  How a Simple Formula Has Been Scientifically Proven to Cure Cancer and Virtually All Diseases
- Highlighting benefits to the reader
  The World's Richest Source of Cash—And How You Can Tap Into It to Start or Grow Your Business
- Explaining exactly what the offer is
  Earn Your Master's Degree Online in 18 Months or Less
- Appealing to the emotions
  Will These Internet Trends Kill Your Online Business?
- Using specifics
  Why the Securities Regulators *Forbid* Me to Tell You How to Consistently Earn 151.8% to 301.02% Returns on Your Investments—and how a loophole can enable you to still cash in on these astronomical returns
- Arousing curiosity
  Words That Command People to Do Your Bidding
- Calling out to a specific target audience
  The Sales-Closing Techniques of a Self-Made Billionaire
- Making an announcement
  $2 Million Scientific Project Unlocks the Secret of Aging: How You Can Become Biologically Younger
- Asking a question

> Does Coral Calcium Really Reverse Aging, Extend Your Life Span, and
> Cure Degenerative Diseases Like Cancer?

- Beginning with the words *how to*
  > How to Control the Mind of Your Prospects—And Influence Them to
  > Buy What You're Selling

Building Block 1

Web headlines differ from advertising headlines because a web headline doesn't always explain what the offer is. Instead, it wraps the offer in an editorial cushion. Like the body copy, the headline should not read like an ad; rather, it should read like an editorial. Remember that, according to Ted Nicholas, *five times* as many people read editorials than messages that scream out, "I'm an ad!" If an advertorial is prepared in a way that lends credibility, it can pull up to 500 percent more in sales!

Building Block 2

When writing a headline that highlights benefits, remember that there are obvious benefits as well as hidden ones. An obvious benefit is one that is immediately apparent. Even then, the obvious must be articulated in a way that conveys value. For example, say you are trying to convey the money-saving benefit of joining a buyers discount club. Instead of writing a bland headline like "Save 20 Percent on All Your Purchases," I'd write the following:

> Discover How to Give Yourself a 20 Percent Pay Raise—Without Having
> to Squeeze a Single Cent from Your Boss

Do you see the hidden benefit? When you save 20 percent or more on everything you buy as a discount buying club member, it's the equivalent of getting a 20 percent pay raise (and you don't have to pay taxes on that pay raise!). I've stated the obvious in a creative way and added emotion and drama to it by using the action words *discover* and *squeeze*.

A hidden benefit is one that is not immediately apparent and, at first glance, may not seem to be a reason for buying your product or service. "A Tax-Deductible Vacation in Las Vegas" is a hidden benefit of attending a seminar in Las Vegas.

Building Block 3

According to master copywriter and marketer Ted Nicholas, who reportedly spent more than $100,000 testing to find out which copy elements boost response rates, an ad headline draws 28 percent more attention if framed in quotation marks! The ad appears much more important because the impression that someone is being quoted adds credibility, which in turn makes it more riveting and more likely to be read. For example, "You, Too, Can Pick Winning Stocks—with 95 Percent Accuracy."

Building Block 4

Whenever possible, use the imperative in your headline, which is a grammatical mood that (as its name implies) influences the behavior of another or expresses a command.

Land a Better Job
Create Your Own Channel and Share Video Online
      [courtesy of MaxCast.com]
Put an End to Migraines
Broadcast Yourself [courtesy of YouTube]
Erase Your Negative Credit Marks
Share Your Photos. Watch the World. [courtesy of Flickr.com]
Cancel Your Debts
Stop the Flu Dead in Its Tracks

An online advertisement for Windows Mobile phone uses four such imperative statements in succession, as follows:

Get more done, stay more connected, explore more places, have more fun.

The imperative mood commands, leads, or empowers your prospect to do something. It starts with an action verb such as *blast, impress, improve, create*; it assumes the subject is you and ends with the object of the action. If your verb is *blast,* the question is "Blast what?" And the answer is "Your competition."

The headline is "Blast Your Competition." If your action verb is *impress,* the question is "Impress whom?" Answer: "Your friends." The headline is "Impress Your Friends."

Building Block 5

There is another powerful but underutilized way of crafting a headline that rivets attention in a subtle way. It is a device named the *self-empowering nuance* by Fred Catona, founder of Bulldozer Digital, a leading direct-response advertising agency that effectively fuses radio advertising with online marketing.

Back in 1998, Priceline.com was a start-up company with a simple business model: It is a commercial website that helps users obtain discount rates for travel-related purchases such as airline tickets and hotel stays. Having a limited marketing budget, its founder, Jay S. Walker, hired Fred's advertising agency to run direct-response radio ads because radio had the power to reach virtually everybody, and it had a very low cost compared to TV and print. Priceline.com was launched on radio using William Shatner as its spokesperson. They tested various headlines, such as "Get the Lowest Price on Your Travel" and others that conveyed the discount travel rates that Priceline.com offered. But it wasn't until they tested the headline "Name Your Own Price" (for hotels, flights, rental cars, etc.) that the audience began flocking to Priceline.com in droves.

Within 14 days of the company's marketing launch via radio, 2.2 million people visited the Priceline.com website. Within 120 days, Priceline had become the second-biggest e-commerce brand, behind Amazon.com. And in 18 months, Priceline had made a billion dollars in sales—faster than any other company in history had hit the billion-dollar mark. Priceline's primary method of marketing was *95 percent direct-response radio advertising.* Only after the company went public and was valued at more than $20 billion did Priceline switch to TV advertising.

One of the main factors that contributed to the success of Priceline.com was the use of the self-empowering nuance headline "Name Your Own Price." That headline has since become a registered trademark of Priceline.com.

The reason for the effectiveness of a headline that uses the self-empowering nuance is quite obvious. With a headline like "Name Your Own Price," you literally hand all the power to the customer. The subtle psychology at work is this: Customers don't just obtain the lowest prices on travel, *they are actually given the power* to name their price.

The self-empowering nuance is also the reason that headlines such as "Start Your Own Business with as Little as $25" and "Make Your Own Website in One Hour or Less" cause people to respond to an ad. They give people a taste of power and make them feel in control.

Fred launched FreeCreditReport.com also using primarily direct-response radio advertising. The interesting thing is that all their test radio ads, which used headlines such as "Get Your Free Credit Report" and "Your Credit Score Is Very Important for Your Future—Send for Your Credit Report Today for Free," failed to make profits for the company. When they were ready to abandon radio advertising altogether, Fred tried one final headline: "Run a Free Credit Report on Yourself." That headline, which utilized the self-empowering nuance, was one of the main reasons for FreeCreditReport.com's rapid ascent to profitability and its emergence as a noted national success.

CHOOSING YOUR WORDS: TIPS, TERMS, AND CONCEPTS

Once you've written your copy, it is vital that you pay attention to how readable that copy is. Short sentences and simple words make your copy more inviting. They also help to cut up huge blocks of text into bite-size paragraphs that are no more than three or four sentences each.

Microsoft Word has a tool that displays information about the reading level of the document, including readability scores. It rates text on the 100-point Flesch Reading Ease scale; the higher the score, the easier it is for people to understand your writing. Aim for a score of 70 or higher. It also rates your writing on a U.S. grade-school level. For example, a score of 7.0 means that a seventh grader can understand the document. When writing copy, aim for a score of seventh- or eighth-grade-level comprehension.

Whenever possible, *dumb down* your writing. As legendary copywriter Eugene Schwartz used to say, "Write to the monkey brain." He made a fortune for his clients and had an 85 percent success rate with his ads because he wrote copy tailored to the monkey brain.

Words to Avoid in Your Web Copy

You already know that you should avoid using intellectual, rational, or right-brained words, opting instead for emotional words, but there are other categories of words you must avoid using.

Don't use euphemisms in an effort to avoid words that might offend. Doing so insults the intelligence of your audience. While you think you are trying to spare your readers' feelings and sensibilities, using euphemisms may backfire and cause readers to be more offended than if you had just been straightforward. For example, don't call overweight people "metabolically challenged" or people who suffer from hair loss "follicularly challenged" or poor people "economic underachievers." People see through these euphemisms and may think you are actually being condescending.

Don't use buzzwords if the buzzwords don't play an integral part in your selling proposition. In other words, don't use buzzwords just to show people that you're cool, demonstrate that you're hip to modern lingo, or impress them with your vocabulary.

Buzzwords sometimes alienate people who don't understand what you are talking about. They may also make you sound pretentious. Even worse, you may be using words that have gone hopelessly out of style (without your knowing it), which makes you appear so outdated.

Don't use corporatespeak. The way you write web copy is distinctly different from the way you would write a corporate communication or even a literary or journalistic work. As I tell my students, "You're not going to win any literary awards for writing excellent web copy, but you are going to win sales." You might pride yourself on writing flowery prose or businesslike correspondence, but those things don't cut it in web copy. For instance, the sentence "We are committed to your success" doesn't mean anything to people anymore. It's tired, it's boring, and it doesn't convey tangible benefits.

Don't use clichés. I believe the avoidance of clichés applies to all genres of writing. They diminish the value of your writing. Clichés make your writing look terribly dated, which in turn may affect how your readers view your offer. If you are behind the times, what does that say about your product or service?

Don't use tentative adjectives. These are words and phrases like *pretty good, very impressive,* or *quite wonderful.* Such words rob your writing of conviction. You must either drop the word or the phrase altogether and simplify your sentence or replace the word with a compelling one that dramatizes the thought you are trying to communicate.

Do communicate. We've all heard the Internet referred to as the "information superhighway." In fact, that's practically a cliché. But information is distinctly different from communication. The Internet is filled with people who can inundate you with all kinds of information; the person who has the ability to communicate is the one who will rise above the clutter and the noise—and actually be heard or read.

Author Sidney J. Harris once said, "The two words 'information' and 'communication' are often used interchangeably, but they signify quite different things. Information is giving out; communication is getting through." In marketing, use words that communicate, words that will create interest, trigger enthusiasm, and motivate people to action.

Words to Use in Your Web Copy

Here are some eye-catching words that create positive or engaging images.

Attention-Grabbing Words

Affordable	Bottom line
Alert	Brain picking
Allure	Bravo
Applause	Breakthrough
Avoiding	Buy
	Buyer's guide
Big	
Billboard	Challenging
Blockbuster	Competitive edge
Bonanza	Comprehensive
Boom	Compromise

Concept

Crucial

Danger

Daring

Destiny

Dirty

Distinguished

Dividends

Dynamics

Eager

Easy

Eat

Economic needs

Effective

Emerging growth

Endurance

Energy

Enterprising

Envision

Epidemic

Excitement

Exercising

Expert

Explain

Exploit

Favorable

Find out

Flex

Flourishes

Focus

Foothold

Forecast

Formula

Fueling

Fundamentals

Funny

Gaining

Gallery

Generic

Get

Giant

Good-looking

Growth

Gut feelings

Happy

Heritage

High-tech

High yield

Hit

Hopeless

Hot property

Hybrid

Huge

Hurry

Idea

Imagination

Inflation-beating

Innovative

Insatiable

Investigative

Just in time

Keep in touch
Kidding

Last-minute
Late-breaking
Launching
Liberated
Lifeblood
Lively
Longevity
Lucky
Luxury

Mainstream
Make
Mania
Marvelous
Masterpiece
Measure up
Medicine
Merit
Monitor
Monumental

Naked
Nest egg
New
Newswire
Next generation
Nostalgic
Novel

Obsession
Opportunities
Overrated

Perspective
Philosophy
Pioneering
Portfolio
Profitable decision
Promising

Recruiting
Remarkable
Reminiscent
Renaissance spirit
Reviewing
Revisited
Revolution
Rewards
Rich
Right now

Sampler
Save
Savvy
School of thought
Scorecard
Security
Show me
Shrewd
Simplistic
Skill
Slash
Smart

Soar	Tell
Specialized	Test-drive
Speed up	Timely
Spiral	Top dog
Spotlight	Traces
Stardom	
Starter kit	Ultimate
Stop	Underpriced
Stubborn	Unlock
Successful switch	Upscale
Surefire	
Surging	Value line
Survival	
	Willpower
Tax-resistant	Word-of-mouth
Tech revolution	
Technology	Young

DOs AND DON'Ts OF WEB COPYWRITING

Do give a compelling promise early in the body copy that the material viewers are about to read is worth their while. For example:

> Be sure to read every word of this because the secret ingredient for turning your small business enterprise into a mega–success story is hidden in this article.

In the next example, I challenge them to read every word, because if they don't, they'll miss that thing they are dying to know.

> Your first step is to read this article in its entirety. Please don't just skim through it—I don't want you to miss a single word, because when I demystify web copywriting for you, you simply cannot fail to create the sales and profits you want on the web.

Another technique I use is to reveal a little-known fact, anecdote, or case study at the beginning, followed by a statement like this:

If you think that's interesting, wait 'til you read what I've discovered.

This statement implies that more interesting information is about to be revealed. In the next example, the promise of solid proof is compelling and makes readers continue reading with anticipation.

The career of writing no longer has to be synonymous with starving. An annual income of $100,000 or more—even on a freelance or part-time basis—is now well within your reach. This is absolutely no hype—and I'll give you solid proof in a moment. And if you think that's exciting, wait 'til I show you how you can do it in as little as 6 weeks.

This is how it works when you put it all together: In your introductory paragraphs, tell your readers what you are going to say with a compelling promise. In the body copy, deliver on the promise, and, in a concluding paragraph, remind them of what you just revealed. This boosts your credibility for delivering on a promise and paves the way toward making your reader welcome your offer.

Do establish early in the copy who is writing the piece and why the audience should believe the writer. This is where your (or your client's) credentials, qualifications, or experience become important. They don't necessarily have to be monumental—that is, you don't have to be the leading expert or authority in a particular field—but your credentials must make you (or your client) believable.

One html trick I use to identify the writer (i.e., the person in whose "voice" the web copy is expressed) early in the piece is to make the writer's name a hypertext link. When visitors click on the link, it opens a pop-up window containing the qualifications of the writer.

Do write in the first person. Whenever possible, remove the words *we* and *our* from your web copy and replace them with *I* and *my*. By speaking in the first person, it is as though one person is talking to another. *We* and *our* sound more corporate, less intimate and friendly. You can't use this technique all the time, but do use it when it's appropriate.

Do use a drop letter (also called a drop cap) when starting your body copy. A drop letter is an oversized (often bold and ornamental) first letter of the first sentence of your body copy. Generally, it drops down two or more lines into the opening text of your body copy. Tests conducted by Ted Nicholas have proven that starting your body copy with a drop cap increases readership because it draws readers' eyes to it, thereby leading them to start reading the body copy instead of clicking away. In his book *Ogilvy on Advertising,* David Ogilvy writes, "The drop capital increases readership of your body copy by 13%." (See Figure 3.4.)

When I applied drop caps to 11 major paragraphs of the copy I wrote for 1MinuteCure.com, not only did readership increase, but sales increased by 251 percent the week after I installed them.

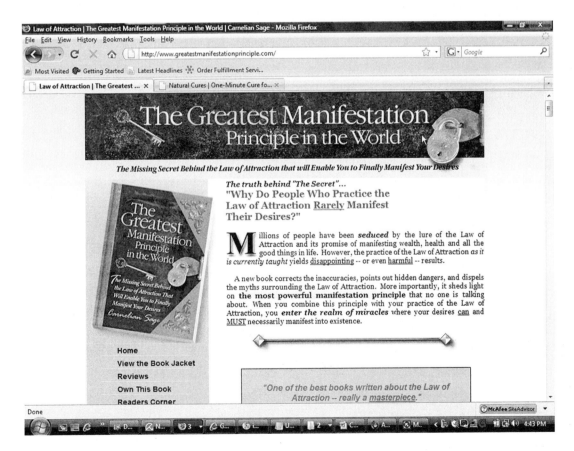

FIGURE 3.4 Drop capital increases readership.

Do use multiple pricing structures. Always remember that people's budgets fall into different price categories. That's why Mercedes-Benz makes cars that cost $30,000, $69,000, $85,000, and more. Most people fail to recognize this when they design their offers. As a result, their offers are static. They usually have just one price and one offer.

Different pricing programs are structured to catch as many people as possible at the level at which they are willing to buy. One technique that works well is to create *good-better-best offers*. Example: When I wrote the copy for TransformationAntiAgingCream.com, I structured the offer as follows:

PREMIUM DEAL

You'll get a **20% DISCOUNT when you order a 3-month supply** of *Transformation Skin Rejuvenating Crème*—three (3) 1-oz. jars—for just $167.94. That's a savings of $41.97! Order the Premium Deal Now.

SUPERIOR DEAL

You'll get a **10% DISCOUNT when you order a 2-month supply** of *Transformation Skin Rejuvenating Crème*—two (2) 1-oz. jars—for just $125.95. That's a savings of $13.99! Order the Superior Deal Now.

TRIAL OFFER

Order a 1-month supply of *Transformation Skin Rejuvenating Crème* for just $69.97. Order the Trial Offer Now.

Here were the results after five months:

	Orders	
Premium Deal—3 Jars	1,150	
Superior Deal—2 Jars	310	
Trial Offer—1 Jar	3,249	$209,689.50

Had we presented a static offer of one jar only (Trial Offer), we would have missed out on the 1,150 customers who bought three jars and the 310 customers who bought two jars of the product. As a result, $111,704.57 in sales would have been lost.

People also gravitate to different income promises: If you run a headline that reads "How to Use Website Metrics to Boost Your Conversion Rates to 10%, 20%—Even 30%" you're likely to get more responses than if your headline reads "How to Use Website Metrics to Boost Your Conversion Rate to 30%." Why? Because a broader spectrum of the audience can relate to—and believe—the three levels of improvement (10, 20, and 30 percent). Some people would have trouble believing anyone could get a 30 percent conversion rate, but they might readily believe that 10 or 20 percent is possible.

Remember that when you write web copy. Say I write the following headline to promote a web copywriting course: "Earn $300 Per Hour as a Web Copywriter." Very few people would read any further. The claim sounds unbelievable, even though it's true. Some people think it's not possible for them to earn that much. If, on the other hand, I write "Can You Really Earn $85, $125—even $235 an Hour as a Web Copywriter?" and a subheadline that reads "The Web Price Index Says You Can," that would make more people read on, wouldn't it?

Do call attention to the flaws or shortcomings of your product or service, but only if you can turn those flaws and shortcomings into benefits. When you admit the drawbacks of your product or service, you immediately increase your credibility. People think you are really up front and honest about the not-so-great aspects of your product, not just touting the good things about it. The key here is that you should not call attention to flaws or drawbacks unless you can turn that "confession" into a benefit. Avis said it this way: "We're Number 2. We try harder" and turned a drawback into a unique selling proposition. I'm sure you've often heard this said: "We're not cheap, but we're the best."

Do ask an opening question. I have already discussed the importance of incorporating compelling questions into your web copy to grab the attention of your readers and to force their brains to answer the questions more imaginatively than you can articulate them. When you open the first paragraph of your web copy with a question, it increases your chances of getting your readers to read on.

A well-designed question causes the prospect's thoughts to focus on what you have to say. Your opening question must, of course, be relevant and important and must speak to the needs of your audience. When crafted skillfully, questions point to the result or benefit of your product or service.

Do craft text links that are engaging and highly clickable. We already know that web visitors often scan the page instead of reading it word for word. When they do, their eyes gravitate to formatting devices such as words in bold print or italics, underlined words, and bullets. Hyperlinks to related websites are also formatting devices. These are even more eye-catching than bold, underlined, or italicized words because they're in another color.

It takes more than a vague "click here" to compel readers to click through to the target destination. In order for the text link to be highly clickable, it must either convey a benefit or employ an embedded command.

> Click here to discover *little-known medical breakthroughs and forbidden treatments.*

Notice that this example contains an embedded command (more on that in Chapter 7), conveys a benefit, and is written in the imperative mood. These kinds of text links are significantly more clickable. "Give it a try, risk-free" as a clickable link is more effective than "Click here to order."

Do use phrases that take the edge off the act of purchasing, that make it look easy, and that, ideally, convey a benefit:

> Submit Your Online Reservation
> Unlock the Cash Vault Now
> Click Here to Get Your Name in the News
> Become an Associate
> Get [*product*] Now
> Attend the Boot Camp
> Own This Book Now

This enhances the editorial approach to writing web copy. If you can avoid using words like *buy now* and *order* inside your editorial web copy, do it.

THE LONG AND SHORT OF IT: HOW LONG SHOULD WEB COPY BE?

I'm often asked if web copy has to consist of multiple pages in order to sell—especially since most people don't read on the web. While there will always be companies, products, and services for which abbreviated web copy is both suitable and adequate, I believe that when you're trying to convince people to invest any amount of money or time (or both), you need to assure them that they are making the right purchase decision.

Most often, you simply can't do that in a single page or less of copy. That would be like expecting a customer to walk into Best Buy and walk out five minutes later with a brand-new computer after spending 60 seconds with a sales-person pitching that particular brand. That's just not how buying decisions are made, and that's just not the anatomy of the sales process.

How long should web copy be? My answer used to be this: "Web copy should be like the length of a woman's skirt—long enough to cover the subject, but short enough to be interesting." Although that answer may sound clever and does hold seeds of truth, a more accurate reply is "Web copy should be as long as it takes to make the sale. Period."

This policy holds true in offline copywriting as well. In his book *Ogilvy on Advertising*, David Ogilvy wrote: "All my experience says that for a great many products, long copy sells more than short. . . . Direct response advertisers know that short copy doesn't sell. In split run tests, long copy invariably outsells short copy."

In his first advertisement for a first-rate luxury car, Ogilvy used 719 words, and he found that the advertisement was thoroughly read. Spurred on by the success of long copy in garnering attention, he used 1,400 words in his second advertisement for the car, also with excellent results. The 1MinuteCure.com web copy used 8,757 words (18 pages), and went on to generate $4.4 million in online sales—without the benefit of bookstore distribution.

Another well-known example demonstrating the effectiveness of long copy is the Schlitz beer advertisement written by legendary copywriter Claude Hop-kins. Hopkins wrote five pages of text, and as a result of that campaign Schlitz moved up from fifth place to first in beer sales.

Seldom have I seen a high-ticket item sold in less than several pages of copy—either online or offline. As a rule, the higher the price of what you are selling, the longer the web copy should be. For example, the web copy I wrote for Jay Conrad Levinson's Guerrilla Marketing Boot Camp took 13 pages to make a $2,500 sale. But when you consider that those hardworking 13 pages sold more than half a million dollars' worth of seminar seats, you begin to understand the value of long copy.

When you learn the principles of writing long direct-response web copy, you will be able to write short web copy easily. It's similar to going to medical school and specializing in surgery. If you were a brain surgeon who later decided to become a general practitioner, you could do that.

However, the length is not always dependent on the price of the product or service you are selling. For example, the web copy I wrote to sell an e-class with a ticket price of $1,500 was only six pages long, while the web copy I wrote for a $27 book took all of eight pages. Both sold very well. It all points back to writing web copy that's as long or as short as it takes to make the sale.

The more practice you have writing web copy, the better feel you will have for the rhythm of the sale and the sentiments of your audience, and you'll know instinctively how long or short your web copy needs to be. The warp-speed copywriting exercise in Chapter 1 will fine-tune your instincts.

Of course, there is also such a thing as web copy that is too long. I've seen a 75-page sales letter used on a website to promote an Internet marketing seminar. There may be people who will read something that long, but, generally speaking, that length overwhelms most people. Above all, don't use long copy as an excuse to babble on and on. Your web copy needs to be a lean, mean selling machine, even if it is disguised as editorial content. It pays to remember what advertising master John Caples once said about the length of copy: "It can't be too long, only too boring."

The Trifecta Neuro-Affective Principle, which is presented in Chapter 6, provides the option of streamlining your copy to just the essential elements that make the most impact. Since the trend on the Internet is leaning more and more toward shorter forms of copy, it is advisable to master the principle so that you, too, can sell any product or service without having to use long-scrolling webpages' worth of copy.

HOW WELL DOES YOUR WEBSITE SELL?

In the years I've spent specializing in web copywriting, I've developed a comprehensive Formula for Mathematically Measuring the Selling Quotient of Web Copy. I coined the term *selling quotient* (SQ), which is the predictor of a website's sales performance based on its web copy.

You can plug this formula into your existing web copy and determine exactly what kind of a selling job your website is doing. You can also use it as a tool for evaluating web copy that you have written following the guidelines in the first four chapters of this book.

This formula allows you to grade your web copy on a scale of 1 to 100. The real beauty in the formula, though, is that even if your website scores low, you will know exactly how to fix it.

Formula for Mathematically Measuring the Selling Quotient of Web Copy

Rate the following components of your website, giving yourself a possible score of 100 points.

First Screen

Does the first screen give the web visitor a compelling reason—in 5 seconds or less—why he or she should stay and read on? (0–7)   _____

Note: Did you make sure that the logo, company name, header, graphics, and other nonselling features did not take up a sizable chunk of the first screen?

Headline

Does the headline stop readers dead in their tracks? (0–7)   _____

Does the headline read like an interesting editorial—instead of an ad? (0–7)   _____

Does the headline incorporate a compelling promise or point to a benefit that's important to the target audience? (0–2)   _____

Does the headline call out to the target audience? (0–1) _____

Does the headline cause the reader to read the subheadline and/or the first paragraph of the web copy? (0–3) _____

Is this the best possible headline for the objective? (0–2) _____

Is this the best possible headline for the target audience? (0–2) _____

Is this the best possible headline for the product or service? (0–2) _____

Does the headline do one or more of the following: (0–1) _____

- Appeal to the emotions?
- Use specifics?
- Arouse curiosity?
- Make an announcement?
- Ask a question?
- Begin with the words *how to*?

First Paragraph or Opening Statement

Does the first paragraph cause the reader to read the second paragraph? (0–3) _____

Does the opening paragraph ask a compelling question that breaks preoccupation, or grabs attention, or points to the result or benefit of the product or service? (0–2) _____

Style and Formatting

Is the web copy written in a conversational style? Does it use contractions, colloquialisms, and easy-to-read language instead of corporatespeak? (0–1) _____

Is it scannable? Does it do the following? (0–5) _____

- Use bulleted lists to summarize content?
- Highlight (i.e., bold, italicize, underline) selected keywords to help scanners move through the web copy?

- Have meaningful subheads (versus amusing or clever ones)?
- Present one idea per paragraph?
- Use the inverted-pyramid style of writing (i.e., key points and conclusions presented first, followed by less important matters and background material)?
- Break paragraphs into two to four sentences?
- Incorporate interesting stories or case studies, significant facts, quotes, or statistics that are set off in boxes?

Body Copy

Is the body copy written in editorial (versus advertising) style? (0–3) _____

Does the body copy lead readers down the intended sales path? (0–3) _____

Was emotion injected into the body copy? Is the body copy built on proven emotional drivers such as anger, exclusivity, fear, greed, guilt, and curiosity? (0–3) _____

Do all the parts of the body copy compel the reader to read from start to finish? Did you employ the questions "What's in it for me?" and "Who cares?" and "So what?" after writing each sentence—and remove all sentences or phrases that don't satisfy those questions? (0–2) _____

Does the body copy employ the linear path—with minimal distractions and minimal clickable links that don't support the sales process? (0–5) _____

Does it use psychological devices that motivate prospects to buy? Have rational words been replaced with emotional words wherever possible? (0–3) _____

Does the body copy answer the question "Will this product really work for me if I use it?" with an unequivocal "Yes!" Were all possible sales objections addressed? (0–2) _____

Is the writer of the website's information identified early in the body copy? Are reasons given for why the readers should believe the writer? (0–2)   _____

Does the web copy convince readers that no other product or service can compare to the one that's being sold on the website? (0–2)   _____

Offer, Testimonials, Bullets, Price, Guarantee, Bonuses, and Close

Is the offer crafted in an irresistible manner? Does it establish a unique selling proposition—and is that USP featured prominently on the webpage? (0–3)   _____

Does the web copy employ the use of testimonials? Are the testimonials strategically placed in areas where they reinforce the selling arguments? (0–3)   _____

Does the web copy employ mouthwatering bullets? Do the bullets first state the benefit that readers will receive, followed up with either (1) a brief scenario of how their life will change when they get that benefit or (2) an injection of emotion, drama, or intrigue that elevates the desirability of that benefit? (0–3)   _____

Are free bonuses or gifts offered as an incentive to buy? (0–2)   _____

Does the close summarize the offer, employ a persuasive call to action, and inject a sense of urgency by giving compelling reasons to act now? Is the close written in a style that assumes the sale? (0–3)   _____

Does the web copy convince the reader that the product or service is worth the price? (0–2)   _____

Does the product or service being offered have a guarantee that removes the risk from the purchase? (0–3)   _____

Other Elements

Is there a mechanism to capture the web visitors' contact information? Does the opt-in offer feature an irresistible and easy way to compel the target audience to give up their contact information? (0–7)   _____

Do the web design layout and graphics support the web copy? (0–1)   _____

Does the order form include the following essential components? (0–3)   _____

- Check box
- Summary of offer, bonuses, and guarantee
- Price
- Assurance of secure ordering
- How the product or service will be delivered—and when
- Testimonial as reinforcement of purchase

TOTAL SCORE _____

Note: To avoid having to manually add up your worksheet score, you can go to www.WebCopywritingUniversity.com/formula.htm. That webpage enables you to simply plug in your scores, and the CGI script automatically calculates the total for you. (The CGI script is courtesy of Paul Galloway, www.PaulGalloway.com.)

Thomas Carruthers once said, "A teacher is one who makes himself progressively unnecessary." This formula is one of the devices I've used to make myself progressively unnecessary to my web copywriting students and clients. It allows you to dissect your own web copy (or your prospective clients' web copy), evaluate its selling ability, and make the necessary improvements—all in one fell swoop.

CHAPTER 4

E-MAIL MARKETING

The Internet's Killer Application

It is not your customers' job to remember you. It is your obligation and responsibility to make sure they don't have the chance to forget you.

—PATRICIA FRIPP

Whenever I refer to *web copy,* I am using an umbrella term that includes not only website copy, but also e-mails that sell, opt-in offers, newsletters, e-zines, online ads, autoresponder messages, free reports or promotional articles, online video or audio, search engine listings, signature files, and other online marketing communications. These can represent as much as 90 percent of the sales you can make online.

Of all the components that make up the web copy mix, e-mail marketing is one of the most important. For that reason, I believe writing e-mail copy is crucial to your online success, whether you are a web copywriter or an Internet marketer.

TRAFFIC CONVERSION: TURNING VISITORS INTO CUSTOMERS

On the Internet, there are two fundamental ways of acquiring website sales: The first is to generate traffic to your website (*traffic generation*), and the second is to convert your website visitors into customers (*traffic conversion*).

Web copywriting is the primary element of traffic conversion. Make no mistake about it, as a web copywriter, your primary function is as a traffic converter. After all, what good is all the traffic in the world if you can't get visitors to your site to do what you want them to do when they get there?

Traffic generators are those things that drive traffic to a website. These include search engine traffic, pay-per-click advertising campaigns, affiliate marketing, media placements, online video marketing, blogging, joint-venture endorsements, and similar devices. There are thousands of ways to generate traffic. When you write marketing communications such as free reports, promotional articles, online ads, newsletters or e-newsletters (or e-zines), SIG files, and search engine listings, you assume the secondary role of traffic generator.

Wagging the Website

Whenever I discuss e-mail marketing, I always mention *Wag the Dog,* a movie starring Robert De Niro as a political operative and Dustin Hoffman as a movie producer, whose characters come together to promote the sagging candidacy of the president. De Niro's character hatches a scheme that, with the help of Hoffman's character and the magic of Hollywood smoke and mirrors, fools the American public and the highest branches of the U.S. government into believing there is a war going on, setting in motion a huge chain of events. Thus, the tail (De Niro's character) is wagging the dog (the United States). The metaphor of the tail (a small, relatively insignificant appendage) wagging the dog finds parallels in web commerce, particularly in the dynamic between e-mail and a website.

On the Internet, what do online businesses pay the most attention to and spend the most money on? The website, of course, because that's the highly visible component of the marketing mix. The website is where a business displays its products and services; it's where you close the sale and take the orders. E-mail, on the other hand, is not glamorous and is therefore viewed as merely a supporting component of the marketing process, which is a big mistake.

Most online entrepreneurs and writers overlook the significance of e-mail, and, as a result, they write e-mails haphazardly, almost as an afterthought. They regard e-mail as something that supports the objectives of the website, or as a vehicle for customer service, or as a way to send out special announcements. In other words, they regard e-mail as a low-cost, inconsequential accessory to their web presence, like the tail of a dog.

While e-mail can and does make a fine supporting actor, used properly it can assume a starring role as the primary sales tool. E-mail can be used to direct what happens on your site, not vice versa. In essence, you can use e-mail to "wag the website."

Why Your E-Mail May Be More Important Than Your Website

I'm not suggesting by any means that a website is *not* important or that you should forget about putting one up. I am saying that if you rely exclusively on a website for your sales without using the power of e-mail to fuel those sales, your Internet business is not going to get very far.

E-mail marketing is a hot item in e-commerce. A layperson may think of commercial e-mail as spam, but to the marketing industry, e-mail is a gold mine that allows companies to speak personally and directly to prospects and customers and to carry on a relationship that contributes significantly to sales.

As you know, chances are that less than 1 percent of visitors to your site will ever buy your product or service. Even the best marketers with the most successful websites seldom convert more than 5 percent of their web visitors into customers when their website is their only marketing vehicle. That's why an opt-in mechanism is vital for capturing your visitors' contact information, developing a relationship with them, and, as a result, dramatically increasing the chance of ultimately making the sale.

In view of this, writing powerful e-mail copy is one of the most important skills required for doing business on the web. You should never write e-mail haphazardly. If you do, you'll be leaving a lot of money on the table. Here's why:

- Virtually every person who is online sends and receives e-mail. E-mail provides greater visibility for any Internet marketer. E-mail is also a far better vehicle than a website for distributing and collecting information, as well as for developing a dedicated following.

- Relationship marketing is at the very heart of all e-commerce. You simply can't build a relationship solely through your website, no matter how many interactive bells and whistles it has. E-mail, on the other hand, builds relationships. To produce an income, a website relies on people visiting and revisiting the site. You may have heard the saying "The money is in the list." What it means is that when you leverage your relationship with the prospects in your database (your list), you are more likely to close a sale. That's because you give people a chance to know you and trust you. Even if your website gets only modest traffic, you can convert that traffic into more money than you can imagine through e-mail.

- While it's true that a website makes the front-end sale, you'll be missing out on 90 percent or more of the potential profits if you don't use e-mail to fan the flames. The real selling starts after the first sale is made, by multiplying that one sale into many, many more repeat sales and upsell and cross-sell offers via follow-up e-mails. This is why the lifetime value of the customer—not the first sale—is paramount.

Lifetime Value of a Customer

How do you calculate the lifetime value (LTV) of a customer? First, you figure out how many years your average customer does business with you (customer lifetime). Next, you estimate how much business you'll get from the average customer over that period of time (sales per customer). Then you factor in the number of referrals the average customer gives your company and multiply that by the percentage of those referrals who become customers. The formula will look like this:

$$\text{Customer lifetime} \times \text{sales per customer} \times \text{number of referrals}$$
$$\times \text{ percentage of referrals who become customers} = \text{LTV}$$

Let's plug in some hypothetical figures for an online bookstore:

Customer lifetime = 10 years
Sales per customer (per year) = $50
Number of referrals made by average customer = 4
Percentage of referrals that become customers = 26%

$$10 \times \$50 \times 4 \times 0.26 = \$520$$

Next, subtract the cost of books sold—say, $403—and that gives the bookstore a gross margin (gross profit) of $117 per customer. That's the LTV of one customer to that bookstore.

If each customer has an LTV of $117, then the bookstore can easily determine how much it can reasonably spend to acquire each new customer and still make a profit over the lifetime of that customer. The profits probably won't come with the first sale. They may not even come in the first year, since the cost of acquiring a customer can be high, but if you build strong relationships and offer quality products and services, over the life of the customer, you should reap handsome rewards.

1. E-mail helps you keep the customers you have. It costs much less to keep an existing customer than to acquire a new one. According to *eMarketer,* it costs five to ten times as much to find a new customer as it does to retain an existing one. Additionally, loyal customers are more profitable to your business because they usually buy more of your company's products, are less sensitive to price, and often refer other customers. They usually take less of your customer service time because they're already familiar with your company.

2. An increasing number of traditional brick-and-mortar companies are discovering that a website is simply not sufficient for success in e-commerce. The Internet's killer application—e-mail—is the primary vehicle for interactive marketing. Why? E-mail is a high-response-rate vehicle because it's in-your-face, immediate, and inexpensive. It sells, promotes, informs, creates buzz, acquires and retains customers, reinforces branding, and provides customer service all in one fell swoop.

   With an estimated 39 trillion pieces of e-mail being sent out each year at the time of this writing, 80 percent of which are spam mails, it makes sense now, even more than ever before, to maximize the impact of your e-mail messages, or you'll be buried alive in the mountains of e-mail that people get.

Having a mailing list of prospects does not mean you will automatically make money. That's *not* what "The money is in the list" means. The money is indeed in the list, but only if you know how to leverage that list through e-mail copy that deepens your relationship with the members of your list—and you have a systematic (and automated) way of making sure none of your list members are left unattended (see Chapter 10).

In your e-mail, you can use psychological devices (as mentioned in Chapters 5, 6, and 7), but if you fail to get your e-mail audience to like and trust you, you won't make sales. It's as simple as that. This is even more true these days when phishing and e-mail scams are rampant on the web.

How many times have you bought products that you didn't particularly like, want, or need just because you liked and trusted the people who were selling them to you?

Dr. Ralph F. Wilson, who, according to the *New York Times,* is "among the best-known publishers and consultants who preach the responsible use of e-mail for marketing," exemplifies this premise. Among the practices he advocates are (1) using a confirmed or double opt-in mechanism to keep from getting bad e-mail addresses or getting unwilling recipients on your list, (2) providing quality content in every e-mail communication, (3) avoiding overpromotion and modulating e-mail frequency, (4) providing e-mail recipients with an easy way to unsubscribe in the event they no longer wish to receive e-mail from you, and (5) safeguarding your reputation in the context of e-mail.

One example of an Internet marketer who provides outstanding content on a weekly basis and practices responsible use of e-mail marketing is Danica Collins, who is well liked, trusted, and respected by more than 250,000 subscribers to the popular e-newsletter *Underground Health Reporter* and its portal website UndergroundHealthReporter.com.

THE FRAME-OF-MIND MARKETING METHOD FOR WRITING E-MAILS

Empathy is defined as the capacity to understand, be aware of, be sensitive to, and vicariously experience the feelings, thoughts, and experiences of another person. Frame-of-mind marketing grows directly out of that feeling of empathy.

While many seem to be born with that ability, the good news is that empathy is not a genetic trait but, rather, a skill that you can easily develop.

The ability to view things from the perspective of your audience is valuable not only in copywriting and marketing, but for all social interactions. The more sensitive you are to people's frame of mind, the more persuasive you can be, the more rapport you can have with them, and, consequently, the more they will trust you and agree with you.

Let's examine the frame of mind of people who are in the process of opening their e-mail. The easiest way to do this is to put yourself in the shoes of your average e-mail recipient. Write down the thoughts that normally run through people's heads as they open their e-mail in-boxes. Here are some examples of typical thought processes:

Okay, who sent me e-mail today? They are curious and eager to receive e-mail. According to AOL's fourth annual Email Addiction Survey, 51 percent check their e-mail four or more times a day, and 20 percent check it more than ten times a day. According to another poll, about 40 percent of people surveyed said they checked their e-mail 6 to 20 times a day.

I'm busy and I just have enough time to read the good stuff. They scan their in-box for (1) important business e-mail, (2) personal e-mail, and (3) other things that they have time to read, usually in that order.

Let me delete all the junk mail so that it doesn't clutter up my in-box. People are inundated with commercial e-mail, free newsletters, and e-zines—and their forefinger is positioned over their mouse, ready to click on the Delete button.

My in-box is my private, personal space, and I don't want strangers and salespeople invading my privacy. Their in-box is a sacred place, and they are protective of it, inviting only friends, relatives, colleagues, and selected business acquaintances to enter. Some people may have additional reasons, but these are nearly universal. Most of us probably feel the same way.

For this reason, the cardinal rule for writing successful e-mail copy is to review the frame of mind of your audience before writing a single word. Clearly, when we want to sell our ideas or products to others, we need to create rapport, and one good way to do this is by aligning ourselves with them, which simply means being like them. People develop a bond with you because they see a reflection of themselves in you. An effective way to do this is by mirroring the language in which your target audience communicates, which allows you to gain instant rapport with them. The result is that they instantly like and trust you, although they may not know why. Can you see how useful this can be in the selling process—online as well as offline?

People online are used to the up-close-and-personal language that is prevalent in e-mail, instant messaging, and text messaging. There is a one-on-one, in-your-face kind of intimacy in e-mail, and you have to work with it and not against it. You must understand who your audience is and speak their language. At the same time, you should make it personal and conversational. Even if you are speaking to CEOs, you don't have to use the language of the boardroom. Speak to your reader's level of intelligence and comprehension, but keep it friendly.

Just as in writing copy for your website, don't begin your e-mail messages with formal corporatespeak: "We at Widgets.com have been in business for 15 years, and we are the industry's premier source of widgets." Not only does that kind of language sound pompous, but it deliberately keeps your audience at arm's length. It's also boring, so your readers are likely to tune out. Furthermore, how does the fact that your company has existed for 15 years fill the needs of your audience? What's in it for them?

Breaking the Sales Barrier

There's another part of the equation that is rarely mentioned: Getting your prospects to like you is important, but what's even more important is letting your clients see that you like them. When that occurs, sales barriers really come down. When we know someone likes us, we believe that they won't cheat, lie to, or take advantage of us, but instead will give us the best possible arrangement or the best possible deal.

For this reason, it's crucial to write your e-mail as though you are writing to just one person that you're fond of, not 1,000, 10,000, or 100,000 at once. Don't speak *at* or *to* your reader, but *with* him or her.

Since your audience's e-mail in-box is a sacred place where only trusted people are welcome and invited, it is also the place where you can create the closest, strongest bond that can be forged between marketer and audience. You must never damage that bond by abusing your readers' trust in you. If they opted in to receive marketing tips from you, and if you don't deliver on that promise but instead give them sales pitches for various products, you blow it. If you treat their e-mail in-box as a dumping place for junk mail, you will also blow it.

People form opinions about you based on the e-mails you send them. Often, you don't know what those opinions are unless people happen to be vocal about them. Sometimes people brag about the size of their mailing list, but as the saying goes, "It's not the number of eyeballs that matter, it's the frame of mind behind those eyeballs that really matters." Just because you have a list of 50,000 or 100,000 e-mail addresses doesn't mean that those people care a whit about you. I'd rather have a list of 1,000 devoted subscribers with whom I have a first-name relationship than 100,000 who couldn't care less about me. That's because I'd be more likely to make a significant number of sales from 1,000 loyal readers than from 100,000 strangers.

THE FUTURE OF E-MAIL MARKETING

Anyone who has been online for any length of time is aware of the alarming proliferation of spam e-mail. The trend is expected to continue, as an increasing number of marketers, eager to cash in on the free marketing medium, exploit the situation without giving any thought to the bandwidth they are wasting and the people they are annoying. Add to that the growing fear of computer viruses, worms, scams, and pornography, and you begin to understand the vigilance that organizations and the government are exercising to put a stop to spam.

The CAN-SPAM Act (Controlling the Assault of Non-Solicited Pornography and Marketing Act), which was signed into law back in 2003 (and revisions to which went into effect on July 7, 2008), sets forth a framework of administrative tools and civil and criminal penalties to help America's consumers, businesses, and families fight spam. In addition, spam and virus filters have become standard on e-mail servers, permanently blocking suspicious and obviously unsolicited e-mail.

A review of spam levels in October 2006 estimated that 75 percent of all e-mail messages were spam. By mid-2010, about 90 percent of e-mails were spam. (Source: Barracuda Central, a 24/7 security center that monitors and blocks the latest Internet threats.)

Some people are predicting that, with the rise of flooded e-mail in-boxes and spam filters that can block even legitimate opt-in messages, the demise of e-mail as a marketing and publishing channel is not far behind.

Is e-mail marketing on its way out? Not by a long shot. There's still a lot of marketing juice left in e-mail.

However, gone are the days when marketers could compose an e-mail message, push the Send button, and expect everyone on their mailing list to receive it. Marketers need to become more sophisticated about the medium in order to make their e-mail marketing as effective as it was prior to spam phobia. The rest of this chapter reveals some of the cybersmarts that you need to navigate the changing e-mail landscape.

HOW TO MAKE SURE YOUR E-MAIL IS DELIVERED

Do you know the most important objective when it comes to sending e-mail? Many experienced marketers say, "Getting your e-mail opened." Actually getting your e-mail opened is the second-most-important thing. The most important is getting your e-mail delivered.

As a service to their users, more and more e-mail providers offer filters intended to radically reduce the amount of spam their users receive. What is a legitimate e-mailer to do? Let's say you send a mailing to your opt-in list, some of whom have e-mail services that block bulk mail and redirect it to the recipient's bulk mail box, the equivalent of sending it to Siberia. This happens frequently, especially if you have a huge mailing list. If your list is large, you may avoid such filters by breaking up your mailings into smaller chunks.

In addition to blocking bulk mail, a majority of e-mail programs allow their e-mail users to filter out spam and other junk mail. People can, for instance, ask to have e-mail that contains certain words such as *sex* or *girls* or *one-time mailing* in the subject line or even in the body of the e-mail filtered from your in-box or sent to the trash bin. More and more people are availing themselves of such filtering capabilities, which is why popular e-mail services such as Gmail and Yahoo! Mail, and e-mail applications like Eudora and Outlook come with built-in filtering capabilities. People can also filter out specific mailers, that is, create a blacklist of unwanted e-mail senders. This is good and bad news, since they can also opt to let certain e-mailers in (i.e., create a whitelist of e-mail addresses or domain names from which an e-mail blocking program allows messages to be received), but this often takes a specific action, and not all recipients are aware of this feature.

Some e-mail programs, like Outlook, automatically filter out e-mail that has the word *free* in all-capital letters in any part of the e-mail. If they find sales@anydomainname.com in the From field, they filter that out, too. Ditto for *extra income* or *for free* with a question mark or an exclamation point.

How to Avoid Spam Blockers

Spam blockers and filters used by the majority of e-mail providers have become increasingly restrictive, and this often causes even legitimate e-mail to be relegated to recipients' bulk e-mail boxes or prevented from being delivered altogether. Therefore, before you press the Send button on your promotional e-mail, newsletter, or e-zine—stop. Give it a once-over and see if it contains any of the following offending words and phrases:

Amazing	Congratulations	Great offer
Amazing stuff	Credit bureaus	Guarantee
Buy now	Dear friend	"Hidden" assets
	Dig up dirt on friends	
Cable converter		Investment
Cash bonus	Free	Maximize
Collect child	Free grant money	Money
support	Free installation	Multilevel marketing
Compare rates	Free investment	
Compete for your	Free leads	New
business	Free preview	No investment

Opportunity	Removes wrinkles	Stock disclaimer
Order now	Reverses aging	statement
		Stop snoring
Powerful	Sale	
Profit	Search engine listings	Tells you it's an ad
Promise	Serious cash	
you . . . !	Special Promotion	Winner

In addition, customary phrases like *Click here, Click below, Unsubscribe,* and *To be removed* are also blocked, because these phrases are frequently used by spammers and other purveyors of spam. Following is a list of other words and phrases that also resemble spam. They may not necessarily be flagged as spam by spam filters when used only once in the body of an e-mail, but it would be advisable to use them in moderation or avoid using them altogether, if possible.

Accept credit cards	Calling creditors	Easy terms
Act now! Don't hesitate!	Cancel at any time	Eliminate bad credit
	Can't live without	E-mail marketing
Additional income	Cash bonus	Expect to earn
All natural	Casino	
Apply online	Cents on the dollar	Fantastic deal
As seen on	Check or money order	Fast Viagra delivery
Avoid bankruptcy	Consolidate debt and credit	Financial freedom
		For instant access
Be amazed	Credit card offers	For just $ (some amount)
Be your own boss	Cures baldness	
Being a member		Free sample (or free anything)
Big bucks	Direct e-mail	
Billing address	Direct marketing	Full refund
Billion dollars	Do it today	
Buy direct	Don't delete	Get it now
	Drastically reduced	Get paid
Call free		Get started now
Call now	Earn per week	Gift certificate

Have you been turned down?	MLM	Once in lifetime
Home employment	Money back	100 percent guaranteed
Human growth hormone	Moneymaking	One-time mailing
	Month trial offer	
	More Internet traffic	Online biz opportunity
If only it were that easy	Mortgage rates	Online pharmacy
Increase sales	Name brand	Only $
Increase traffic	Nigerian	Opt in
It's effective	No age restrictions	Order status
	No claim forms	Orders shipped by priority mail
	No cost	
Join millions of Americans	No credit check	
	No experience	Pennies a day
	No fees	Please read
Limited time only	No gimmick	Potential earnings
Long-distance phone offer	No inventory	Pure profit
	No medical exams	
Lose weight	No obligation	Real thing
Lower interest rates	No purchase necessary	Refinance home
Lower monthly payment	No questions asked	Requires initial investment
Lowest price	No selling	Risk free
Luxury car	No strings attached	Round the world
Mail-in order form	Offshore	Satisfaction guaranteed
Marketing solutions	Offer expires	
Mass e-mail	Offers coupon	Save $
Meet singles	Offers extra cash	Save big money
Member stuff		

If you've included any of these words—or any dollar signs, exclamation points, or anything in all-capital letters, for that matter—in your outgoing e-mail, you may want to rethink what you have written.

That's because SpamAssassin (and other, similar programs, like SpamGuard, which come integrated in e-mail providers like Yahoo! Mail) may inadvertently identify your e-mail as spam and block it from being delivered. SpamAssassin, one of the most popular open-source antispam applications, has several hundred spam filters and allows mail administrators to customize which e-mails get through and which ones are automatically blocked and sent to spam limbo, meaning they are redirected to the recipient's bulk mail bin or purged altogether.

Even if the e-mail you are sending is legitimate opt-in e-mail that the recipient has requested and wants to receive, it can be hijacked by e-mail providers or Internet service providers (ISPs), who are becoming increasingly vigilant about protecting their clients from junk e-mail.

You can see how easy it is to get caught in the crossfire and end up in the same dump as spammers. The sad fact is that some legitimate e-mail marketers and newsletter and e-zine publishers don't even realize that their e-mail is being rerouted to spam limbo, and they wonder why their click-through and conversion rates are dismal.

How do you get around this? You can either play by the rules and not use the offending words and phrases altogether or devise creative ways to conceal the words and phrases from the spam radar. You can insert symbols within the words; for example, use "fr^ee" or "fr*ee" instead of "free." Don't get too creative; your sentence or thought must still be understandable to your readers.

Another matter worth noting is that the deliverability of e-mail is often dependent on the spam-blocking strength of e-mail services or ISPs. Yahoo! Mail, for instance, uses aggressive server-level spam filters that do a great job at reducing the amount of unsolicited e-mail messages, but they also erroneously flag legitimate e-mails as spam and send them to the recipients' bulk mail folder. Other ISPs like MSN Hotmail and Juno, on the other hand, have less vigorous spam filters that allow all but the most blatant spam to reach recipients' in-boxes. It's worthwhile to keep abreast of the major ISPs' server-side filtering so that you can send out e-mails accordingly. For example, if you're planning to send out a promotional e-mail to your mailing list, it might be wise to segment that list by ISP (sort according to their domains, for example, those addresses ending in "@yahoo. com" or "@msn.com" or "@aol.com") and tailor each e-mail for each segment of your mailing list so that each e-mail works within the parameters of each ISP's spam-filtering rules. Although this might seem like tedious work to you, consider the alternative. If you send one universal e-mail to all recipients in a single bulk mailing—without segmenting your list and without taking the spam rules of the receiving ISPs into consideration—the majority of your e-mail could land in your recipients' bulk mail files.

If you want your e-mail to be read and not filtered out as spam or junk mail, you must pay attention to these guidelines and keep up with the constant changes ISPs make.

Does Your E-Mail Test Positive as Spam?

My favorite strategy for sanitizing my e-mail of items that might trigger a false positive is to run it through Contactology.com's Email Spam Checker before sending it out. This is a free service that enables you to receive a Message Quality Score™ (MQS) on any e-mail you're planning to send out. The MQS allows you to quickly determine the quality and test the e-mail deliverability of your message on a scale from 0 (bad) to 100 (excellent). You can find it at www .contactology.com/check_mqs.php.

When you get there, paste your text into the form provided on the website, and you'll instantly get your score. If your score is low, it's an indication that your e-mail strongly resembles spam and might be blocked or filtered by major e-mail providers or ISPs. If it's high, you can be reasonably assured that your e-mail will be delivered without incident.

There currently exists no program, application, or utility that can guarantee with 100 percent certainty that your outgoing e-mail is spam-proof. Even Contactology.com's Email Spam Checker only checks your e-mail against certain spam-filtering rules, but it does not represent the spam-filtering strength of all e-mail services and ISPs. This is why it is necessary to stay informed about the major ISPs' constantly changing e-mail rules.

HOW TO WRITE E-MAIL THAT'S READ

Let's assume your e-mail gets through those e-mail filters. How do you appeal to the actual e-mail recipients themselves? I've read tens of thousands of e-mails, and I've written thousands more over the past ten years. I've found that the e-mails that do a great job of selling contain seven elements.

Seven Elements of E-Mails That Sell

Element 1: A Compelling Subject Line. The subject line must be irresistible and must beg to be opened, *not* because of hype or overly commercial language, but because it is compelling. What's more, your subject line *must not* appear to be an advertisement, which, even if it somehow got through the filters, would have the same effect as asking readers to watch a commercial.

Remember that each of us is bombarded with an average of 3,500 commercial messages per day—from TV, billboards, radio, the Internet, and practically everywhere we turn. The last thing we want to see when we open our e-mail (or visit a website) is yet another ad. Yes, that applies even when we gave a company permission to send us e-mail.

Here's a simple exercise that will give you the best education you can get when it comes to writing subject lines that are impossible to ignore. This exercise puts you smack-dab in your prospects' shoes or, more precisely, in their frame of mind. Go to your e-mail in-box and check your incoming e-mail. You need to actually do this; don't be tempted to just do it mentally or you'll defeat the purpose of the exercise. This is positively eye-opening.

Once you have your e-mail in-box in front of you, what do you see? You see the sender, the subject, and—depending on which e-mail service you use—you might also see the time, date, and size columns. Where do your eyes go first? Some people glance at the sender column, but if you're like most people, you'll tend to scan the subject column to see which e-mail you want to open first, right? Which subject lines are you most likely to open first, and why? All the tests I've been involved in show that e-mail recipients from a confirmed opt-in list are at least five times more likely to open those that have the appearance of personal e-mail versus commercial e-mail, and those that have a friendly tone rather than a corporate, businesslike tone. Which of the following e-mails would you open first?

Subject: Online Marketing Gazette
Subject: Avon Spring Specials

Subject: Are the rumors about you true?
Subject: 30% Discount on Eyewear!
Subject: Holiday Bonanza
Subject: You got me worried
Subject: Save up to 70% off at Overstock, 40% at Amazon, and more!

I'm betting you'll open the e-mail with the subject line "Are the rumors about you true?" or "You got me worried" first.

It's obvious which e-mails are personal and which are commercial, and it's easy to see that if the subject line of your e-mail looks like it's coming from a friend, it's more likely to be opened first.

Here are a few more examples of subject lines that give the appearance of personal e-mail:

Subject: This got my attention . . .
Subject: Did you get my message?
Subject: This finally came . . .
Subject: Not sure if you got this?
Subject: I'm not quite sure about you . . .
Subject: Okay, I'm guilty . . .
Subject: Here's what I promised . . .
Subject: Here's the formula . . .
Subject: I almost forgot . . .
Subject: Sorry, I goofed . . .

When your eyes zero in on the subject line, they also dart quickly (if not peripherally) to the Sender field of the in-box. Therefore, the subject and the sender must agree with each other. Suppose you craft a subject line like the following in an attempt to trick the recipient into thinking it is a personal e-mail:

Subject: Hey, was that you I saw?

If the name in the Sender field is "Internet Profits Weekly," your otherwise friendly and curiosity-provoking subject line is negated when your recipient realizes it's a ploy. Above all, be real.

Some say that this technique is deceptive because the recipient is not really your friend but, rather, a prospect, a customer, a subscriber, or just someone who has opted into your list. The fact is, your e-mail recipient *should* perceive you as a friend. That's the heart of relationship marketing. That's the reason you ask viewers for their e-mail addresses in the first place—to start a relationship with them so they can get to know you, trust you, and eventually buy from you.

There's a very thin line between creating a riveting subject line and one that is deceptive. The new rules of the CAN-SPAM Act require that the subject line of any commercial e-mail not be deceptive. Therefore, do not use the bait-and-switch ploy of using a subject line that is designed for shock value or for the sole purpose of getting recipients to tear open your e-mail if the content of the e-mail bears no relevance to the subject line. Furthermore, if you use trickery to get recipients to open your enticing message, they may bite once or twice, but when they recognize the pattern, the game's over. They're likely to ignore all future e-mails from you, they may ask to be removed from your list, they could report your e-mail as spam, or they might blacklist your e-mail address via their spam filter, preventing your message from getting through to them. There are no hard-and-fast rules in e-mail. When you do your own intelligence work, the frame of mind of your audience will become apparent to you, and writing subject lines that are noticed will be a snap.

It would serve you well to know the hidden rules that spam filters use to discourage unsolicited commercial e-mail senders from trying to fool their recipients by using subject lines that appear to be coming from a friend. For instance, if you send out a personal e-mail to a friend, with the subject line "Here's what I promised . . . ," it wouldn't be tagged as spam. But if you sent out an e-mail broadcast with that subject line, every word that has four letters or more must be capitalized, as follows: "Here's What I Promised . . ." or it may be labeled as spam. This is just one way e-mail recipients are able to differentiate between personal e-mail and commercial e-mail.

When you get a feel for the language used in e-mails that get maximum readership, you've won half the battle. Reading this, you might think that creating a personal-sounding e-mail does not seem difficult. After all, you e-mail your friends all the time. Shouldn't it be a simple task to write marketing e-mails the same way? One would think so, but it's not. Somehow, when we sit down to write marketing e-mail, many of us try to be clever and creative or we inject a big dose of marketese and, as a result, lose our friendly, personal tone, as we subconsciously switch to writing in a commercial or corporate style. That puts us way off the mark when it comes to e-mail communications.

To make matters interesting, I'm going to throw you a curveball. I recently wrote a successful subject line that read "Why the FDA Is Suppressing the One-Minute Cure for All Diseases." That doesn't sound friendly or conversational at all. It's a straightforward, "what's contained within," editorial-style subject line.

When sent to the appropriate target audience, it works because it suggests a benefit to the reader and arouses curiosity (what is the one-minute cure and why is the FDA suppressing it?). Furthermore, it reads like an editorial, not an ad (even though the body of the e-mail promotes a book titled *The One-Minute Cure*). This subject line appeals to the audience's information-seeking mindset. Again, there are no hard-and-fast rules—only guidelines. What is true is that it's essential to pay attention to the frame of mind of your audience and the medium in which they will be viewing your message, and to assess the impact you're making. Here are a few examples of editorial-style subject lines designed for specific target audiences:

Subject: Venture Capitalists Explain How to Get Funded
Subject: Warren Buffett's Favorite Foreign Stock Picks
Subject: This Company May Be the Biggest Threat to Your Family's Health
Subject: Vitamin E Linked to Cancer

Personalizing E-mails—Not All It's Cracked Up to Be. We've established that, above all, e-mail subject lines need to be as friendly, human, and personable as possible, but do they need to be personalized? I have long advocated personalizing subject lines, but I was in for a shock when I opened my e-mail in-box and found five e-mails from five different senders with the following subject lines:

Subject: Maria, this Friday
Subject: Maria, will you be part of this test?

Subject: Will you be near a phone tomorrow, Maria?
Subject: Maria, your account
Subject: Maria, last chance!

The e-mails came from five different senders. That was a real eye-opener. I realized that the tactic of using the recipient's first name as a way of personalizing the subject line had become so widespread that instead of making me want to open the e-mails, it made them candidates for deletion! Any one of these subject lines on its own might have been an effective device for getting people to open your e-mail, but when viewed in the context of the recipient's in-box, it lost its punch.

This may seem minor, but it has major repercussions for your marketing, not only in terms of this particular device but as it applies to other techniques that might, over time, become overused.

What would happen if you weren't constantly in tune with your audience's frame of mind or weren't paying attention to the trends as they emerge? If you rely on what others are doing and continue to blindly use the same tactic, your e-mails will fail miserably and you might never know why your response rates dropped.

About two years ago, I received an e-mail from a well-known Internet marketer whose subject line was as follows:

Subject: It's not _____ that made Bill H. an online millionaire,
it's _____ . . .

At first, I thought the subject line was brilliant because it made me tear open the e-mail to satisfy my curiosity. It's interesting to note that the Internet marketer who sent out the e-mail is also a professional teleseminar host who always makes it a habit to distribute advance teleseminar handouts filled with intriguing, fill-in-the-blank statements—statements to be completed with information presented at the teleseminar. That seemed to me a terrific strategy for getting people curious enough to attend the teleseminar (see the bullet point "Incomplete thoughts" under "Crafting the All-Important Subject Line" later in this chapter)—and the fill-in-the-blanks subject line he employed was equally effective in getting the reader to open his e-mail. Just as I predicted, the e-mail did, indeed, get a high readership and a high click-through rate. But after the fill-in-the-blank tactic was repeated a few times (and copied by dozens of other Internet marketers to boot), the e-mails that employed the tactic were no longer being opened and, instead, were largely ignored. There was nothing intrinsically wrong with the psychological device used, mind you, but its execution (fill in the blanks) became overused, and that rendered it ineffective.

Part of deciphering the frame of mind of your prospects is observing what they're wising up to, what they're becoming immune to, and which tactics are no longer working. You will be well served if you also observe what e-mail spammers are doing. Spammers often resort to devices that attempt to disguise the fact that their e-mails are unsolicited (such as using phrases like *at your request*). Those devices start becoming recognizable to your target readers, who then begin ignoring or deleting the messages. If those devices start to resemble yours, you need to adjust lest your e-mails be mistaken for spam.

Crafting the All-Important Subject Line. Recall that I mentioned the most important element of a website: the *first screen*. In an e-mail, the subject line is the most important element.

Direct magazine reported that an American leatherware company sent out a marketing e-mail to its mailing list and accidentally omitted the body copy. The e-mail was sent to the entire list with nothing but the subject line. Much to the company's surprise, that mailing generated the largest response rate it had ever had!

When writing subject lines, keep these things in mind:

- *This.* The word *this* in the subject line of an e-mail is proven to get recipients to open their e-mail.

    Subject: This is what I was talking about . . .

    This is so powerful because it arouses the recipients' curiosity, and they must open the e-mail to find out what *this* is. Of course, not all subject lines containing the word *this* will be opened. For example, "This is the best moneymaker in the world . . ." would most likely be recognized as spam and immediately deleted. Other powerful e-mail openers are *here* and *about your . . .*

- *Ellipsis points.* Whenever possible, I use ellipsis points at the end of my subject lines. This creates a sense of incompleteness, which makes readers want to rush to open your e-mail.
- *Incomplete thoughts.* Presenting an incomplete thought in the subject line, especially about a topic of particular interest to your target audience, causes what I call a "brain itch." Scientifically, it arouses the reticular activating system (RAS) in the brain, which is the part of the brain that dislikes incomplete information and does not rest until it finds the information it needs to close a topic. This "brain itch" can be relieved only when the reader opens the e-mail to complete the thought. The thought, of course, must relate to the topic of your e-mail. Otherwise, recipients will click open your e-mail just to satisfy their curiosity, then click away when they realize it was simply a ploy to get their attention.
- *Why, what, and how.* When used properly in a subject line, the words *why*, *what*, and *how* pack a powerful punch. Again, this is because they arouse the e-mail recipient's curiosity and cause that "brain itch" which compels them to open the e-mail. Examples of these types of subject lines that have pulled high open rates are:

   Why a Man Who Discovered a Cancer Cure Got Jailed
   What Your Overworked Liver Is Dying to Tell You
   How Bees Produce a Cure for AIDS
   How Thoughts Spontaneously Heal Disease—Including Cancer
   Why Joint Pills Don't Work
   How Touching Your Ear Can Help You Kick the Smoking Habit

Words to Avoid Putting in the Subject Line. Strangely enough, some of the attention-grabbing words that you would use on a website are some of the very words you must avoid in an e-mail subject line:

Buy	Power
Discount	Powerful investment
Free, Maximize	Profit
Money opportunity	Sale
New	Special

Words like these reek of advertising or commerce, when your goal is to appear friendly and personal. While these are the magic words advertisers and direct marketers swear by and use liberally in their copy, they are not effective when used in e-mail. This is an area in which what works well in offline marketing (direct mail, radio and TV, print ads, or infomercials) does not work well on the web. Chances are, these words will fail miserably on the web, not to mention that they might be censored by spam filters.

Permission-Based E-mail: Not a License to Be Bland. I'm often asked whether it is advisable to put the name of the company or newsletter in the subject line of an e-mail. My answer is that permission-based e-mail doesn't give you the liberty to be bland.

Much has been said about the recipient's permission being the foundation of e-mail marketing. Back in 2001, Brann Worldwide, a marketing agency, conducted a national survey and found that 92 percent of U.S. consumers feel positively toward companies that ask their permission before sending them information. But that was in 2001, and the online population's attitudes have changed since then. Most people dislike e-mails they once gave permission to but now no longer wish to receive. Q Interactive, an online marketing services provider, and Marketing Sherpa, a marketing research firm, conducted a joint e-mail survey about how people's definition of spam has changed from *unsolicited* e-mail to *unwanted* e-mail. One of the most striking findings is that 56 percent of the survey participants no longer regard spam as simply e-mail that violates permission-based regulations but now include any e-mail that causes consumer dissatisfaction. Therefore, most people now consider the following types of e-mail to be spam: (1) marketing messages from known senders if the message is just not interesting to them, (2) too frequent marketing messages from companies they know, and (3) e-mails that were once useful but aren't relevant anymore.

The majority of marketers are as yet unaware of this change in people's attitudes toward e-mail; therefore, they continue to operate on the premise that their e-mails are welcome as long as their recipients have given their permission. Proceeding on this inaccurate premise, some marketers believe that the subject lines of their e-mails must identify who they are in order to remind the recipients that the e-mails contain requested information.

In an environment where most e-mail recipients can't remember whether or not they asked for this or that information, you don't have the luxury of playing it safe by using a bland subject line that consists of nothing but the name of your company or newsletter. The objective of the subject line is to give the recipient a compelling reason to open your e-mail *now*. Instead of using the all-important subject line to state *who* you are, it's far better to use the Sender field or the first sentence to identify yourself.

Element 2: The First Sentence. The next thing you need is an opening line that identifies who you are and establishes rapport. Your e-mail must have a real person behind it; it can't be a faceless piece of communication. You can start by saying something that you would say to a friend. I've seen an Australian newsletter publisher, for example, start an e-mail by describing the wonderful weather they were having in Australia and briefly describing the idyllic setting where he lives and works. A famous Internet marketer started an e-mail by saying that he just got back from a successful trip, followed by a short description of that trip. Brevity is the key; just a couple of ice-breaking sentences should suffice.

Some copywriters and marketers skip this seemingly insignificant gesture because they want to get to the point and not waste their audience's time. As a result, they miss the opportunity to bond with their readers and gain rapport with them. Some of the most successful e-mails are the ones that elicit the reaction from people that makes them say, "I feel like I know you!" This is your opportunity to get your audience to like you, and if they like you they're more inclined to buy from you.

Element 3: Stay on Point. This is the gist of your marketing message or the promise of a benefit to come. A good way to do this is by using a journalists' device called the *inverted pyramid* (an upside-down triangle, with the narrow tip pointing down and the broad base at the top). The broad base represents the most significant, newsworthy information, and the narrow tip the least important information. Following this method, you put the most important information at the beginning and the least important information at the end of your e-mail. As with most journalism, brevity and clarity get high marks, so get right to the point. Your readers are busy, and they don't want you wasting their time.

Whatever you do, don't make the mistake many Internet entrepreneurs make and start your e-mail with a lengthy reminder that the e-mail is not unsolicited, that the recipient has agreed to receive your mailing or newsletter, and then offer instructions on how to opt out. While this statement acknowledges the permission-based aspect of your relationship, it wastes the first screen of your e-mail, which is the prime area for starting your sales process. Put instructions for opting out at the end of your message.

Element 4: Just One Message. Don't litter your e-mail with a slew of subjects and topics (unless your e-mail is a newsletter). Stick to a single message so that you can lead your reader down your intended sales path.

When average recipients receive an e-mail, particularly a lengthy one, they don't read it sequentially. They scan it looking for things that may interest them. If three or four topics grab their attention, they make a mental note of them and start reading the one that interests them most. As they read that part of your e-mail, their brains are unable to pay full attention to what they're reading. Various other ideas start competing for attention. This can easily work against you, especially if you are trying to sell something. Not only will you not have your readers' full attention, but also they are not likely to go down your intended sales path or take action of any kind, because the brain is compelling them to read the other things that attracted them.

Multiple messages in a single e-mail, combined with the fact that readers have short attention spans, make for an unholy alliance when it comes to e-mail marketing.

Element 5: Provide Value. Give your e-mail recipients something of value in return for their undivided attention. This could be something free or at a discount, or some useful information or a special offer.

Element 6: The Benefit. It's not enough just to tell your readers what your offer is; you must demonstrate how it will benefit them. An easy way to do this is to state the offer and follow it up with " . . . so that you can [*fill in the blank*]." A travel website, for instance, can say, "Try our complimentary fare-tracking service so that you can be informed weekly of all the unpublished, hard-to-find bargain fares to Boston—without having to scour the web."

Element 7: A Call to Action. Many e-mail marketers go to great lengths to create well-crafted e-mails that make a compelling selling argument about their product or service, but at the last moment, when the prospect is just about ready to take the next step, they drop the ball by failing to ask the prospect to take action. The action can be a request to click, sign up, register, or buy, but whatever it is, you must make sure you tell the reader what to do next. This is true not only for your e-mails but for your website and all marketing communications.

PUT THE COMPETITIVE EDGE INTO YOUR E-MAIL MARKETING

Forrester Research analyst Jim Nail underscored how important it is for e-commerce players to use e-mail to create a dialogue and deepen intimacy with customers in order to maintain the response rates that e-mail marketing often enjoys. He emphasized the importance of starting slowly and gradually building rapport, which allows you to gain additional personal information that in turn helps you fine-tune your marketing and sales message.

Creating a dialogue, deepening intimacy, and building rapport take us back to frame-of-mind marketing and the importance of knowing your prospects' and customers' frame of mind. Once you've identified and written down all the aspects of your own list members' frame of mind, you are ready to write an effective e-mail.

The following technique takes the struggle out of writing e-mail.

Step 1: Write down the three words that best describe the message you're trying to convey. Not a three-word sentence, mind you, but three individual words or phrases that summarize the thought you are trying to communicate—for example, a smell, a benefit, an emotion, a color, a mood, a texture, a sound, a flavor, or an adjective that describes your message. If I were writing an e-mail about a hair restoration product, I might choose patent, scientific, and side effects. Or I might choose clinical, success rate, and track record. (See Chapter 6 for a more detailed explanation of the magic of three.)

Your three words help narrow your focus and keep you grounded. After you select your words, start writing your e-mail, paying attention to these simple rules:

- Focus on the frame of mind of your audience, and write in a way that appeals to that frame of mind.
- Write the way you speak.
- Don't try to be creative or formal.
- Write the letter as though you're writing it to one person only—and that person is your friend.

Step 2: Give yourself five minutes to write the letter, making sure you use your three keywords in the letter. Don't edit the e-mail as you write. Here's a trick that makes editing your e-mail painless: When you are finished writing, e-mail it to yourself. The perspective you'll gain from this experience is priceless. You'll see firsthand how you'd perceive your subject line relative to other subject lines in your in-box. Would you pick it out among the rest of your incoming e-mail? Would you open it and read it? You'll read it in a whole new light: from the point of view of your recipient. With every sentence, ask yourself, "Is this something that I would say to a friend?" If the answer is no, revise what you've written.

Similarly, you will discover the nuances of language and whether you've succeeded in gaining rapport and persuading your prospects to take the action you want them to take. All the rough areas that need work will become apparent, and you will see exactly what needs to be fixed.

Adapt as Your Audience's Frame of Mind Changes

When you send a series of e-mails to your list, the recipients' frame of mind is slightly altered with each mailing, as your previous communications influence their expectations and predispositions. They may have warmed up to you and begun to trust you more, or, if you have misread their frame of mind, maybe just the opposite.

All too often, marketers assume that each e-mail gets the same kind of attention as those that went before. This is a mistake. You must never write in a vacuum or regard each e-mail as an isolated piece. You must think of each e-mail as part of a conversation in an ongoing relationship.

When you have a good grasp of your prospects' frame of mind at every stage, you are in a better position to monopolize their attention. Since you know what your prospects' predispositions and expectations are, you have the opportunity to find ways to engage them. For instance, you can use the element of surprise to delight or intrigue them, or you can find ways to arouse their curiosity in order to make them look forward to future e-mails.

The variations are practically infinite. Just consider the unique frame of mind of your own list members and you can come up with ideas that may have never occurred to you before and that are custom-made for your list.

Using E-Mail to Get Attention

Earlier we discussed the reticular activating system (RAS) in relation to subject lines of e-mails and the brain's need for closure, its need to complete incomplete thoughts. The RAS, in essence, is the attention center in the brain. It is the key to turning on the brain and is considered the center of motivation. It determines what we pay attention to.

Here's an example of how the RAS works: Do you remember the last time you decided to buy a new car? Let's say you decided that you wanted to buy a Ford Explorer. All of a sudden you started seeing more Ford Explorers than you'd ever seen before. That's not because people are buying Explorers in record numbers; it's because the RAS of your brain made you aware of them, whereas previously you ignored them.

The RAS receives thousands of stimuli and messages every second, and since it is not possible for the brain to pay attention to everything, it filters or blocks out most of the messages, allowing only certain ones to come to our attention. You can immediately see how valuable it would be if you could get your e-mail messages to rise above the avalanche of messages that your recipients receive. Here are some of the ways you can stimulate your prospects' RAS in order to transition them to a receptive frame of mind:

1. *Ask your reader to write something down.* The act of writing something down helps trigger the RAS. In her book *Write It Down, Make It Happen* (Fireside, 2000), Henriette Anne Klauser writes, "Writing triggers the RAS, which in turn sends a signal to the cerebral cortex: 'Wake up! Pay attention! Don't miss this detail!' " What you ask readers to write down depends on the nature of the product or service that you sell. I have a client who is a director of a discount buying club that offers up to 18 percent in rebates whenever members purchase from among 200-plus online stores with more than 250,000 products. An e-mail I wrote to encourage members to shop in these stores included the words "I'm sure you're eager to get started, so make a list of all the things you need to buy in the next three months, such as [*I listed a dozen items*]" and concluded with the words "Go ahead and write them all down."

   The simple act of writing down the items puts them at the forefront of your readers' minds and makes them receptive to going the next step and doing what you ask them to do. Think back on your own experience. Isn't it true that whenever you had a written list of things you needed to buy (whether you carried that list with you or not), your mind subconsciously zeroed in on those items when they came into your field of vision? Your mind may have tuned out those things had you not written them down.

2. *Create a small, but entertaining or interesting, activity.* This provides a refreshing diversion from the usual barrage of commercial e-mail. Make sure the activity leads up to a well-crafted marketing message that invites readers to click through to your website or otherwise carries them along your intended sales path. When you lead off with a noncommercial activity, you get recipients to agree to something. When you subsequently get them to click through to your website, that's another *yes*. In effect, you are breaking a large buying decision into several manageable steps to which the reader can say "Yes!" Professional salespeople use this technique all the time.

   One marketer who sells software for installing website audio sends out an e-mail inviting recipients to send a free personalized audio postcard to three friends. It is an ingenious (and fun) activity that also demonstrates the ease of producing an audio recording, displays its excellent sound quality, and thereby paves the way to the sale of the software.

Another marketer, who sells a book for dog lovers and owners titled *Your Dog's Love Letter,* sent out an e-mail inviting the members of her list to view a heartwarming video on YouTube about a dog trainer who sings five puppies to sleep in less than a minute.

Subject: This dog video is priceless—a must-see . . .

Hi [FirstName],

I hope this letter finds you well and enjoying the summer.

I just thought because you're a dog lover, that you'd enjoy this 1½- minute video. You won't believe it 'til you see it. This is a must-see for dog owners. http://www.youtube.com/watch?v=G4KWZJ4tOsA

Let me know what you think of it.

All good wishes,
Coy Meadows

As a result of sending this e-mail to the 145 people on her mailing list, the video she uploaded to YouTube was viewed by over 8,571 people in just 14 days. As of the time of this writing, 73,376 people have viewed the video. Apparently, her e-mail recipients had forwarded the video link to other dog lovers and owners. The interesting thing is that she didn't even own the video. It belonged to someone else who already had the video on YouTube and had received over 4 million views. All she did was ask permission to use the video and repurpose it for her marketing campaign by embedding her website address in it. Viewers of the video caused her website traffic to spike and sales of her book to increase significantly—even though there was no call to action in the e-mail whatsoever.

3. *Invite your recipient to participate in a quick poll or a one-question survey.* This is an involvement device that gets your readers to pay at-

tention to a subject on which you want them to focus. The subject of the poll or survey should be one that is of particular interest to your list members, one that gives them a chance to interact with you and express an opinion about something that is important to them, as well as one that gives you the opportunity to segue into your marketing message. As an incentive, you might offer to give participants access to the poll or survey results. (Create e-mail surveys at www.surveymonkey.com, or go to www.freeonlinesurveys.com to create surveys for free—see Chapter 12 for details.)

4. *"Please forward."* The Association for Interactive Marketing (AIM) discovered a technique for encouraging pass-along readership of its newsletter. AIM simply added "Pls. Forward" to the end of its newsletter subject lines. The association reports that this little device has more than doubled its circulation numbers.

What *Really* Works on the Internet Sometimes Doesn't

There are rarely absolute truths when it comes to Internet marketing. There are only conditional truths, based on the frame of mind of the marketplace or your audience. What was true yesterday, last week, or last year may not be true today. This is especially true in the changing online climate of Web 3.0.

With direct mail, when you track and test your mail pieces and identify your control piece, you can roll out the control piece and virtually predict how much money you will make with mathematical certainty. On the Internet, results are not as predictable, because things change rapidly. While I'm an advocate of tracking and testing online, my test results may or may not apply to you, and you should be wary of those who offer sweeping generalizations.

No one website strategy, e-mail tactic, or marketing message works all the time. Ultimately, you alone can determine what does and does not work, depending on the frame of mind of your own audience and the results of your own tracking and testing. There are e-mail marketing services that have the ability to evaluate the effectiveness of your e-mail campaigns by tracking how many of your e-mails were opened, replies, length of time opened, specific links clicked on, bounces, unsubscribes, and even orders completed. In my opinion, these services are invaluable not only because they show unequivocally what's working and what's not working, but because they also enrich your knowledge of your audience's frame of mind in real time.

SIG File: Your Online Business Card

A signature file, also known as a SIG file, is, quite simply, your digital signature. It's the part of your e-mail message that appears at the very bottom and tells your story—who you are and what you do—or features whatever product or service you are promoting. A SIG file can be delivered in html or plaintext.

Think of it as your online business card, which you can use as a marketing tool because it gives you the opportunity to advertise your website, your product, or your services with every e-mail you send, at no cost to you. Most free e-mail service providers such as Gmail, Yahoo! Mail, and MSN Hotmail enable users to load their SIG files onto the e-mail account settings so that the digital signature is automatically appended at the end of all outgoing messages. Likewise, most e-mail applications like Eudora and Outlook enable users to create a SIG file that is appended to each outgoing e-mail, and they also give options such as graphics, stylized text, and even a virtual business card.

Example

Bob Grant, L.P.C.

"The Relationship Doctor"

http://www.RelationshipHeadquarters.com

E- mail: bob@RelationshipHeadquarters.com

= = = = = = = = = = =

Get your F.R.E.E. Report: "The Mistakes Women Make That Cause Men to Leave Them." How many mistakes are you making? Send a blank e-mail to mistakes@domain.com and the report will be sent to your e-mail box instantly.

How Your E-Mail Reputation Affects E-Mail Deliverability

Clearly, e-mail marketing still offers one of the best dollar-for-dollar returns on investment (ROIs) in the entire field of marketing, although ROIs are diminishing rapidly.

While the sales generated from each dollar spent on e-mail marketing still compares favorably to those resulting from offline marketing media (including direct mail), open rates have dipped to all-time lows, and e-mail recipients have become all too eager to click the Report As Spam button on commercial e-mails.

The main reason for this growing animosity and lack of responsiveness, of course, is that the number of commercial e-mails being sent out every day (including those that are unsolicited and unwanted) has reached record highs. Internet users are tired of being inundated and have begun tuning out instead of being responsive the way they used to be. Moreover, people are tired of being sold to, talked at, or pitched practically every minute of the day by marketers. Today's consumer is not only a victim of information overwhelm but is also becoming increasingly guarded when it comes to marketing. For your e-mails to impact this audience, it's imperative that they be engaging, informative, and beneficial, as suggested by the guidelines contained in this chapter.

There is a practice prevalent among ISPs to block not only incoming e-mails that resemble spam but also e-mails coming from specific e-mail senders whom they identify as spammers. According to the ClickZ Network, AOL routinely blocks and deletes around 75 percent of incoming e-mail it identifies as spam. This points to yet another issue that e-mail marketers need to pay special attention to when it comes to ensuring e-mail deliverability—and that is one's *e-mail reputation.*

E-mail reputation is similar to the conventional concept of reputation except that it has to do with your e-mail-sending practices and behavior. ISPs use your online reputation score to decide whether or not to deliver the e-mails sent by you. Online reputation has two fundamental aspects:

1. *Recipient reputation.* This represents your track record with your e-mail recipients and incorporates such factors as including a readily identifi-

able sender in the From field, ensuring the appropriate frequency of e-mails, providing relevant content, sending only to people who opted in or subscribed, providing an easy way to unsubscribe, and honoring unsubscribe requests on a timely basis.

2. *ISP reputation.* This is your track record with ISPs that monitor whether the e-mails you're sending are addressed to accurate, live e-mail addresses, that there is a consistency in the From addresses and IP address(es), and that your e-mails are opened by and clicked on by recipients.

Companies like IronPort and Return Path regularly monitor hundreds of millions of e-mail senders daily—their infrastructure, e-mail-sending behaviors and practices, whether or not they're blacklisted by the major ISPs, and a multitude of other e-mail-related factors. You could be blacklisted by the major ISPs due to some e-mail behavior you exhibited in the past and not even know it. If you're blacklisted by an ISP—Yahoo!, for instance—all e-mail you send to recipients who use Yahoo! Mail will be blocked. Unsuspecting marketers often have low open rates and click-throughs on their e-mail campaigns because they have poor e-mail reputation scores.

How sure are you that your e-mail is making it to your recipients' in-boxes? How do you find out what your e-mail reputation score is? There are a variety of ways. SenderScore.com offers detailed e-mail reputation reports. It also has Blacklist Lookup, where you can check whether your IP address or the e-mail server sending your messages is included in the Reputation Network Blacklist due to past behavior. If so, it may be difficult for your e-mail messages to be delivered to some recipients.

Just as your credit score determines whether or not creditors will extend credit to you and what interest rate you'll get on your loans, your e-mail reputation score determines whether ISPs will allow your outgoing e-mails to be delivered to your recipients. Sometimes ISPs like AOL even go to the extent of restricting member access to sites run by spammers and locking down accounts that generate spam.

So how do you prevent yourself from getting a low e-mail reputation score—and what should you do if you discover that you already have a low reputation score? Following are a few tips for improving your e-mail reputation and, consequently, your e-mail deliverability:

1. Use confirmed opt-in lists (or double opt-in, whenever possible) to ensure that only willing recipients subscribe to your list and to prevent the accumulation of inaccurate, inactive, or fake e-mail addresses.

2. Make sure your e-mail content is relevant to the interests of your list members and that it coincides with the topic that they gave you permission to send them. Irrelevant e-mail content may cause your recipients dissatisfaction and result in your e-mail being deemed spam, thereby degrading your e-mail reputation.

3. Limit the frequency of your e-mails. When subscribers receive an excessive number of e-mails from you, they might not unsubscribe, but they will begin to ignore most of them. ISPs such as AOL, MSN Hotmail, Yahoo!, Gmail, and AOL are able to track both open rates and click-through rates—and fewer opened e-mails and click-throughs will hurt your e-mail reputation.

4. Send e-mail in smaller chunks to keep excessive volume from being blocked by ISPs. ISPs do not like large numbers of e-mails to be sent simultaneously because not only do excessive e-mails take a heavy toll on bandwidth but large mailings are usually characteristic of spam. You are likely to be suspected of being a spammer if you don't get into the practice of sending your e-mail in smaller segments.

5. Instruct your subscribers to whitelist the e-mail address from which you routinely send your e-mails. A *whitelist* is a list of e-mail addresses or domain names from which an e-mail blocking program allows messages to be received. Important: Because most people do not know how to whitelist an e-mail address and the instructions are not always easy to find within the e-mail account, you must provide specific instructions.

6. Consider paying for e-mail reputation management services such as Return Path, or send out mail via a third-party professional e-mail service. E-mail reputation management services like Return Path help ensure that your e-mails adhere to industry best practices, and as a re-

sult your e-mail reputation improves and your in-box deliverability is maximized.

7. Refrain from sending commercial e-mail to mailing lists other than your own. Most marketers are unable to resist the temptation of buying third-party opt-in lists, especially when they don't have sizable lists of their own. Third-party opt-in lists are big business these days. Those who build and sell these lists usually entice people to join their list by offering them a reward such as a travel certificate, a chance to win a grand prize, a gift card that can be used at a store or restaurant, or one of many other freebies. When people opt into these lists, they usually fail to read a notice in fine print that says the company has the right to sell or trade its e-mail addresses with others, or they just blindly agree to continue receiving e-mails from the company and other third parties in exchange for the freebies. Therefore, when you buy such third-party opt-in lists and send commercial e-mail to them—even including a reminder that they've agreed to receive information from third parties—you have unwilling e-mail recipients who have usually been bombarded by all the other commercial enterprises who also bought those lists. There was a time when third-party opt-in lists might have worked to legitimize your unsolicited e-mails, but these days, as ISPs become overzealous about open rates, click-through rates, and spam complaints from e-mail recipients—even though the list you bought is a confirmed opt-in list—you could land on the blacklist of the major ISPs with a single mailing. If that happens, your e-mail reputation score will plunge, which will render most, if not all, of your subsequent e-mails undeliverable.

8. Make it easy for your list members to unsubscribe from your list. Although including an opt-out notice is now a requirement under the new rules of the CAN-SPAM Act, it is even more important for you to ensure that the mechanism for unsubscribing is easy. It should be no more difficult than sending a reply e-mail or visiting a single webpage. Although every e-mail marketer dreads having list members opt out of their list, if you don't make it easy for them to unsubscribe, the Report As Spam button is infinitely easier for your e-mail recipients to click. Al-

ways remember that a list member's request to unsubscribe from your list does not affect your e-mail reputation, but a spam complaint will. In the final analysis, you won't want to keep unwilling recipients subscribed to your list anyway because they're not likely to respond to your offers.

9. Include your postal address with all your commercial e-mails. The rules of the CAN-SPAM Act require senders of commercial e-mail to include the sender's current physical address. This need not be the actual physical address of your business, but according to the new rules under this act, a post office box or private mailbox is acceptable. This requirement is intended to ensure that both e-mail recipients and law enforcement authorities are able to contact senders. If you don't comply with this requirement and an ISP decides to take issue with it, or a recipient complains about your noncompliance, you risk not only getting a poor e-mail reputation but also incurring federal penalties.

Now that you've learned the key strategies for writing web copy and online marketing communications, it's time to learn how to make your web copy even more compelling through the use of psychological devices that can turn skeptical prospects into willing buyers.

CHAPTER 5

USING PSYCHOLOGY TO MOTIVATE PROSPECTS TO BECOME PURCHASERS

What power there is in a drop of ink, which falling like dew upon a thought produces that which makes thousands, perhaps millions think.

—LORD BYRON

Step 4 of our web copy blueprint called for adding the psychological devices that transform readers into buyers. These are tactics that fly beneath the radar of your readers' perception, producing an almost hypnotic effect that actually makes them want to buy what you are selling—often without knowing why. These devices are extremely powerful and, if used inappropriately, can be dangerous. I urge you to use them judiciously, responsibly, and ethically.

Using psychology to sell is not about conning people into giving you their hard-earned money. It's not about manipulating people to do something against their will. It is about using your understanding of human nature to make your readers voluntarily and willingly become happily involved in a buying decision that you have made painless, even enjoyable. The fact is that all the psychological devices and triggers in the world won't amount to anything if you fail to speak to the needs of your target audience—and your target audience's frame of mind.

THE "REASON WHY"

In his book *Influence: The Psychology of Persuasion* (rev. ed., Collins Business, 1998), Robert Cialdini, Ph.D., discusses an experiment conducted by Harvard social psychologist Ellen Langer in which she demonstrated that people like to have a reason for doing something. Her experiment was simple. People were waiting in line to use a copy machine at a library. Langer's colleague asked those waiting if she could go ahead of them, saying, "Excuse me, I have five pages. May I use the Xerox machine because I'm in a rush?" Interestingly, 94 percent of those asked complied. Note the word *because,* which introduced a reason for the request.

The experiment was repeated with a new group. This time Langer's colleague said, "Excuse me, I have five pages. May I use the Xerox machine?" Only 60 percent agreed, a significant decrease. When the requester did not offer a reason, significantly fewer people complied.

They repeated the experiment a third time, saying, "Excuse me, I have five pages. May I use the Xerox machine, because I have to make some copies?" Although the reason was not a convincing one (everyone in line had to make copies), 93 percent of those asked said yes. Just the semblance of a reason introduced by the word *because* was enough to persuade people to comply.

In selling a product or service, always tell your readers why they need to do what you're asking them to do. For example: "You must watch this eye-opening video now because your life—or the life of a loved one—may depend on it." Sometimes, something as simple as "You must act now because this offer expires on December 31, after which we can no longer accept orders" is sufficient.

THE ZEIGARNIK EFFECT

The Russian psychologist and theorist Bluma Zeigarnik (November 9, 1900–February 24, 1988) is best known for having discovered a phenomenon called the Zeigarnik effect. She first took an interest in the phenomenon when her professor, Gestalt psychologist Kurt Lewin, observed that waiters at a local eatery had better recollections of orders that had yet to be served than of those that had already been served. From that observation, she theorized that people have a tendency to remember things that are unfinished or incomplete. The Zeigarnik effect refers to the state of mental tension and unbalance caused by uncompleted tasks.

When website visitors arrive at a website and are met with many options and links leading to various items of interest, mental tension and unbalance occur for as long as they aren't able to complete the task of clicking on those items of interest. When applied to writing web copy, this means that you shouldn't litter your website (or your sales webpage) with a slew of subjects and topics that will distract your reader. You must stick to a single message so that you can lead readers down your intended sales path. This is the *linear path* method of writing web copy.

To understand this better, let's examine the thought processes of website visitors: When web visitors arrive at your site, they scan through the entire site looking for things that interest them. If several buttons and links grab their attention, they make a mental note of them and start reading the one that interests them most. Now, here's the interesting thing: While they are reading that page, the Zeigarnik effect takes over, creating the mental tension and confusion that come from uncompleted tasks, which, in the case of your visitor, is the urge to click on those other buttons or links.

Since the brain is unable to pay full attention to the topic at hand until those other tasks are completed, this can create a problem, especially if you happen to be in the middle of making a selling proposition when the effect takes over. Not only will you lose your readers' attention, it is unlikely they will go down your intended sales path or take action of any kind, because their brains are compelling them to do the other tasks. That's why it's advisable to minimize the number of unnecessary links and buttons on your website or sales webpage—to keep your reader on the linear path.

Likewise, mental tension may appear when, in the course of reading your copy, your readers come across unfamiliar concepts or terms. To combat this, I employ small pop-up windows to explain concepts that might create mental tension. That way, readers can click on the link, quickly relieve the tension by reading the brief explanation in the pop-up window, and continue reading what

I want them to read. The other way, they might be tempted to click away, never to return.

Both the linear path concept and the Zeigarnik effect are very powerful concepts that many web copywriters and website owners fail to understand. If you're ever tempted to include advertising banners on your website, or Google AdSense ads, or reciprocal links with other websites, or links to other unrelated pages in your website that don't contribute to the sales process, remember that you are violating the linear path concept and allowing the Zeigarnik effect to kick in.

THE CLIFFHANGER

The cliffhanger is one of my favorite devices. If you've ever watched the season finale of a TV series, or heard teasers for TV news or newsmagazines that say things like "Is green tea the new miracle cure for cancer? Film at eleven," you already understand the concept.

This is a variation of the Zeigarnik effect. The uncompleted thought demands our attention. As a result, we eagerly sit in front of our TV sets to see the season premieres of our favorite shows just to find out what happens next or listen to an entire news broadcast just to hear that 30-second snippet that answers the question that's been bugging our brains.

You can imagine the impact this principle has on web copy. Whenever I break my copy into multiple webpages and it's essential that readers click through to the next page, I use a cliffhanger to get them to click. For example, "The secret ingredient of branding that can single-handedly turn a small business enterprise into a mega-success is hidden in Tommy Hilfiger's story. Did you catch it? Here it is . . ." (followed by a button designated Next Page).

You can also apply the cliffhanger device by presenting a small sample of what you're offering (in order to get them involved and wanting more)—and then dangling an enticement that makes it difficult for them to resist the rest of your offer. Example: "Now that you've learned the first natural remedy for lowering blood pressure, discover 9 more powerful methods for curing hypertension naturally—and free yourself from a lifelong dependency on HBP prescription drugs—by watching this video now."

HYPNOTICALLY PERSUASIVE LANGUAGE

Neurolinguistic programming (NLP) is the science of how the brain codes learning and experience. This coding affects all communication and behavior. NLP involves the use of proper syntax (or language). Using it properly can make all your written communications more persuasive. There are several NLP devices that I often use in writing web copy. Among them are embedded commands, presuppositions, linguistic binds, and reframing.

Embedded Commands

The objective of web copywriting is to generate a response of some kind, such as getting your readers to pick up the phone and call your business, subscribe to your newsletter, sign up for your mailing list, or buy your product or service. Using embedded commands entails crafting the action you want your reader to take and wrapping it in the cushion of a casual, innocent-looking sentence.

Consider the following sentence:

I wonder how quickly you are going to buy this product.

It seems harmless enough. Your reader might consciously take it as a hypothetical comment. But notice the embedded command, which is quite hypnotic in effect: *You are going to buy this product.*

Using embedded commands in speaking calls for altering your tone of voice. You would lower your voice and speak the command part of the sentence more slowly for emphasis and to produce a hypnotic effect.

In writing, however, you can use boldface, quotation marks, italics, or even a different color to set off or delineate your command. When you write "I wonder how quickly you are going to buy this product," use boldface type for the command "You are going to buy this product." The bold type plays a role in how effectively the command is communicated. A person will respond to that part of the sentence as a command and will follow the command without consciously realizing it.

In this way, you gain compliance effortlessly. Your readers don't even perceive that they've been given a command. Typically, they will obey your command as though they had received it directly, without any resistance whatsoever. Clearly, this is a very powerful tool. Because embedded commands evade the scrutiny of the left brain (the critical, logical side of the brain), readers are not aware of what is causing their desire.

Embedded commands motivate people to take action and compel readers to come to a quick decision. Advertisers have known this for years, and that is why they write slogans like "Aren't you glad you use Dial? Don't you wish everybody did?" The embedded command, of course, is "use Dial." The same is true of "Wouldn't you really rather have a Buick?" Of course, the embedded command used in the sentence is "have a Buick."

Writing Embedded Commands

Start by constructing your command. This is usually three to seven words articulated in the imperative mood; that is, you begin with an action verb that presupposes the subject "you."

Some examples of commands are

Get your hands on this [*name product*].
Act on my advice.
Say yes to this offer.
Learn this secret.
Pick up the phone.

Next, simply embed the command in a sentence and set it off in bold type. For example, if the action you want your readers to take is to "read every word of this article," your sentence could go like this: "As you **read every word of this article,** you will discover advanced psychological tactics that will boggle your mind."

Presuppositions

Powerful as the brain is, it usually can focus on only one major thing at a time. Therefore, when bombarded by multiple thoughts, it is forced to presuppose (assume) and accept suggestions as facts. This is why using presuppositions in your web copy is such a powerful technique.

The question "What will you do with the extra $2,500 you'll earn next month?" is an example of a presupposition. Your brain is asked the question "What will you do . . . ?" By its very nature, the human brain is compelled to answer it. It's an involuntary, spontaneous reaction. When your brain is asked a question, it instantly goes to work in search of an answer. If you've ever had the experience of waking up in the middle of the night with the answer to a question you were thinking about earlier in the day, then you've experienced the profound effect questions have on the brain. The brain keeps working on the question subconsciously until it comes up with an answer (if not verbally, then mentally). The answer may not always be correct, but the brain is satisfied only when it has produced an answer that it considers valid.

The question "What will you do with the extra $2,500 you'll earn next month?" assumes that you will earn $2,500 next month simply by asking what you're going to do with it. This is called an *adjacency pair,* and the reader's/listener's brain pays attention only to the first part ("What will you do . . .") of the pair. A significant percentage of language processing takes place subconsciously. To understand a question or sentence, we must subconsciously make assumptions in order to make sense of what is being asked or said. Therefore, in order to answer the question, your brain has to assume that the second part of the question, "the extra $2,500 you'll earn next month," is an established fact. Do you see how smoothly that just slides into your consciousness?

Presuppositions are often seen in the leading questions prevalent in courtroom dramas, as well as police interrogations. These leading questions imply the existence of something when, in fact, its existence has not been established. Consider the following question:

Why did you steal the money?

The question assumes the existence of a sum of money. It further assumes that the money has been stolen, that you have stolen it, and that you have a reason for having stolen it. When questions such as these are delivered by a lawyer or law enforcement officer skilled in the syntax of presuppositions—especially when fired in rapid succession (stacked presuppositions), the listener is often forced to tacitly accept the implied meaning of the questions, even when the adversarial questioning was designed to introduce damaging arguments.

Here's another example of a presupposition: What will you do when the government imposes a five-cent surcharge on every e-mail that you send out? The brain focuses on the first part of the adjacency pair ("What will you do . . ."), which means it has to presuppose that the latter part of the sentence (about the government imposing a five-cent surcharge on every e-mail that you send out) is an established fact, when it actually is nothing but a rumor.

Here's another example: "Are you one of the 325 million people in America who's tired of the nine-to-five corporate grind, who wants to start her own business?" The question presupposes that there are 325 million people who want to start their own business in America, when that fact hasn't been established. Heck, that figure even exceeds the total population of the United States!

Not all presuppositions come in the form of questions. You can use presuppositional phrases like "As you know," "I'm sure you know," and "Everybody knows . . ." and presuppositional words like *clearly, obviously, evidently, undoubtedly, easily, readily, automatically,* and *naturally.* Any statement you put after any of these words is more likely to be received or accepted by your reader without resistance. For example, "Obviously, these triggers usher in a revolutionary—and immensely more effective—era of selling that you simply can't miss out on," or "Clearly, investing in ViralVideoWizard.com's services is the fastest way to get Page 1 Google rankings and send massive traffic to your website in as little as 24 hours."

Clearly and all the other presuppositional words and phrases impart a halo of credibility around what you are saying and lead the reader to assume that the ensuing statement is true. It makes the statement take on the appearance of fact and therefore makes your sales argument go down smoothly.

I am not suggesting that you use this device to tell lies, use weasel words, or slip your readers a Mickey. I believe in telling the truth in advertising and abide by the adage "Advertising is truth well told." As with any powerful psychological device, you have to use presuppositions ethically and judiciously.

Linguistic Binds

A linguistic bind is a form of syntax that makes your reader say, "Why, of course, what you're saying is true!" and is another powerful tool in the art of persuasion. Let's analyze this linguistic bind: "While you're sitting there reading this letter, you begin to understand why you can't afford to waste any more time getting less than everything that life has to offer."

It consists of two parts. Part 1 states something obvious ("you're sitting there reading this letter"), and part 2 states what you want your reader to think, say, or do. It is the command. Curiously, this pattern makes your reader believe that what you are saying is logical when, in fact, parts 1 and 2 of your sentence are not linked by logic at all. Nevertheless, this device can make people agree with practically anything you say.

Here are some more examples of linguistic binds:

"Now that you've read this special report, I'm sure you realize that you must get a copy of *The One-Minute Cure: The Secret to Healing Virtually All Diseases* now so you can find out how to heal yourself and your loved ones."

"As you sit there reading this, I know that you're thinking about all the ways you can turn your book into a bestseller as a result of attending Mark Victor Hansen's Book Marketing University."

"As you think about what you really need in your business, you begin to realize that you have only one choice to make, and that is to invest in this [*product or service*]."

There are other variations of linguistic binds. One is "The more you A, the more you B" syntax. For example:

"The more you understand the power of this one psychological trigger, the more you'll realize that you need to get all 30 of Joe Sugarman's *Psychological Triggers*."

"The more you read, the more you won't want to be without this incredible product."

Another is the cause-and-effect syntax: "Taking advantage of this free trial of our water purifier in the comfort of your own home will cause you to fully understand why buying bottled water is simply not the way to go."

Reframing

Reframing is the process of altering one's perception of a person, place, or thing by changing the context in which it is viewed. Consider reframing in its literal sense. Imagine an ordinary photograph in a plain metal frame hanging on a wall. You would probably not regard it with any more importance than, say, a typical poster. Now imagine that same photograph reframed in an ornate museum-quality, solid-hardwood frame with custom moldings. Suddenly, you perceive it as a photograph of distinction, significance, and importance.

Our perception of a person, place, or thing is altered simply by changing the context—the frame—in which it is viewed. In verbal or written communication, perception can be altered by using the technique known as *reframing*.

Reframing in the context of copywriting is a technique for communicating a flaw, a shortcoming, an imperfection, or a disadvantage in a way that transforms its meaning to one that is pleasant, desirable, or advantageous. Advertisers often abuse this concept by saying misleading things like "When you purchase this camera, you will also get as a free gift this genuine, handsome, imitation-leather carrying case." There is nothing genuine about imitation leather. One advertiser tried to elevate the value of a plain plastic comb (which was being given away as a free gift) by describing it as a "hand-finished, saw-cut shower comb." Don't reframe in this way because it insults the intelligence of your audience.

The key to successful reframing is to shift the reader's focus to a desirable, sometimes hidden, aspect of a disadvantage and turn it into a plus. You may be surprised to discover how just about anything can be reframed into something desirable when you look at it in a different light or, more accurately, with a fresh set of eyes.

Reframing is an excellent tool to use to justify the price of what you're selling. In the following example, reframing was used to justify the $1,595 price tag for a one-day speakers' workshop:

What price can you put on learning how to get as many speaking engagements as you can handle? $25,000? $15,000? $10,000? (Believe it or not, that's how much other speaker trainers charge!)

If you paid me my standard consulting fee of $625/hour for the 7½ hours I'm giving you at the Speakers' Workshop on October 18, it would cost you $4,687.50.

Would you believe it if I told you the workshop won't even cost you $4,000? No, not even $3,000. Your investment in your speaking career—*and* your life—is only . . .

$1,595.

You'll most likely earn at least **twice** that much on **your very first speaking engagement.**

Here, the price of the workshop ($1,595) is compared to: (1) how much other speaker trainers charge ($25,000, $15,000, or $10,000), (2) the cost in consulting fees to receive an equivalent 7½ hours of training ($4,687.50), and (3) how much the buyer would earn on his or her first speaking engagement (twice as much as the price of tuition to attend the speakers' workshop). When reframed in this context, what could appear to be a prohibitive amount of money to spend on a one-day workshop suddenly seems reasonable—even inexpensive.

The preceding example also illuminates an interesting aspect of consumer psychology. When a prospect is presented with a high-priced product or service, followed by the presentation of a second, lower-priced product or service, the latter will be deemed *considerably less expensive* than if it were presented all by itself without a basis of reference. For example, if you're selling a software program that is available in a Standard Version (priced at $49) and a Professional Version (priced at $79), and you present the higher-priced Professional Version first, followed by the lower-priced Standard Version, prospects are likely to think the Standard Version is a bargain because they're comparing it to the price of the Pro Version. Had you presented the Standard Version all by itself, it wouldn't have seemed like a bargain at all because they would have no basis for comparison.

Applying this to web copywriting, in order to appeal to this aspect of consumer psychology, you should simply mention the higher-priced option first, if one exists, before you present the price of the actual product you really want the prospect to consider buying. In the minds of your prospects, the higher-priced option would be the expensive version and the lower-priced model the low-cost or cheaper version. Now, just when you think you've got your prospects all figured out, and you predict they'll choose the lower-priced product, they may choose the more expensive model instead. This actually happens a significant percentage of the time, and it's because prospects are often propelled by an inexplicable psychological compulsion to buy the deluxe version instead of settling for the cheaper one. Either way, you win because prospects are more likely to buy one version or the other.

Another way to apply this concept in copywriting is by elevating the *value* of your offer in your prospects' eyes before mentioning the price. That way, they will expect it to be priced at a premium and will be pleasantly surprised to know it's much less—that is, a bargain. For example:

> What would you expect to pay for a software program that combines the functionality of the best html editors plus 12 of the most popular Internet marketing applications? You would have to buy 15 products to match the power of WebGenius—and they would cost you more than $850. But WebGenius doesn't even cost half of the combined cost of all those products. Your investment, including lifetime upgrades, is only $99. That's only a small fraction of the cost of all those other programs that don't do half as much as WebGenius does.

THE APPEARANCE OF CONSISTENCY

Humans have a nearly obsessive desire to be—or to appear—consistent to others and to ourselves. Once we've subscribed to something, voted for something, bought something, or taken a stand on something, we are under tremendous pressure to behave consistently with that commitment in order to justify our earlier decision.

I use this technique in writing web copy by first helping my readers express a firm stand or opinion about something, then presenting my product in a way that plays to the stand my readers have taken. I first construct a question to which readers could not possibly answer no, such as "If I could show you a way to double or triple your sales closing rate—and teach you how to sell 50 to 100 percent of all prospects you come in contact with—are you willing to spend an entertaining 63 minutes to learn it?"

By asking this question I have, in effect, extracted an unspoken commitment from the readers, even if I receive no audible reply. Next, I tell them to read the rest of the article, where I give the details of my offer. After I've given the sales pitch, I say something like:

> Earlier on, I asked you the question: "If I could show you a way to double or triple your sales closing rate—and teach you how to sell 50 to 100 percent of all prospects you come in contact with—are you prepared to spend 63 minutes to learn it?"
>
> Since you're still reading this, I'm going to assume you answered, "Yes." Well, now that I've shown you unequivocally how Brian Tracy's 24 Techniques for Closing the Sale can deliver on that promise—and have also shown you Brian's first-rate credentials and the rave reviews he's received—it's time for you to act on this.

As you can see, I remind readers that they need to behave consistently with the commitment they've made. This is one of the most powerful weapons of influence.

CONTRADICTORY THINKING

The best way to explain this concept is to tell you a story—actually, a fable. You probably remember this Aesop's fable. There once was a fox who tried in vain to reach a cluster of grapes dangling from a vine above his head. Although the fox leaped high to grasp the grapes, the delicious-looking fruit remained just beyond his reach. After several attempts, the fox gave up and said to himself, "These grapes are sour, and if I had some, I would not eat them."

This fable illustrates what former Stanford University social psychologist Leon Festinger called *cognitive dissonance*. Cognitive dissonance (or contradictory thinking) is the distressing mental state in which people "find themselves doing things that don't fit with what they know, or having opinions that conflict with other opinions they hold."

The fox's withdrawal from the pursuit of the grapes clashed with his thinking that the grapes were tasty. By changing his attitude toward the grapes, however, he was able to maintain an acceptable explanation for his behavior.

You can put this to effective use in your web copy by giving your readers a compelling reason to buy early in the sales process. This, in turn, makes them more likely to buy when confronted with the actual buying decision. Your readers have to be able to take ownership of that promise and cling to it so tenaciously that no other thought can pry it away from them. Any doubts or obstacles that may occur to them during the sales process are overcome by the original belief, paving the way to a home-run sale.

Robert Cialdini once wrote about a presentation he attended where two presenters tried to recruit new members into a Transcendental Meditation (TM) program. The presentation began with a compelling selling argument. However, when it came to the question-and-answer portion, an attendee demolished the presenters' arguments, and the presentation collapsed. The rest of the audience, however, instead of being turned off, rushed in record numbers to plunk down their $75 deposit to attend the TM program.

Cialdini thought that the other attendees hadn't quite understood the arguments or the logic of the dissenting attendee, but after interviewing those who signed up, he learned that they had had good reasons for considering signing up for the TM program before attending the presentation. Apparently, the dissenter's remarks, instead of dissuading them, compelled them to sign up; otherwise, they might go home, think about the dissenter's arguments, and never sign up, which would have contradicted their original commitment to TM.

Driven by their needs, they were desperately searching for a way to solve their problems, and they very much wanted to believe that TM was their answer. Rather than face the tedious task of finding another solution to their problems, they opted for the comfort of staying with their original belief, despite evidence to the contrary.

How can you use cognitive dissonance in your web copy? In the beginning of your web copy, you have to get your readers to say, "Yes, that's exactly what I need!" You can do this by crafting a well-articulated promise and inserting it very early in the body copy. Next, get readers to take ownership of that promise and cling to it so tenaciously that no one can pry it away from them. That way, any doubts or obstacles that might arise during the sales process will be squashed by the original belief, thus paving the way to clinching the sale. Here are examples of well-articulated promises:

> By the time you finish reading this article, you will know how to consistently pick the hottest stocks that are on the upswing right now—so you can make a killing on the stock market every time.

> What if I told you I could show you how to increase your ability to ethically influence others, naturally, without sounding like you're making a sales pitch? How much more money and success could you create with that skill?

THE CYRANO EFFECT

The value of emotion in web copy cannot be overemphasized. I've repeated the principle "People buy on emotion and justify with logic" often—for good reason. Emotion is such a powerful element of the online sales process, one that is intricately connected with the psychology of the Internet buyer, that it would require an entire book to devote to its intricacies. I've encapsulated those intricacies into one psychological device that I call the Cyrano effect.

If you were to ask a sports car owner why he bought his car, he might tell you something along the lines that the car is a technological marvel, that it goes from 0 to 60 in five seconds, that the engine represents a breakthrough in German engineering, that the car has won many awards—or that he got a good deal for it. What he probably won't tell you is that the real reason he bought it is because of how he *feels* when he steps behind the wheel of the car—that it makes him feel powerful, virile, young again, and maybe even superior to others. Neither will he tell you that he bought it because it would make him feel good to be the envy of his neighbors, to impress women, or to get the respect of his associates. Then there are other subconscious emotional reasons that he may not even realize, much less verbalize—some of which have roots that go back to his childhood.

The preceding example indicates that to a great extent, a sale is made based on the salesperson's ability to stir as many emotions in the prospective buyer as possible. This is true in auto sales as well as in virtually all selling situations, and even more so in selling online, where attention is difficult to capture. Inasmuch as emotion is the single most important reason why people buy, the most important objective of a salesperson, marketer, or copywriter is to deliver an *emotional experience* during the sales presentation—or the test drive (in the case of auto buying). When people visit your website, for instance, they buy the vivid emotions you give them with your web copy. People have the need to be stimulated, not just intellectually but emotionally. In an increasingly technological world, they want to be taken out of their ordinary, day-to-day existence and temporarily transported to a place where they can feel alive, victorious, proud, accomplished, gratified, noble, responsible, or just plain happy.

This certainly goes hand in hand with what John Naisbitt, author of runaway bestseller *Megatrends* (Warner Books, 1982) wrote in his book *High Tech High Touch* (Broadway Books, 1999): "Focusing on the effects of technology in reshaping society, the book brings together a mountain of evidence implicating technology in relentlessly accelerating our lives and stirring profound yearnings for a more emotionally satisfying existence."

Now, here's the important lesson that you must learn from this glimpse into human nature: Although buyers want physical satisfaction, which they hope to obtain from the benefits of your product or service, what they really desire is emotional satisfaction. When you're able to satisfy them emotionally during the sales process, the virtues of your product or service become secondary.

When you engage your prospect's imagination successfully, it often eclipses the gratification they get from actually having your product or service. It is to the illumination of this concept that I've coined the term *Cyrano effect*. This is derived from the title character of a French play written by Edmond Rostand, *Cyrano de Bergerac*. Cyrano was an ordinary-looking man with an overly large nose, who wooed the beautiful Roxanne on the behalf of his handsome but less articulate friend Christian de Neuvillette by writing beautiful letters that made Roxanne swoon. The story of Cyrano de Bergerac actually shines the light on this truth about advertising: An extraordinary product without emotionally engaging copy may have only a slim chance of selling well, while an ordinary product with emotionally engaging copy can sell incredibly well.

When marketers and advertisers speak of adding value to their offers to make them irresistible (as I've suggested in earlier chapters), one might think they're appealing to their prospect's logical mind, which knows a good deal when it sees one. Actually, when you dissect the matter further, the desirability of anything you offer for sale still boils down to how well you make your prospect's heart beat a little faster. Again, it's the emotional experience that you're really selling, and a value-added offer that your prospect "simply can't resist" is only an offshoot of the emotion you've successfully stimulated.

I've seen the Cyrano effect in action on countless occasions, both in my personal experience as well as in the experiences of many online marketers that I know. On one occasion, I wrote the copy for a company that sells a turnkey business-in-a-box that is licensed to market a variety of downloadable audio-books on the web. I didn't find the product particularly exciting at first, but as I began to develop the copy, I renamed the product a *franchise* to replace the bland business-in-a-box concept. Almost as soon as I called it a franchise, my imagination took flight. I found a sudden spark of inspiration that enabled me to write an emotionally driven copy piece. The peculiar thing about it was that I myself became excited about it and even planned to buy one of the franchises for my stepdaughter, but decided to wait until later. The product was launched at noon on November 16, 2006, a buying frenzy ensued, and 2½ days later the franchises were all sold out and my client had made $1 million! In fact, there was not a single franchise left for me to buy for my stepdaughter, and I regretted having waited too long. Looking back, it dawned on me that the excitement generated by the prospect of owning a franchise captured people's imaginations (including my own!), and what people actually bought was that emotional buzz, that temporary high that made them feel how they wanted to feel. For a considerable percentage of the buying population, that buzz is worth any amount of money you could ask for. This is reminiscent of the old sales aphorism "Sell the sizzle, not the steak."

Is this deceptive advertising then? Of course not. It's simply marketing that takes the psychology of online buyers into consideration. As I've mentioned earlier, I prescribe to the maxim "Advertising is truth well told." Advertising is not about telling lies, misrepresenting the virtues of one's product or service, or dispensing hype or exaggerated claims—although many unscrupulous advertisers have given advertising that reputation. It is actually contingent upon advertisers and copywriters to position their product or service in the best possible light so that it becomes desirable to their target audience. There's no deception in that. In truth, you're actually giving your customers what they *really* want—an emotional experience.

Now, here's an interesting phenomenon that happens as a result of providing an emotional experience in your web copy or sales process: Once you've successfully engaged your prospects' emotions, and your prospects consequently buy your product or service, more often than not the satisfaction they experience after the purchase has very little to do with the product or service they bought. The satisfaction persists even if buyers never use the product or service! Mind you, this phenomenon does not happen in most buying situations. We all know countless people who have bought products from emotion-driven infomercials and end up being remorseful and unhappy about their purchases. The satisfaction phenomenon happens only when you skillfully provide your buyers with an indelible emotional experience and, more important, you've succeeded in getting customers to *like* you. This goes hand in hand with the principle discussed in Chapter 4 (in the subsection entitled "Traffic Conversion: Turning Visitors into Customers") about how people often buy products that they don't particularly like, want, or need just because they like and trust the person who is selling the product to them.

Joe Girard, who was named the World's Greatest Salesman by Guinness World Records, operated on the tandem concepts of this satisfaction phenomenon. He sold an average of 6 cars a day, sold a total of 13,001 cars at a Chevrolet dealership in Detroit between 1963 and 1978, and was inducted into the Automotive Hall of Fame. Joe accomplished this not because he sold the most desirable cars in the world, not because he worked in the only car dealership in town, and not because he was the stereotypical fast-talking salesman. He did it by giving his prospects an emotional experience and getting them to like him. He made it his policy to tell every prospective customer who came into the dealership that he liked them, sometimes by admiring something about them, something they were wearing, their attitude, their smile, and so on. People like people who like them. Joe's prospects felt flattered (emotion!); they instantly liked Joe and wanted to do business with him because he liked them. He also made it a point to tell them, "I'm not excited about selling you this car today. You know what will excite me is if you come back and buy from me a second time." This made people feel that Joe cared more about making them happy (more emotion!) than merely selling a car. Joe was also famous for sending out greeting cards every single month to every person who ever bought a car from him (more emotion!), and he constantly assured them that he would take care of any auto service needs they might have. With the twin practices of providing an emotional experience and getting people to like him, Joe became the only car salesman in history who sold cars by appointment only. Customers had to wait between seven and ten days to book an appointment with him just for the privilege of buying a car from him. That's because they had heard about how he treats his customers and they, too, wanted to have that emotional experience.

I've seen this satisfaction phenomenon firsthand countless times, but the instance that I will never forget is the case of an Internet entrepreneur, whom I will call Peter, to protect his privacy. Peter offered a career counseling program on his website consisting of 15 audio CDs that he sold for $900. Since I was hired to write his website copy, I set about creating excitement for his prospects, giving them a remarkable emotional experience just from reading the copy. (Stimulating emotions is even more indispensable when it comes to selling high-ticket items.) As a result, Peter sold over 500 copies of the program in less than three months. It wasn't until after they started shipping out the audio sets to his customers that Peter learned of the serious error made by the company that produced the audio CDs for him. Apparently, CD #5 was completely blank! Instead of sending out an apology to all the people who had bought the program, he waited for customers to complain about the blank disk and planned to send a replacement CD only to those who asked for it. Out of over 500 customers, only 8 notified Peter that CD #5 was blank and asked for a replacement! And not a single customer returned the program for a refund.

This case study illustrates that when web copy successfully delivers emotional satisfaction *before* the purchase is made, this often translates to satisfaction *after* the sale—even in cases where there may not be sufficient reason to be satisfied. Emotionally satisfied customers are also likely to ignore or underestimate the faults of a product or service. Naturally, there also exists the possibility of buyer's remorse once the customer climbs down from the emotional high, but, by and large, buyers remember the emotional experience that caused them to buy in the first place, and that effect stays in place once they own or use the product or service.

Those who are experts in branding know this effect all too well. The De Beers diamond cartel launched a branding campaign over 70 years ago with the slogan "A diamond is forever" and supported it with the emotion-stimulating theme that diamonds are the symbol of enduring love, which is how they justified the high cost. Who could put a price on eternal love after all? Then came the brilliant slogan "She already knows you love her. Now everyone else will, too." As a result of manufacturing a relationship between emotion (love) and diamonds, 80 percent of American grooms give their brides diamond engagement rings, which average $3,000 in price. Women who receive a diamond engagement ring, or any gift consisting of diamonds, often float on a cloud of emotional satisfaction—and they feel "like a million bucks" long after they receive the expensive gift that proved to them how much they are loved. And the men who gave them the diamonds derived their emotional satisfaction from the feeling of proving their love through the gift of diamonds, not to mention the happy reaction they received from the women. In reality, the emotional satisfaction that both the men and the women experience has little to do with the intrinsic value of the diamond. The desirability of natural diamonds is emotional, not rational. A large part of diamonds' allure is their high cost and supposed rarity. In actuality, diamonds are plentiful and would probably cost no more than semiprecious stones were it not for De Beers's stockpiling them, rather than selling all of them, in order to prevent prices from falling. So in the final analysis, the only thing De Beers is really selling is not rare, expensive gems; they're selling emotional satisfaction, which endures long after the purchase is made.

When you consider how De Beers built a trillion-dollar business by simply fabricating preciousness out of people's emotions, you begin to realize how powerful emotional satisfaction is in driving sales. This is worth paraphrasing Ralph Waldo Emerson's famous saying "Build a better mousetrap and the world will beat a path to your door" as "Stimulate people's emotions and the world will beat a path to your website." If you fail to provide emotional satisfaction, you fail to make the sale.

So how do you create an emotional experience and provide emotional satisfaction in web copy?

You can do it by articulating your target audience's 3 Ps—their problem, pain, or predicament—as accurately as possible, or you paint a picture of what their lives could be when their problem, pain, or predicament is eliminated. Consider the following headline:

What Will You Do When Your Family's Assets Are
Wiped Out to Pay for Nursing Home Expenses?

Another thing you can do is install involvement devices in your copy that engage your website visitors emotionally. Here's an example of an emotional involvement device employed by a client of mine who sells a Career Success Manual. (The screen capture on the next page is courtesy of UltimateCareerGuide.com.)

Which of the following statements describe you?
(Check all that apply.)

- ❐ Your career is **unfulfilling** or you're stuck in a **dead-end job** where you're not growing professionally or personally.
- ❐ You **don't know exactly what you want** in a career, but the work you're doing now certainly isn't it!
- ❐ You're eager to get promoted or advance within your industry, but you're **having trouble "breaking through."**
- ❐ You're **dissatisfied with your job,** and you want a way out—but you don't know how to go about it.
- ❐ You're **unemployed** or afraid you might be **laid off** soon, and you want to find a new—and better—job as soon as possible.
- ❐ You feel **burned out, overworked, or underpaid,** and you want to find an enjoyable job that pays what you deserve.
- ❐ Your **career is not a good fit**—and you yearn for work that would more closely match your interests, personality, and skills.

In the preceding example, the emotions you're trying to stimulate are frustration, dissatisfaction, defeat, and even despair. You not only effectively get your website visitors involved with your website, causing them to stay there longer, but also get them to identify themselves as your prospects when they check the items that apply to them. Most important, you stir up emotions in them that will go a long way toward keeping them glued to your web copy.

A client of mine who has the reputation of being a stock-trading whiz kid offers a service called First Hour Trading, which is a type of day trading wherein he pinpoints "Bull Trap" stocks that have the highest probability of experiencing price movements during the first hour of the trading day. He and the subscribers of his service who follow his trades average at least 1 percent returns on their investments every day. However, because he's prohibited by the Securities and Exchange Commission (SEC) from making income promises to prospects, I installed the following Earnings Calculator in his web copy.

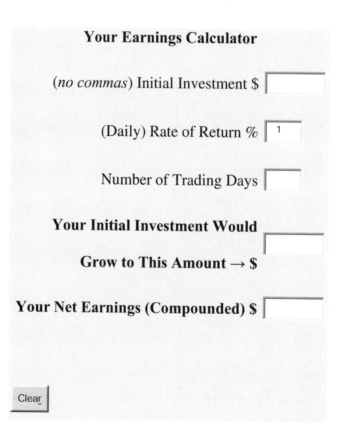

✦✦✦

NOTE: Type "$25,000" in the Initial Investment field (this is the minimum investment amount for day trading). To calculate how much you'll earn in a month, type "22" in the Number of Trading Days field (since there are *22 trading days a month*).

When website visitors type in the amount of their initial investment and the number of trading days, they're effectively involved in the sales process already. When the form automatically calculates their potential earnings for the month, it comes to $4,894 per month even on the minimum investment amount—and compounded yearly earnings of $256,612! If that doesn't get their hearts pounding faster and make them emotionally involved, I don't know what will. The best part is that we didn't have to make any income promises. We simply gave the website visitors a tool with which to do their own math.

Another method you can use to create an emotional experience is to get your website visitors to imagine for themselves how it would feel to own or use your product or service. Here are a few examples:

Service: Weight Loss Clinic
How *proud* will you feel when you attend your high school reunion being in the best shape of your life? Imagine the look on your former classmates' faces.

Service: Interior Design
Imagine having an interior designer who can create your living environment in a way that transforms . . .
. . . the way you view the world when you wake up in the morning
. . . the mood you have throughout the day, and
. . . even what you dream of at night.

Product: Day Trading Workshop
How will your life change when you begin getting a 10%, 12%—even 15% return on your investments every month? What kind of car will you be driving? In what part of town will you live?

Product: Time Management Seminar

How much more quality time will you have with your family and the people you care about when you discover how to get your job done in half the time?

Product: Language Learning Program

How *confident* will you feel when you arrive in Rome able to speak Italian fluently?

Product: Business Opportunity

How *satisfying* would it feel to be able to do the things you never had time to do before—the things that are truly important to you—and still be making the kind of income you want?

In my experience, I've seen website sales double or even triple with the judicious use of any one of the devices I've described in this chapter. This is why psychological and linguistic devices are an integral part of your web copy. Strategically employing these devices wherever possible in your copy is essential if you want to maximize the sales generated.

CHAPTER 6

THE ART OF CHANGING YOUR PROSPECTS' MINDS

At any given point in your online sales process, your prospect has a level of interest that ranges from apathy through mild interest, medium interest, strong interest to sold. (See Figure 6.1.)

Your prospects also have various levels of skepticism ranging from extremely skeptical to distrustful, reserved, accepting, believing, and, again, sold. (See Figure 6.2.)

The Trifecta Neuro-Affective Principle that I present in this chapter is designed to take your prospects from wherever their present interest or skepticism levels may lie and transform them into not only enthusiastic believers but willing buyers. When used on your target audience in tandem with the five-step blueprint in Chapter 2, this principle can accelerate your prospects' decision-making process, thereby dramatically minimizing the time it takes for them to buy what you're selling.

What exactly does it take for your prospect to change his or her mind about your product or service—and act on the basis of that mind shift?

I wish to emphasize that it is not my intention to teach you how to cause your online prospect to think favorably of your product or service—and consequently want to buy what you're selling—through compulsion, nor through deceptive or manipulative approaches.

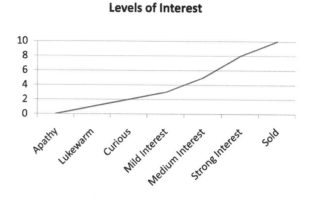

FIGURE 6.1 Levels of interest.

Having stated that, the secret to changing your prospect's mind—or any other person's mind, for that matter—is to produce a shift in his or her mental representations. A mental representation in the context of this discussion is defined as a presentation to the mind in the form of an idea or image. It's the specific way in which an individual perceives, codes, retains, and accesses information in the brain.

One extremely powerful method of changing someone's mind is by present-

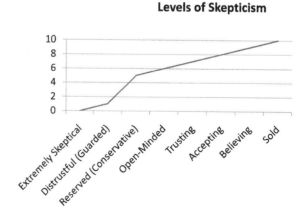

FIGURE 6.2 Levels of skepticism.

THE TRIFECTA NEURO-AFFECTIVE PRINCIPLE

The term *trifecta* is derived from a type of horse-racing bet, in which the bettor must select the *first three finishers in exact order.* In like manner, it is contingent upon web copywriters and online marketers to select which three representations of their sales proposition they should use—and in which sequence—in order to make the sale.

The word *affective* means "arousing feelings or emotions," and *neuro* refers to the billions of nerve cells in the brain (called *neurons*). The term *neuro-affective,* therefore, denotes the *connection between the mental and emotional states.*

To the extent that you arouse emotions in human beings, you also alter their mental representations of reality, effectively changing their minds. I owe this insight to philosopher and scientist Alfred Korzybski (July 3, 1879–March 1, 1950) and his work on general semantics, which states that a person's experience is not reality but a representation of it, based on the structure of the human nervous system and the structure of language.

ing multiple versions of the same concept. In my experience, as well as in most cases that I've observed, the optimum number of versions that has the highest likelihood of making an impact is three. When three forms of representation are offered, especially when each of the three conveys a well-rounded spectrum, a change erupts dramatically in the consciousness of your prospect as a result of the subtle mental-emotional processes that crystallize.

Consider the following: Ken Kragen, who successfully managed the careers of some of the world's most important entertainers, including Kenny Rogers, Lionel Richie, Trisha Yearwood, Olivia Newton-John, the Bee Gees, and the Smothers Brothers, uses the *magic of three* to catapult his clients to stardom. He determined that it takes three highly visible media events occurring within a short period of time to take a person from obscurity to fame. It's clear to see why this is so. Imagine hearing about an up-and-coming actress three times this week. The first time you hear about her is in a feature article written about her in *People* magazine, the second time as a guest on *The View,* and the third time on *Entertainment Tonight,* where she's shown walking down the red carpet at a movie premiere accompanied by a famous actor. When these three things happen in the span of one week, you don't just sit up and take notice—you're likely to think she's someone who matters in Hollywood, and you might be led to believe she's an A-list actress, even if you've never heard of her before this week. The buzz around the water fountain at work may now even include her: "That actress whom Dylan Maynard is dating now" or "I heard she led a rally against the resumption of commercial whaling" or just casual banter like "Did you see the Armani dress she wore at the premiere?" If the actress happens to have a movie coming out in theaters this weekend, you might go see it, even if you would never have considered seeing it had it not been for the three-event strategy engineered by her brilliant manager!

The magic of three has captivated our imagination not only in Hollywood but also in the stories we've read or been told since childhood, as well as in titles of bestselling books, idiomatic expressions, and advertising slogans.

"Goldilocks and the Three Bears"
The Three Musketeers
A Christmas Carol (and its three spirits of Christmas)
Diners, Drive-Ins and Dives
"Scams, Scoundrels and Scandals" (tagline of the TV show *American Greed*)
"Hear no evil, see no evil, speak no evil"
"Three Blind Mice"
Eat, Pray, Love (bestselling book by Elizabeth Gilbert)
"I came, I saw, I conquered" ("*Veni, vidi, vici*"—Julius Caesar)
Be, do, and have
Healthy, wealthy, and wise
Snap, Crackle, and Pop
Send. Sign. Done. (trademark of EchoSign)
"Spray, brush, and go"
"Hire specialists. Work together. Pay for results." (tagline of Elance.com)
Play. Love. Grow.

Why is a series of three so powerfully persuasive?

One reason might be because three is the most abbreviated way to convey a spectrum—such as in the threesomes of good, better, best; morning, noon, night; thoughts, words, actions; minimum, maximum, optimum; birth, life, death. The spectrum, which also delineates a continuum, then affords us a sense of completion, and anything more would be superfluous. We get the whole picture already, albeit in shorthand.

Another reason might be because three is the minimum number that human perception considers a pattern. If something happens once, it's merely a fluke. If it happens twice, it's a coincidence. But if it happens three times, people begin to draw conclusions. Are you beginning to perceive the unlimited usefulness of threes in web copywriting—and even sales and marketing in general?

For example, three powerful testimonials strategically delivered one after another in succession makes a reader think, "Hmmm . . . three people raved about this product, so it must be great!"

The principle I'm about to teach, however, goes way beyond just the power of threes.

Our brains are wired to respond to threes because three represents a digestible bite. It's also easy to remember a sequence of three. This may be due to the oral tradition by which information was handed down long before the age of the written word. We can remember the joke about the rabbi, the priest, and the minister walking into a bar, but if we add a fourth guy, he may fall just outside the parameters of our memory and tends to weaken the impact of the triad altogether.

In the realm of online selling, when you present three irrefutable sales arguments to your prospect, it causes subtle processes in the brain to coalesce into an emotional experience, and that emotional experience in turn goes a long way toward advancing the sale. (See Chapter 5 for an in-depth discussion of emotional experience and the Cyrano effect.) Since people buy on emotion and justify their purchases with logic, when your buyers are prompted to give a reason why they bought your product or service, it would be easy for them to declare, "I had three good reasons," and then recite them quite effortlessly. This memory goes a long way toward cementing customer satisfaction. A surprising side effect of this exchange is that when your customer recites the three reasons to other people, those reasons may resonate with the other people because they, too, will feel a sense of completion. It might convince those other people to buy your product or service because further considerations would seem superfluous. And it may even cause them to recite the three reasons to other people as well, thereby creating a snowball effect. Following is an example of three sales arguments presented in one digestible bite:

> *The One-Minute Cure: The Secret to Healing Virtually All Diseases* will show you . . .

- → a remarkable, *scientifically proven natural therapy* that creates an environment within the body where disease cannot thrive—and enables the body to cure itself of disease.
- → why over *6,100 articles in European scientific literature* have attested to the effectiveness of this simple therapy in not only killing diseased cells but also simultaneously revitalizing and rejuvenating healthy cells, thereby creating vibrant energy and well-being.
- → how this *safe, inexpensive,* and *powerful* healing modality has been administered by an estimated *15,000 European doctors, naturopaths, and homeopaths* to more than 10 million patients in the past 70 years to successfully treat practically every known disease.

WHAT ROLE DOES EMOTION PLAY IN MIND CHANGING?

Emotion plays a reciprocal role in both the installation of beliefs and the replacement of old beliefs with new ones. The more emotional your prospect's commitment is to an existing belief, the more difficult it is to change his or her mind. Conversely, the more emotionally engaging your web copy is, the easier it is to install a belief that endears your product or service to your prospect.

Some of the most influential people in the world, including political leaders, evangelists, public speakers, authors, and sales professionals, instinctively employ the Trifecta Neuro-Affective Principle—often without even knowing that their use of the principle is the reason they're successful at changing the minds of large numbers of readers, voters, educational institutions, and even nations.

How can you employ the Trifecta Neuro-Affective Principle in your web copy and online marketing communications? The formula that is most effective for changing prospects' minds on the web is the use of multiple entry points—ideally, three. You need to streamline your concept, topic, or sales proposition to the essential triad. When you distill it in this manner, you'll find an extraordinary concentration of power that can produce extraordinary results. Your concept will shine like a raw diamond stripped of all its debris, and it will have optimum impact.

The key to harnessing the power of the Trifecta Neuro-Affective Principle is to determine which three of the many possible presentations you should employ. This may take some deliberation because you face the challenge of becoming ensnared in your own personal preferences instead of those of your target audience (which was the primary shortcoming of using the five-step blueprint). The mind-changing encounter can be successful only when you set aside your own point of view and, instead, engage the psyche of your prospect. The more you know about the mental representations and resistances of your target audience, the more you can engage them fully, and the more likely you will be successful in changing your prospects' minds in your favor.

THE THREE PRINCIPAL TRIGGERS OF MIND CHANGE

Different people have different ways of processing information that is presented to them—and different people may find one representation easier to decode and embrace than others. It would be a futile endeavor to tailor one's web copy to cater to all the diverse triggers of mind change. However, a shift of mind is likely to coalesce when you employ three principal triggers. Precisely calibrating the delivery of your concepts with the use of these triggers literally alters your prospects' behavior and increases the likelihood that they will act in favor of your product or service.

The three principal triggers of mind change are resonance, redefinition, and resistance.

Emotional Resonance

Whereas logic and rational thought stroke the cognitive side of the human brain, resonance arouses the emotional side. Therefore, when an emotional trigger is employed, that's when your prospects feel they *resonate* with you or your message. That also means your concept, topic, or sales proposition feels right or is a good fit for their particular situation, and it convinces your prospects that they need look no further than your product or service to fulfill their needs. That feeling often happens at an unconscious level.

Another aspect of the resonance trigger is the phenomenon that psychologists call *identification*. When your prospects perceive similarities between themselves and you (or your spokesperson or representative), they identify with you, tend to resonate with your ideas, and sometimes even model their behavior around yours. Therefore, to the extent that you're able to have your prospects believe that you're just like them or that you understand their problems, pain, and predicaments, you have the power to influence what they will believe and how they will act. Skilled copywriters and marketers are able to exploit the phenomenon of identification in order to bring about the mind shift and action they want from their prospects.

Redefinition

Your sales proposition becomes convincing to the extent that you can redefine the prospects' understanding of a concept such that it causes them to see things in a brand-new way—that is, *your* way. It becomes even more convincing when it lends itself to representation in a variety of forms, with each form reinforcing and rounding out the others. Since every human being has multiple intelligences, entry to the belief system via a number of different routes corresponding to our different human intelligences is essential. For example:

- *Narrative:* consists of telling a story or case study related to the sales proposition or the people and circumstances surrounding it
- *Quantitative:* consists of using finite, measurable examples that support the sales proposition

- *Logic:* consists of identifying the key elements or factors that come into play and exploring logical outcomes that support the sales proposition

See Figure 6.3.

Other possible forms of representation include graphic, linguistic, humorous, aesthetic, numerical, experiential, and even existential. If you can present a concept in three ways, each one appealing to a different sensibility or intelligence, you make your concept accessible to more people. After all, some of your prospects are more likely to embrace concepts explained to them in a narrative fashion, for instance. Others may be moved primarily by argument, with its logically ordered propositions, while still others might relate to quantitative entries.

Resistance

While the triggers of resonance and redefinition represent factors that facilitate mind change, there also exists one important factor that hinders the progress

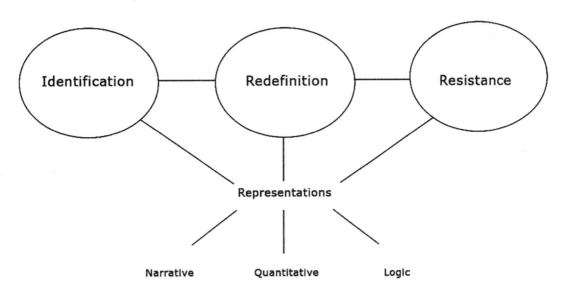

3 Triggers of the Trifecta Neuro-Affective Principle™

FIGURE 6.3 Trifecta schematic: narrative-quantitative-logic.

of mind change. The major paradox in getting a prospect to change his or her mind in favor of your product or service lies in the strong beliefs, views, and perspectives that are resistant to unfamiliar, contrasting, or opposing propositions. Therefore, identifying objections or resistances and overcoming them is essential in enabling the facilitating factors of resonance and redefinition to create the mind-changing effect you want.

When the triggers of resonance, redefinition, and resistance are engaged, and they are represented in three forms that reinforce and round out each other, that combination creates the perfect storm of mind-changing conditions. The "perfect storm" refers to the simultaneous occurrence of events that, taken individually, would be far less powerful than the result of their deliberate combination. Likewise, the triggers constituting the Trifecta Neuro-Affective Principle, taken individually, do not yield the effect of changing people's minds that their combined power produces.

Sales professionals who possess the uncanny ability of turning even the coldest prospects into enthusiastic buyers usually hit upon this perfect storm by chance and without realizing they're employing any principle at all. Knowing the elements of the Trifecta Neuro-Affective Principle enables you to utilize it with conscious deliberation, thereby making the sale a probable occurrence and not a stroke of chance.

I've examined many successful sales processes of companies, professional salespeople, and marketers, both online and offline, and analyzed what made them successful. Invariably, I'd find a *trifecta* that causes people to buy from them, usually without any hesitation or second thoughts. Every one of them had employed a variation of the Trifecta Neuro-Affective Principle.

Here's a real-life case study that shows the precise and successful use of the Trifecta Neuro-Affective Principle. The actual name of the entrepreneur in the following case study has been changed to protect his privacy.

Product: The product was a one-day seminar in Chicago introducing a breakthrough weight loss program. (No physical product was actually being sold—just information regarding the revolutionary weight loss methodology presented by one person.)

Particulars: Erik Morgan, a famous and highly respected bestselling author of seven books and a well-known consumerist known for exposing the unethical practices of the Food and Drug Administration (FDA) as well as pharmaceutical companies and the food industry, sent out a one-page e-mail on April 17. In the e-mail, he told the personal story of how, after struggling with excess weight all his life and trying diet after diet that didn't work, he suddenly lost 25 pounds in less than two weeks and has kept the pounds off for almost a year without dieting, exercising, or taking drugs or fat-burning pills. He said that he did it through a revolutionary breakthrough that many people are calling the greatest nutritional discovery of the century. It makes people lose up to 10 pounds in 48 hours and at least 30 pounds in 30 days without dieting, exercising, or taking weight loss drugs or fat-burning pills. He further claimed, "This discovery is the best, fastest, easiest, and most powerful way to get you to lose unwanted pounds and keep them off forever. This is the miracle I have been looking for my whole life." He went on to say that the drug companies are scrambling to hide this unbelievable way of losing unwanted pounds from the public because they are trying to turn this discovery into a drug that they can patent and sell for billions of dollars. He also stated that the government won't allow him to sell this nutrient, but that the discovery is so powerful, safe, and effective that it makes people lose the unwanted pounds so fast that they end up needing a completely new wardrobe just a few weeks after starting on the program. Erik said the only way he could provide the information about the discovery was through a one-day (12-hour) seminar to be held in Chicago on May 27. The seminar tuition fee was $1,000, and for those who couldn't attend the live seminar, reservations could be made to buy the audio CDs of the seminar recording at a price of $250.

Results: On the basis of that e-mail alone, which consisted of only six paragraphs (473 words), hundreds of people gladly forked over $1,000 to attend the seminar, sight unseen. The one-day seminar was scheduled to be held 40 days into the future at an undisclosed venue in Chicago. No one except those who paid the $1,000 were given the location of the venue. There wasn't even a webpage giving additional details about the seminar—just the one-page e-mail with a link to the online order form. From what I could ascertain, that e-mail campaign generated over $320,000 in seminar tuition fees, not including another $65,000 in revenues from the advance orders of the $250 CD set.

Analysis: It's not my objective to make a judgment call about the quality of the underlying products (seminar and audio CDs) that were sold by Erik

Morgan in this example. My only goal is to illustrate the anatomy of a successful mind change and identify the factors present in Erik's e-mail campaign that squashed people's skepticism and dramatically increased their interest to the point that they were willing to make a $1,000 buying decision (or $250, in the case of the audio CD set) in the time it took them to read the e-mail. Those kinds of results, of course, are the stuff that marketers' dreams are made of—that is, to be able to convey just three things in the right sequence and consequently cause people to fall all over themselves to buy whatever you're selling. I'm not at all surprised by the phenomenal response Erik got, because the Trifecta Neuro-Affective Principle was firmly in place. Here's how the three principal triggers were engaged.

Resonance: The recipients of Erik's e-mail were able to identify with Erik's lifelong struggle with being overweight because they themselves battled excess weight. They got excited hearing about Erik's weight loss—especially the part about maintaining the weight loss without having to diet, exercise, or take diet drugs or pills. Furthermore, they regarded Erik as a respected authority figure, one whom they could look up to and emulate. Since Erik had the reputation of being a consumerist, he was credible to them. They couldn't imagine him fabricating his story about permanent weight loss. Any skepticism that they might have entertained upon hearing this too-good-to-be-true news dissipated. First base.

Redefinition: Erik redefined the accomplishment of weight loss and positioned it as the greatest nutritional discovery of the century. He also mentioned that the drug companies are scrambling to hide from the public this unbelievable way of losing unwanted pounds because they are trying to turn this discovery into a drug that they can patent and sell for billions of dollars. This logically ordered proposition tallied with what they already knew about Erik as someone who exposes the hidden tricks that drug companies employ to fool the public. Therefore, it passed through to their belief system with no resistance. Second base.

Resistance: Erik stated in his e-mail that the government won't allow him to sell the weight loss nutrient, but that the discovery is powerful, safe, and effective. This addresses the objections prospects might have had about the danger of ingesting this new nutrient. Since Erik also said the *only* way he could provide the information about the discovery was through a one-day seminar in Chicago, they were able to justify the high price tag in their minds because the information wasn't available anywhere else. And if they couldn't afford the $1,000, Erik had given a less costly option: the $250 audio CDs. Third base.

With all the triggers engaged, the only question left for the prospects to answer was which one they should opt for—the seminar or the audio CDs? Whether they chose one or the other, the e-mail campaign was a home run for Erik.

Here's something interesting that happens when you employ the Trifecta Neuro-Affective Principle. More often than not, you simultaneously satisfy the five-question blueprint for writing killer web copy (see Chapter 2). The answer to Question No. 1 (What's the problem?) is stubborn excess weight that won't go away. The answer to Question No. 2 (Why hasn't the problem been solved?) is that diets don't work. The answer to Question No. 3 (What is possible?) is that permanent weight loss is now possible without the need for diet, exercise, weight loss drugs, or fat-burning pills. The answer to Question No. 4 (What's different now?) is that now there's a revolutionary breakthrough that many people are calling the greatest nutritional discovery of the century, which makes people lose up to 10 pounds in 48 hours and at least 30 pounds in 30 days without dieting, exercising, or taking weight loss drugs or fat-burning pills. Finally, the answer to Question No. 5 (What should you do now?) is this: Sign up for the $1,000 seminar in Chicago or reserve your copy of the seminar recordings for $250.

One important thing to remember is that putting the Trifecta Neuro-Affective Principle in place is not necessarily equivalent to writing web copy in its entirety. Rather, it is a shortcut strategy for presenting the most salient points of your sales proposition in the most compelling manner in the least amount of time. There may be times that fleshing out your copy further, presenting other benefits and testimonials, or including other copy elements is called for (see Chapter 3 for a discussion of the other essential components of winning web copy). What the application of the Trifecta Neuro-Affective Principle does is successfully grab the attention, maximize interest, create desire for your product or service, and, of-tentimes, cause your prospect to act (i.e., buy, order, or purchase), thus complet-ing the AIDA cycle in a single pass. At other times, the Trifecta Neuro-Affective Principle may capture attention, interest, and desire, but your prospects might still need to acquaint themselves with all the details of your offer before they actually buy. At the very least, when they do click through to your order page (or a page that gives the details of your offer), they arrive in a presold frame of mind and with a willingness to buy your product or service if the price is commensurate with the perceived value of your offer and is affordable to them.

Following is another example of how the Trifecta Neuro-Affective Principle can be applied to yet another product by engaging not only the three triggers but also three forms of representation:

Product: A book that teaches companies how to use the 80/20 principle to maximize the return on their advertising dollar.

Target audience: Companies that have an advertising budget of $50,000 a year or more.

Analysis: The copy starts off with a quote that expresses the "secret sorrow" of practically every advertiser—that of wasting advertising dollars and not knowing what to do about it. More emotions are aroused later in the copy when it is established that there is nothing safe about casting a wide net when it comes to advertising. This employs the resonance trigger, because the readers know that problem only too well—and identify with it.

To convince readers of the applicability of the 80/20 principle when it comes to advertising expenditures, an ordered list of ten advertising media employed by Silhouette Cosmetic Surgery Centers is presented in Figure 6.4, followed by a description of the principle in words, and, finally, a bar graph. Presenting multiple versions of the same concept is an extremely powerful way of turning something abstract and elusive (such as the 80/20 principle) into something familiar and accepted. That's because it's expressed in various depictions (numerical, linguistic, and graphic)—and it is likely that one, two, or all three of them will resonate with readers (see Figure 6.5). Additionally, the simple act of repeating a concept three times in different contexts is often sufficient to install and ingrain a concept into someone's belief system. This then employs the redefinition trigger because it paints a picture of the principle in a compelling way that the reader hasn't encountered before.

Finally, the objections that the reader probably has would run along the lines of "I've seldom been able to pinpoint exactly which of my advertising works and

"I know that half of the money I spend on advertising is wasted, but I can never find out which half."

-- John Wanamaker, the *Father of Modern Advertising*

Most advertisers operate under the unconscious "50/50 principle" of spreading advertising dollars equally across various media. In 1897, Italian economist and sociologist Vilifredo Pareto discovered what has since been called the "80/20 principle," which states that in most situations, 80% of the output will be generated by 20% of the input. Translated in advertising terms, **80% of the desired revenues an advertiser earns as a result of advertising will be generated by 20% of the advertising budget.**

That means John Wanamaker's assertion that half of the money spent on advertising is wasted is actually conservative. It's actually more than half.

Consider the case of the Silhouette Cosmetic Surgery Centers in the following illustration:

The 80/20 Principle - Revenues Generated by Advertising
Silhouette Cosmetic Surgery Centers

Type of Advertising	Percentage of Total Revenues Generated	Percentage of Advertising Dollars Spent
Direct mail – Postcards	31%	6%
Co-op Advertising - Val-Pak Coupons	27%	6%
Direct mail – Salesletters	23%	7%
TV – Cable Stations	5%	16%
Radio	3%	9%
Internet Advertising	3%	10%
Outdoor Advertising - Billboards	3%	8%
Outdoor Advertising - Bus Stop Benches	2%	9%
Print Ads - Magazines	2%	11%
Print Ads - Newspapers	1%	18%
TOTAL	100%	100%

It's apparent from the above list that **81% of the company's revenues** were generated by only the 3 of the advertising media (postcards, co-op advertising and salesletters) which only comprised **19% of the advertising spending**. It's also interesting to see that newspaper advertising, which represents 18% of all advertising spending contributes the least (1%) to the company's revenues. The company is therefore losing a significant amount of money in not just one, but two ways: 81% of their spending is wasted on ads that don't yield maximum revenues; and **they're also losing 400% additional revenues they could be generating** if they allocated all their advertising budget on direct mail and co-op advertising!

The sobering truth is that most advertisers don't have a clue as to whether their advertising is cost-effective or not. They often *play it safe* by "casting a wide net" hoping they'll have a big catch. What they don't realize is that there is nothing safe about casting a big net!

As illustrated above, chances are, only 20% of your advertising buys are adding significantly to your bottom line – and the rest are not only a poor investment of money, but they also prevent you from re-allocating those precious advertising dollars towards the revenue-generating 20% of your advertising campaigns.

Percentage of Advertising Dollars Spent   Percentage of Total Revenues Generated

Thankfully, in this age of technology, we're no longer as helpless as John Wanamaker was a century ago. Today, we have a wide array of mechanisms at our disposal that allow us to **measure people's responsiveness to our advertising messages** – both on and off the Web -- and enable us to track and test the effectiveness of our advertising.

Wouldn't you want to find out which 20% of your advertising buys are working, and the 80% which aren't? How would your company's profitability change when you do more of what's working and eliminate all the wasted advertising – and consequently get a substantially greater return on your advertising dollar?

The Pareto Advertising Model is the only book that shows you how to use the 80/20 Principle to maximize the return on your advertising dollar -- whether you want to **spend less** on your advertising while **earning more revenues** for your business – OR spending the same amount on your advertising and **generating up to 400% more revenues**. No matter how you look at it, it's a *win-win situation*. *The Pareto Advertising Model* reveals little-known tools and resources that enable you to identify your company's advertising campaigns that make you money and cause you to lose money, so that you can **spend less and earn more**. Any one of the tools or resources you learn from this book could pay for its price thousands of times over. When would you like to maximize the sales results you get from your advertising dollars?

FIGURE 6.4 80/20 copy.

3 Triggers of the Trifecta Neuro-Affective Principle™

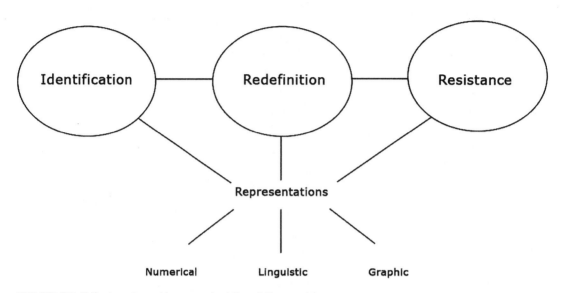

FIGURE 6.5 Trifecta schematic: numerical-linguistic-graphic.

which doesn't. What would I learn from the book that I don't already know?" That unspoken objection is countered by the statements that convey that there is now "a wide array of mechanisms at our disposal" and that the book reveals "little-known tools and resources" that enable one to identify advertising that makes the company money or causes it to lose money. This then employs the resistance trigger.

Notice that the copy in Figure 6.4 doesn't contain much of a sales pitch. There are no psychological devices, involvement devices, or other essential copywriting elements employed. That's because when you complete the trifecta, prospects arrive at a point where they realize that further explorations are not necessary—you've told them enough. Then a peculiar thing happens: Prospects actually sell themselves on your product or service. That's the power of the Trifecta Neuro-Affective Principle in action.

I was recently interviewed by a top public relations professional, whose company is the leading provider of experts and authors to the media. During the interview, she voiced her dislike for overly long sales letter types of copy that she considers overkill. "I don't need to read multiple pages of web copy for me to make a buying decision," she said. "I want to be given just the facts, then I'll decide whether I'll buy or not. Some marketers just write pages and pages of words when they already had me at hello."

There are many reasons why a copywriter would find it necessary to write long copy as opposed to short copy (see Chapter 3). It usually has less to do with the copywriter's preference and more to do with the nature of the product or service, the target audience, the price point, the competition, and many other considerations. However, when short copy is identified as the best route to take, the Trifecta Neuro-Affective Principle can be used to deliver just the facts to your prospects in the most compelling method and sequence. Yes, you can have them at hello. Everything else after that is just details.

THE TRIFECTA NEURO-AFFECTIVE PRINCIPLE IN SHORT COPY

Blaise Pascal, the seventeenth-century French mathematician, physicist, and religious philosopher, once wrote: "I have written you a long letter because I did not have time to write a short one." This goes along the same lines as something Mark Twain once said: "It usually takes me more than three weeks to prepare a good impromptu speech." Most outstanding and impactful presentations—especially sales presentations—require much time and preparation, no matter how easy or spontaneous they might look. Anyone with the gift of gab can fill an hour's worth of speaking time at a moment's notice, but only someone who's well prepared and who knows the key principles of communicating succinctly, clearly, and memorably can give a three-minute presentation that has maximum impact. That's why when individuals are about to be interviewed on a national TV program they often need a media trainer to teach them how to speak in sound bites.

On the Internet, there is also a need for this kind of brevity in a number of copywriting applications, such as product descriptions on catalog-style websites, banner ads, pay-per-click ads, blog posts, and other marketing messages where there are space restrictions and a limited amount of text allowed. How can you make an impact with words in such marketing environments? By presenting information in *cyber bites*. I've coined this term to mean web copy in bite-size pieces that pack a powerful selling punch.

Just like sound bites, cyber bites must make the maximum impact in the minimum number of words or characters—but they also need to accomplish one more thing that sound bites are not necessarily required to do. They have to *sell*.

So how do you go about writing cyber bites that sell? If you were put to the task of writing product descriptions for a catalog-style website, for instance, how would you choose, from a long list of specifications and benefits, which highlights to include in the catalog entry? If you were asked to write an advertisement of 50 words or less, how would you whittle a voluminous amount of information down to the essential information that would cause your prospect to want to buy your product or service, or at least take a closer look for the purpose of making a buying decision? If you were allowed to include only three benefit bullets among the dozens that your product or service offers, which three would you choose?

The answer most copywriters would give is invariably one that involves your personal judgment or opinion. No matter how experienced you are in marketing or copywriting, or how well you know your product or service, using your own judgment seldom hits the mark. The way to increase the likelihood of hitting the bull's-eye is by applying the Trifecta Neuro-Affective Principle.

Before you attempt to apply the Trifecta Neuro-Affective Principle in writing a cyber bite, however, you must first put on your customers' hat so that you can gain consumer insight—what your target consumers are saying and thinking and what truly matters to them. As Robert Collier once wrote, "You must *enter* the *conversation* that's *already* happening in your *prospect's mind*." Only when you have this consumer insight can you develop a unique selling proposition (USP) that highlights the benefit sought by your target customers, and one that speaks to their needs. (See Chapter 3 for a complete discussion on USPs.) This USP then becomes the central concept that you need to present compellingly via the three principal triggers of the Trifecta Neuro-Affective Principle.

Following is an example of an effective cyber bite:

Permanent Hair Removal <u>Without</u> the Pain of Electrolysis —and at a Fraction of the Cost of Laser Hair Removal

- Patented handheld hair removal appliance sends a painless radio frequency to the hair shaft, deadening the hair at the root—unwanted hair is gone forever and won't grow back!
- Approved by the FDA as Medically Safe Technology
- 5,000 of these appliances sold out on QVC in less than 5 minutes!

It's easy to see why this advertisement is irresistible. It not only articulates its unique selling proposition in the headline but also employs the resonance, redefinition, and resistance triggers in its three benefit bullets.

The ad redefines the technology of permanent hair removal (a radiofrequency that deadens the root), causes readers to identify with the 5,000 people who bought the appliance on QVC, creates excitement and a sense of urgency through the mention of how fast the appliance sold, and addresses the common objections to permanent hair removal—that is, pain, cost, and safety.

Following is a cyber bite for WebGenius (a software program presented here for example purposes only—it's not an actual product). The cyber bite is presented in two lengths: a bulleted product description and a 50-word advertisement.

Here's how a cyber bite would look in a bulleted product description:

WebGenius is the only website development software that lets you build a high-performing website equipped with powerful Internet marketing functionality—in as little as 15 minutes. Your website will practically market itself!

- Users call this "the most intelligent website creation software ever designed for Internet marketers."
- 83% of users switched from using Dreamweaver because of WebGenius's powerful and easy-to-use suite of applications no online entrepreneur can do business without.
- Combines the functionality of the best html editors on the market and 12 Internet marketing programs and applications—you'll never need to hire costly programmers or web designers again!

This copy presents its unique selling proposition in the first two sentences and then employs the three triggers in the benefit bullets. The reader identifies with the users who called WebGenius "the most intelligent website creation software ever designed for Internet marketers" because the prospect is an Internet marketer himself. Further resonance is established with the mention of the 83 percent of users who switched from using Dreamweaver, since there's a very high likelihood that the target audience is using that program and is wondering why someone would want to switch to another website creation software program. The ad redefines website creation by mentioning that the software combines the functionality of the best html editors on the market and 12 Internet marketing programs and applications. The prospect's resistance is countered by the presentation of the "easy-to-use" technology and the possibility of creating a high-performing website "in as little as 15 minutes." The final bullet addresses another unspoken concern of the Internet marketer: the cost and hassle of hiring a website designer and programmer to get his website to look and function the way he wants it to.

Here's how this cyber bite can be abbreviated into a 50-word advertisement that still employs the three triggers:

> "The most intelligent website creation software ever designed for Internet marketers." 83% of users switched from using Dreamweaver. WebGenius combines the functionality of the best html editors and 12 Internet marketing applications. Easy-to-use, intuitive—lets you create a website in 15 minutes. You'll never hire web designers/programmers again.

It bears repeating that, whenever possible, you must present a concept in three ways—not just *any* three ways but *the* three ways in the right sequence that give people a sense of completion. Together, they must hit the main cornerstones that constitute a satisfying purchase decision. And those cornerstones are the three principal triggers of the Trifecta Neuro-Affective Principle.

Take a look at the following three bullets that a copywriter might consider using to convey the benefits of owning the WebGenius website creation software:

- Create a high-performing website in a small fraction of the time it currently takes you. What would normally take *10 hours* per website in Dreamweaver or another web design package will take 1/10th of the time with WebGenius.

- Optimize your new websites to rank well with the search engines, increase your websites' "findability" on the web—and drive a consistent flow of traffic to your website.
- Make changes to your website with the greatest of ease. With the Page Layout section of WebGenius, make all the changes you wish to make—and all the changes will be instantly reflected in all your existing pages and any new pages you create.

While these bullet points convey benefits that the prospect might find desirable, they're all leaning toward employing only the redefinition trigger (i.e., they redefine what website creation would be like with the use of WebGenius). Since the bullets don't attempt to cause the prospects to *identify* with the product or its users, nor do they overcome the objections that might be lurking in prospects' minds, they will get a sense that something's missing. They may not be able to put it into words, but it's the vague feeling that you haven't told them enough for them to take the next step toward buying. It is that incompletion that renders your sales arguments powerless. If, on the other hand, you convey your benefits in a way that employs the three triggers (such as in the cyber bite examples given in the previous pages), you cause a subtle but powerful mind shift that prompts your prospects to change their minds in favor of your product or service. And when that happens, they are more likely to act on the basis of that mind change.

In many ways, the Trifecta Neuro-Affective Principle is similar to debate procedure in that it encompasses more than just logical argument and the presentation of research findings; it also includes persuasion that appeals to the emotional responses of the audience. In a debate, the central topic that the opposing sides seek to resolve is called the *proposition* or *resolution*. In selling situations, its counterpart is the unique selling proposition of a product or service. The arguments of those in favor—the affirmative side—in a debate are very much like sales arguments that utilize the Trifecta Neuro-Affective Principle. The principal objectives of both the debater on the affirmative side and the salesperson/marketer/copywriter are

- To support, prove, and defend their respective propositions through reason buttressed with research (redefinition)
- To destroy the opponent's arguments (resistance)
- To appeal to the audience's emotions (resonance)

Successful completion of the three objectives constitutes the critical mass that wins the debate or closes the sale.

CHAPTER 7

INCREASING SALES THROUGH THE USE OF INVOLVEMENT DEVICES

The real voyage of discovery consists not in seeking new landscapes but in having new eyes.

—MARCEL PROUST

nvolvement devices are devices that get people involved with your copy. They move people to read every word of your copy. Getting your website visitors to read your copy is job number one if your objective is to sell them something. When you use involvement devices, you effectively own your audience; that is, you hold your audience captive.

In the first two editions of this book, involvement devices were featured in the same chapter as psychological devices. However, due to the escalating challenge of getting people's attention in the overcrowded streets of cyberspace, involvement devices have become more important than ever before and warrant a chapter all their own. If the struggle to gain attention on the information superhighway was fierce back in 2009, it has only become even more so now that the number of indexed websites has multiplied exponentially! As of June 30, 2012, the estimated number of webpages indexed by Google, Bing, and Yahoo! Search totals 7.38 billion pages. You need to know about every involvement

But first, I want you to name the **top 3 things** you desire to have, or wish to improve, in your life right now -- examples: money (name the *specific* amount you want), a loving relationship, an ideal job, perfect health, your dream house, a brand new car, etc.

(Type the 3 things you desire in the box below.)

Okay, are you done typing the 3 things you want?

What if I told you that there's a way that you can achieve those 3 things -- *and anything else you desire* -- by using the power of your computer for just **10 minutes** a day.

In the next few minutes, I will show you an **advanced technology** that enables you to manifest everything you want through the results-amplifying use of *computerization*. This information is not available anywhere else on the Web -- or the world, for that matter. So I urge you to **read every word** of this article because the secret that can single-handedly turn your desires into reality is **hidden** in this web page -- and I don't want you to miss it.

FIGURE 7.1 Example of an involvement device.

device that will cause your website visitors to stay longer than the eight seconds a website is usually accorded. Nowadays, I rarely write copy that doesn't include the use of one or more of the involvement devices discussed in this chapter.

I tested an involvement device on the website of a client who sells affirmation software. This client's web copy had a decent conversion rate, so I rewrote his copy and added the involvement device shown in Figure 7.1. I installed this involvement device in the first screen of my client's website, and his sales tripled the next day. During subsequent weeks, he maintained sales that were 200 to 300 percent more than the previous daily sales—including days when he sold six times as much product as he had previously.

The original headline, "Learn how to be prosperous, successful and happy in just 10 minutes a day," was an attempt to get at what he thought were the hot buttons of his target audience, but, although reasonably successful, the headline sounded vague, and it definitely was not riveting. It didn't call out to the real desires of his target audience.

The involvement device asked readers to identify their wants, needs, and dreams. What could be more riveting to your target audience than their specific dreams, the dreams they might not dare tell another living soul? The involvement device asked them to name their dreams, and it gave them a safe place to do it because they knew that no one would ever see their responses. Bringing the readers' desires into focus allowed us to present the product (affirmation software) as the means of achieving those desires.

Do you see how powerful that is? Involvement devices break people's preoccupation with other things. At any given moment, a person's attention is occupied with dozens of things—everything from how they're going to pay for their children's college education to what they're going to have for dinner that night. Think of your prospect's mind as an antenna that receives signals from everywhere. Like a radio tuner, an involvement device gets people tuned in to only one signal, one station, or one channel—in this case, your sales message or your web copy. Getting someone's attention on the Internet is probably the biggest challenge you face, because attention is in short supply—with over 7.38 billion webpages clamoring for it.

In an effort to capture attention in the overwhelming marketplace of the Internet, an increasing number of websites in various industries have begun to employ involvement devices. For instance, I've seen a retailer of loudspeakers feature a Home Theater Wizard on its website. The Home Theater Wizard asks a few simple questions of the web visitor, about budget, room characteristics, listening preferences, and equipment setup. The web visitor clicks on check boxes to answer the brief questionnaire, thereby becoming effectively involved. Based on the answers given, the Home Theater Wizard recommends one of the company's preconfigured home theater systems customized to the customer's wants and needs. Since there's no way the company could know what web visitors are looking for in a home theater system, and it offers more than 350 different combinations of speakers from which to choose, the involvement device gets visitors to participate in customizing a system for their needs. In the process, the device causes casual web visitors to stay on the website (instead of clicking away) and take a close look at its product offerings.

The Jewelry & Watches division at Amazon.com employs a similar involvement device. Its website uses a wizard that enables visitors to create a diamond ring to their specifications by answering four questions (visitors click on radio buttons to select their preferred shape, number of carats, type of metal for the setting, and the setting style). When a web visitor answers all four questions, he or she can preview the ring, then select the diamond quality and ring size. The wizard recommends a ring from the jewelry inventory and gives the price of the ring and ordering instructions. This is a more effective approach to choosing a diamond ring than viewing hundreds or thousands that are available.

Figure 7.2 shows an example of an involvement device used on a website that sells a real estate investment course. The quiz does two things: It gets prospects involved and makes them curious enough to click on a text link ("Click here for correct answer") to learn something they don't know—something that whets their appetite for the product being sold. When respondents click on the text link, a small pop-up box reveals the answer. They are not taken to another webpage, which potentially could take them away from the intended sales path. This is essential when designing a device like this one. You won't need to know anything about programming in order to create involvement devices. Your web designer can usually help you install simple devices, or you can post the job you want done on freelance websites like Elance.com, Freelancer.com, or VWorker

What's your Real Estate IQ? Take this **simple eye-opening quiz** -- then learn **specific, cutting-edge** secrets for making **instant cash in real estate**. Answer True or False:

1. In order for you to accumulate a fortune in real estate, you need excellent credit or a lot of money.   TRUE ☐   FALSE ☐

Click here for the correct answer.

2. **Clearly,** real estate investing has created more millionaires than any other industry known to man, but it's a slow process - taking years to acquire massive wealth.   TRUE ☐   FALSE ☐

Click here for the correct answer.

3. 99.32% of today's **elite real estate millionaires** made their fortunes by buying/renting single-family homes.   TRUE ☐   FALSE ☐

Click here for the correct answer.

FIGURE 7.2 A questionnaire-type involvement device.

.com. In the Project Description, you can specify whatever kind of interactivity you want in plain English, and you will receive bids from programmers all over the world, who'll do the work for you inexpensively and even install the device on your website, if you wish.

The website www.1MinuteCure.com utilizes an involvement device (Figure 7.3) in which website visitors are asked to check the boxes next to the diseases that they or the people they know are suffering from. This device effectively compels website visitors to raise their hands and identify themselves as being the prospects for the book the website is selling. This is a superior way to grab visitors' attention rather than simply making a catch-all claim that the information in the book could potentially cure the whole gamut of diseases. When you nar-

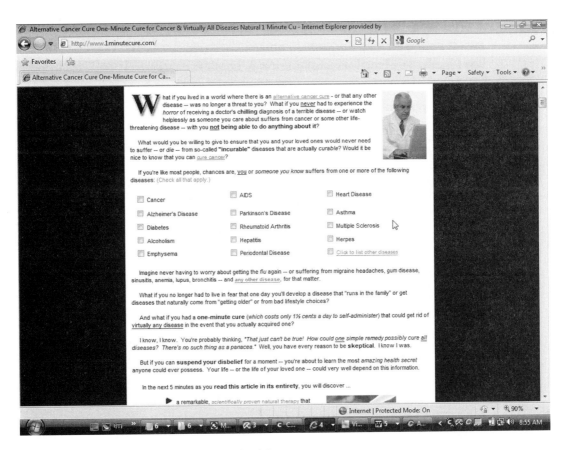

FIGURE 7.3 An involvement device using check boxes.

row their focus on their specific problem you make them believe you're speaking to their particular needs, and they're more likely to pay attention to your sales message. This type of involvement device does not entail programming at all, since the check boxes are simply graphical and do not cause anything to happen other than the placement of a check mark in the check box selected. The only purpose of the check boxes is to involve the website visitors with your copy and compel them to pay attention to your message.

The same website employs a second involvement device in the part of the web copy where an attempt is made to close the sale.

> Now, the only decision you need to make is *this*: Which of the following would you rather entrust your healing (and the healing of your loved ones) to? Check *one*.
>
> ❐ Pharmaceutical drugs that alleviate only the **symptoms** and the **pain** of diseases, but *don't* cure (and often *harm*)
> ❐ Elaborate, *expensive* and often *invasive* treatments and procedures offered by organized medicine
> ❐ A simple, ***low-cost*** therapy based on a *natural* oxygenating substance that is *easy* and ***painless*** to use at home—and which is ***scientifically proven*** to prevent and cure virtually all diseases <u>*without adverse effects*</u>
>
> For your sake, I hope you'll make the right decision in partnership with your doctor or a qualified health care professional.

In the preceding example, when website visitors click on the third check box signifying that they've made their decision in favor of buying the book, they are taken directly to the order page. This type of simple interactivity can be accomplished by installing one line in the html code of your website, which any website designer or anyone with a working knowledge of html can do for you if you're unfamiliar with html.

Interactive software programs are now available through which you can have a multiple-choice involvement device, such as the preceding one, on your website. When your website visitor checks one of the options, the ensuing copy on the webpage *dynamically changes* and is personalized with appropriate benefits and an offer suitable for that specific target audience. One example of such software is called *Interactive Sales Letter,* developed by interactive software developer Scott Stevenson. Using my Web Copywriting Mastery Course as an example, I could conceivably use the following involvement device on my website:

> Countless people from all walks of life wish to learn the skill of writing killer web copy for a variety of reasons. What is your reason? Select one below . . .
>
> ❐ I am an Internet marketer, entrepreneur, or website owner who sells (or plans to sell) a product or service online.
>
> ❐ I am a writer (or copywriter) who wants to transition to the lucrative specialty of web copywriting.
>
> ❐ I am a marketing professional who's in charge of my company's online sales operations.
>
> Go ahead—click on one of the radio buttons . . .

With the interactive software installed, when a website visitor clicks on one of the radio buttons, the software loads a prewritten copy piece designed to speak to the specific needs of that website visitor, depending on which radio button he or she clicked on. This is far more powerful than trying to create one web copy piece for a diverse array of target audiences.

The sky's the limit when it comes to involvement devices. You're limited only by your own creativity. The Earnings Calculator featured as an emotional mechanism in Chapter 5 (see "The Cyrano Effect" section) is yet another example of a device that effectively involves people with your copy, giving them another reason to stay at your website and find out what you have to offer.

In a custom lift letter that I wrote for *Underground Health Reporter,* I used a fill-in-the-blanks questionnaire type of involvement device (See Figure 7.4). The product that was being advertised was Natural Health Dossier, a subscription-based health publication featuring powerful health breakthroughs researched and compiled by doctors and research scientists. Since there was a massive amount of information being presented on Natural Health Dossier's

Transform Your Health and Well-Being -- and Add Years to Your Life with 11 New Breakthrough Cures

How many of these health breakthroughs have you heard of?

[Fill in the blanks ... and then scroll down to the bottom of this e-mail to get the answers that will enable you to enjoy optimum health, freedom from disease and maximum longevity.]

1) The safe way to literally **burn cancer out of your body** that's *14 times more effective than chemotherapy* alone -- without the side effects is ... ==> [   ] .

Hint: This technique has been practiced safely for thousands of years but you won't hear about it in mainstream media and most health publications.

2) What is the natural herb discovered by a biopharmaceutical company that has the potential to **stop the aging process** -- and **enable humans to live longer**? Answer: ==> [   ]

Hint: In double blind, placebo-controlled studies, they found that when test subjects consumed this herb ... their *immune systems were measurably boosted and strengthened* ... their *eyesight was measurably improved* ... they reported an *improvement in their s*e*x*u*a*l performance* ... and their *skin became youthful and smooth.*

3) There's a **million-year-old volcanic mineral** which literally sucks the heavy metals out of the calcium in your arteries, thereby *eliminating one of major causes of inflammation*. It's called ==> [   ] .

Hint: This volcanic mineral is also being hailed as one of the most effective approaches to *treating heart disease,* according to a renowned doctor who has never lost a patient to stroke or heart attack in 20 years.

4) The natural hormone that is the **single best way to fight cancer** is ... ==> [   ] .

Hint: Next to smoking, not getting enough of this hormone is the **No. 2 risk factor of cancer!** Every year, 30% -- or two million people worldwide (200,000 in the U.S. alone) -- could be spared of dying from cancer if they would just take the proper amounts of this hormone.

Did You Know All The Answers to the Questions Above?

To get all the answers -- and **discover 11 powerful health breakthroughs** that you're not likely to find elsewhere, watch this F*R*E*E video. The information presented in this eye-opening video was thoroughly researched and compiled by the brightest doctors and research scientists at *Natural Health Dossier*. This video could transform your health and well-being -- and add years of healthy living to your life. It might even save your life, or the life of a loved one.

This video will be available online only for a limited time, so watch it now while you still can. Click here to watch this video now.

FIGURE 7.4 An involvement device using a fill-in-the-blanks questionnaire.

Now that you know that Megabolic Weight Loss is the surefire way of losing all your
unwanted weight, now all that's left is for you to do what it takes to succeed. In order
to do that, you need to **get leverage on yourself**.

Quite frankly, *Megabolic Weight Loss* simply cannot fail when it is implemented exactly
as prescribed. But no weight loss program, no matter how powerful, will work if there isn't
the **power of commitment** behind it.

So **type your name, the number of pounds you want to lose, and the reason/s
you want to lose the weight** in the blanks below, and read the completed statement
out loud to reinforce the commitment that will lead to your ultimate success:

I, _____, have decided I want to lose ____ pounds,
because _____" and I'm committed to following
the *Megabolic Weight Loss Program* until I reach my desired weight.

FIGURE 7.5 An involvement device that uses the power of commitment.

sales landing page, I decided to distill that information into four intriguing
fill-in-the-blank questions that not only got readers involved but also made them
curious to learn the answers to the questions. This was such a successful custom
lift letter that the advertiser immediately ordered $22,000 worth of additional
advertising with *Underground Health Reporter* and ran that letter multiple times
over the next several months with great results.

Figure 7.5 shows an involvement device that uses the power of commitment.
Why is this powerful? According to Robert Cialdini, "Writing is believing."
When you ask your readers to write down (or, in this case, to type out) the things
they desire, they admit the need for your product or service. In addition, a written commitment is more lasting than a mental commitment. When you write out
a commitment, you have a greater likelihood of following through than if you
don't write it. Notice that I also make readers close the sale themselves by making Megabolic Weight Loss part of their commitment statement.

INVOLVEMENT DEVICES AND THE RECOVERY PRINCIPLE

An involvement device I invented several years ago makes use of the recovery
principle of marketing. It not only gets people involved in the sales copy and
makes them raise their hands and prequalify themselves as your target audience

but also captures their contact information. The recovery principle is not new. It's something used often in direct-response marketing.

Here's how it works: If you fail to sell your web visitors on your primary product at the full price but succeed in selling them the same product (or perhaps a different product) at a lower unit of sale, you recover the effort and cost of getting viewers to your website and plug them into your income stream. Even if you don't make as much profit on each of these sales, you recover costs, which adds to your overall profitability. More important, you turn someone who might otherwise never have done business with you into a customer, and, of course, those customers have a lifetime value since they will be buying future products from you. (See Figure 7.6.)

The recovery involvement device that I used on a website that sells a $2,650 water ionizer accounted for over 115 additional sales to customers who were given a 25 percent discount. That amounted to $228,562 in sales they would never have made if the recovery involvement device had not been installed. Once

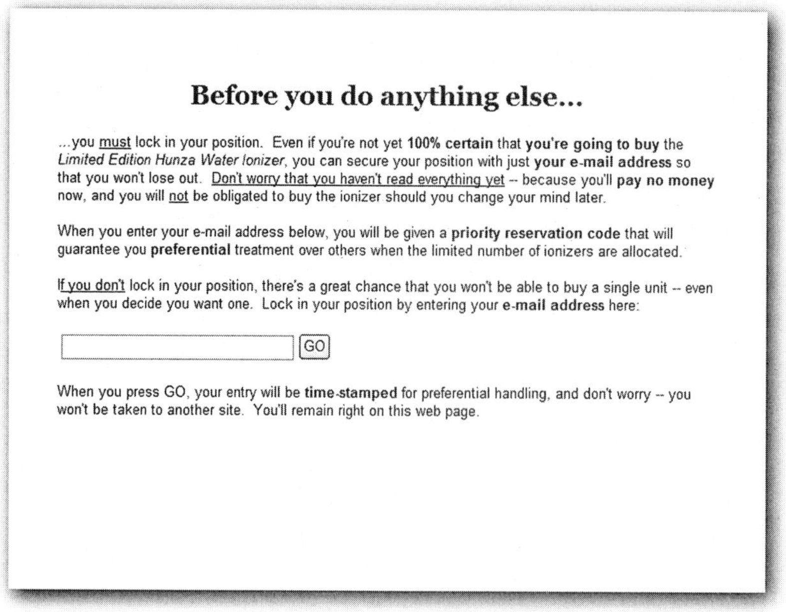

Before you do anything else...

...you <u>must</u> lock in your position. Even if you're not yet **100% certain** that **you're going to buy** the *Limited Edition Hunza Water Ionizer*, you can secure your position with just **your e-mail address** so that you won't lose out. <u>Don't worry that you haven't read everything yet</u> -- because you'll **pay no money** now, and you will <u>not</u> be obligated to buy the ionizer should you change your mind later.

When you enter your e-mail address below, you will be given a **priority reservation code** that will guarantee you **preferential** treatment over others when the limited number of ionizers are allocated.

<u>If you don't</u> lock in your position, there's a great chance that you won't be able to buy a single unit -- even when you decide you want one. Lock in your position by entering your **e-mail address** here:

[_____] GO

When you press GO, your entry will be **time-stamped** for preferential handling, and don't worry -- you won't be taken to another site. You'll remain right on this web page.

FIGURE 7.6 A recovery involvement device.

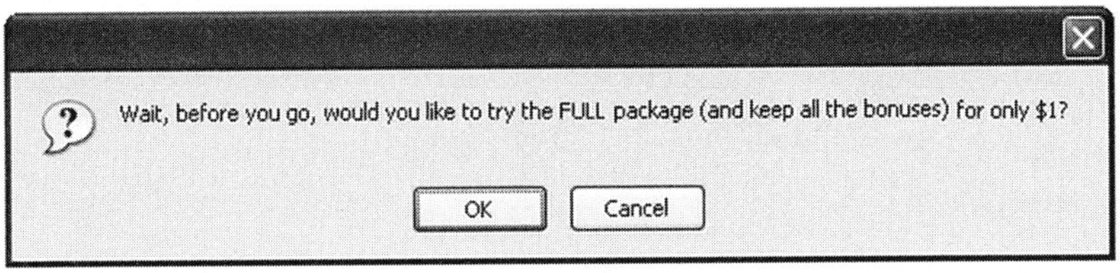

FIGURE 7.7 Recovery pop-up.

you understand that you don't have to offer your product at only one price but you can adjust your offer on the fly, you can make far greater profits than if you had not employed a recovery device, which can dramatically improve your website's profitability.

Another example of a recovery involvement device is one that I saw on a website that was selling an online video submission service package for $97 a month. If the visitor attempts to leave the website without signing up for the service, the window shown in Figure 7.7 pops up.

A prospect who clicks on the OK button is given a 14-day trial of the $97-per-month service for just $1. The company is willing to forgo half a month's revenues (approximately $48.50) in the hope that once prospects try their video submission service, they will become subscribers paying $97 per month.

A software developer named Dave Guindon took the recovery involvement device to a whole new level by creating an automated chat solution called Virtual Smart Agent. Once you have the software installed, a virtual agent appears whenever a website visitor attempts to leave your website without having bought your product or service. The virtual agent offers your departing visitor any discount that you want to extend. (See Figure 7.8.) When this happens, up to 40 percent of your prospects are saved and converted to happy customers. Even if you don't make as much profit on each of those discounted sales as you'd like, you still recover costs and generate revenues, which contribute to your website profits.

According to an *eMarketer* report, acquiring a new customer costs five to ten times more than retaining an existing one. Therefore, every effort must be made to keep customers. Some companies use the recovery approach to increase

1) Visitor reads your sales page, probably all the way to the order form, then decides to leave the page...

2) Upon attempting to leave, the Virtual Smart Agent gives more information to the visitor (for example, a special offer).

3) The Virtual Smart Agent "closes the deal" and sends the visitor to an order page.

4) Many sales are "saved" and you're putting more money in your pocket without doing any more work!

FIGURE 7.8 Virtual Smart Agent.

customer retention and minimize product returns. A software company sends out the following e-mail to those who want to return a product:

Dear [name of customer],

Thank you for your recent order of [*name of software*]. I'm sorry to hear that you've found it necessary to return the software for a refund.

We've gone to great lengths to make sure that [*name of software*] meets the needs, and exceeds the expectations, of entrepreneurs like you. Therefore, unless you're dissatisfied with the way [*name of software*] performs, we'd like you to continue enjoying the benefits and convenience of owning it. In this regard, we'd like to offer you the rebate of $68.50—that's 50% of the price you originally paid for it. We're offering you this special accommodation because we certainly don't want to lose you as a customer, and look forward to serving you for years to come.

Simply reply to this e-mail, and a check in the amount of $68.50 will be mailed to you immediately. Please understand that your acceptance of this rebate signifies your decision not to return [*name of software*] at some future date. Should you not wish to accept this rebate offer, and choose to return [*name of software*], please place it in the original packaging (or another appropriately sized box), send it back to us insured (for your protection), and we will issue a full refund of your purchase price within 4 weeks of receiving the product.

Sincerely,
Name of customer service representative

Marketing communications such as this one go a long way toward retaining customers, as well as recovering the effort and cost of getting them to buy in the first place. AOL uses a similar recovery approach when its "free trial" members call in to cancel their memberships. Instead of just letting potential customers go without a fight, AOL offers every member wishing to cancel the opportunity to continue enjoying AOL at no charge for another month—sometimes two or more. The company is justified in thinking that if members become accustomed to using AOL, eventually they won't want to cancel.

The key to the recovery principle is that no offer has to be static. Any of its parts—the price, the duration, the warranty, the privileges—should be flexible enough to meet the needs of customers. Even if the profit margins from the downsell are considerably less than the standard margins, every unit of sale adds to the company's bottom line, helps to recover costs, and keeps customers in the company's income stream. When you consider that repeat customers spend 67 percent more—and after ten purchases, the average customer has referred seven people—every attempt to exercise the recovery principle is well worth the effort.

CHAPTER 8

ONLINE MARKETING COMMUNICATIONS

It's What You Do After People Visit Your

Website That Counts

If you advance confidently in the direction of your dreams and endeavor to
live the life which you have imagined, you will meet with a success unex-
pected in common hours.

—HENRY DAVID THOREAU

Online marketing communications play a low-profile but nonetheless pivotal role in the Internet marketing arena. Principal among these communications is the opt-in offer, the crafting of which is often more important than website copy for reasons that will become clear as you progress through this chapter. Irresistible autoresponder e-mails are yet another essential aspect of online marketing communications, because effective follow-up frequently spells the difference between mediocre and outstanding sales. Finally, learning how to write free reports, promotional articles, newsletters, e-zines, online ads, signature files, and banner copy enables you to complete the basic components that constitute the web marketing mix. This chapter looks at each of these marketing communications and how to create killer copy for each.

THE OPT-IN OFFER: YOUR MOST IMPORTANT ASSET

Converting web visitors into customers is rarely completed during the website visit, but by crafting an irresistible opt-in offer and following up with e-mail messages designed to build rapport and a relationship with the prospects, conversion rates of 15 to 25 percent (and sometimes greater) can be achieved.

I have seen websites that attract only a few hundred unique visitors per day, but because of their brilliant opt-in offers, they are able to get more than 20 percent of their web visitors to sign up to receive their offers. Naturally, if they have constructed a series of follow-up autoresponder e-mails effectively, they could conceivably amass considerable monthly revenues from their website.

An opt-in page I created (www.1minutecure.com/registrationtotbp.htm) gets an outstanding 36.7 percent opt-in rate. That's because the opt-in page features a powerful six-minute video that uses the cliffhanger device (see Chapter 5) and gives just the right amount of riveting information (but keeps viewers wanting more); it also employs a compelling opt-in offer, which uses the Trifecta Neuro-Affective Principle (see Chapter 5). The 36.7 percent who opted in were then sent a series of seven follow-up e-mails via autoresponder, and the resulting click-to-sale conversion rate (i.e., the percentage of people who bought after clicking through to the www.1minutecure.com website) ranged from 8.92 percent to 15.1 percent.

Capturing contact information is fundamental to the success of any business enterprise. As web marketer, entrepreneur, or copywriter, your primary goal, at the very least, should be capturing your web visitors' e-mail addresses. Without this information, you have, in effect, wasted all the time, money, and effort it took to get them to your website. For this reason, I can't overemphasize that constructing your opt-in offer is infinitely more important than crafting the offer for your primary product.

It's apparent, therefore, that you need to make your opt-in-offer copy as compelling as possible in order to convince visitors to give you this personal information. A good way to do this is by providing a benefit that gives visitors an incentive to give you their e-mail address. One method is to ask them to sign up for a free report (with an irresistible title), a free newsletter, a free course, free

> **"How to Pay Less for Almost Everything"**
> The world's best *bargain hunters* and haggle hounds reveal their **secrets** for easily finding the *lowest prices* on things you buy everyday. Once you learn these simple, but **ingenious** strategies for getting more and spending less, it's like having given yourself a **20% (or more) pay raise** -- *tax-free*!
>
> Send for this **FREE report** today. Simply fill in your name and address in the form below -- and this **valuable** report will be sent to your e-mail box automatically *within minutes*!
>
> [Your contact information will be handled with the *strictest confidence*, and will never be sold or shared with third parties.]

☐ **Send me my FREE report now.**	
Email address:	
First Name:	
Last Name:	

Add Address

FIGURE 8.1 Opt-in offer.

product, free chapters of your book—or just ask them to sign up to "Get the Full Story." In other words, something that requires no financial commitment.

The opt-in offer in Figure 8.1 was designed as an exit pop-up (a window that pops up when the visitor leaves the site). The objective of this opt-in offer is to capture the contact information of as many web visitors as possible so that, through a series of follow-up autoresponder e-mails, prospects can be encouraged to sign up for a DHS Club discount buying membership.

"How to Pay Less for Almost Everything" is a title that appeals to the target audience of the DHS Club website, which consists of people who like to save money on everything they purchase. The opt-in offer is designed to prequalify prospects. In this case, it means that anyone who signs up to receive this free report is interested in getting discounts and saving money on purchases and therefore is someone who might also be interested in signing up for a paid membership to the discount buying club to get even more discounts on a wider variety of products and services.

Five Keys to an Opt-In Offer That's Impossible to Refuse

In addition to creating an offer that prequalifies prospects, there are five elements that winning opt-in offers contain:

1. Compelling title that speaks to the needs of your target audience
2. Appealing benefits
3. Instant gratification
4. Assurance of privacy
5. Form for obtaining an e-mail address and, at least, a first name

Notice that the opt-in offer for the DHS Club satisfies all of these:

1. It has a compelling title ("How to Pay Less for Almost Everything") that speaks to the needs of the target audience (people who like saving money on all their purchases).
2. It offers appealing benefits the recipients will receive (secrets for easily finding the lowest prices on things they buy every day).
3. It offers instant gratification. (The valuable report will be sent to their e-mail in-boxes automatically within minutes.)
4. It offers an assurance of privacy. (Their contact information will be handled with the strictest confidence and will never be sold or shared with third parties.)
5. It includes a form that captures the e-mail address and the first name.

A free subscription to a newsletter or e-zine is the most common item featured in online opt-in offers. There was a time when free subscriptions were desirable, but because practically everyone is offering a free newsletter or e-zine nowadays, people are not as eager as they once were to sign up for them. A growing number of people regard free newsletters and e-zines as contributors to their already cluttered e-mail in-boxes, particularly since the content of most leaves a lot to be desired.

Since the objective of an opt-in offer is to get as many web visitors as possible to sign up, you must offer something irresistible that people can't wait to get their hands on right away, something that offers instant gratification instead of a promise of monthly (or weekly) issues of publications of dubious value. An example of this is the opt-in offer used for The Healing Codes (see Figure 8.2). The offer was for a report titled *6-Minute Antidote to Stress*. The information in the report provided an opportunity to prove and demonstrate the power of The Healing Codes by teaching one of the codes. Proof and demonstration are extremely powerful. Once prospects learn how simple, easy, and effective the code for alleviating stress is, this goes a long way in convincing them that they should buy the entire Healing Codes package.

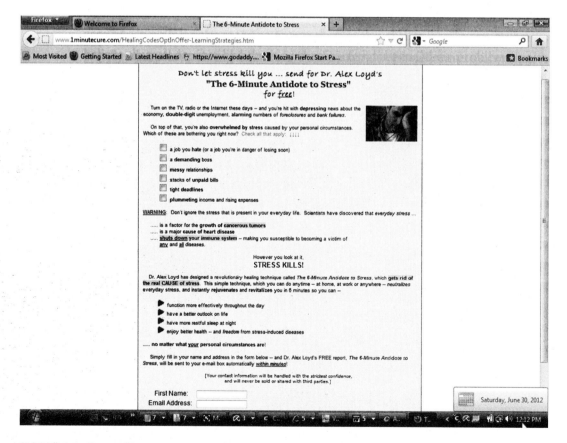

FIGURE 8.2 Opt-in offer.

You conceivably could offer a free newsletter that presents irresistible content, but I don't recommend it as the primary opt-in offer. I don't mean to imply that newsletters and e-zines are no longer viable marketing vehicles. On the contrary, when written effectively, not only are they a major marketing communication by which companies can stay connected to their prospects and customers but they can also be a vehicle that can generate considerable revenues. However, for the purpose of capturing the contact information of as many web visitors as possible, they should be regarded as secondary opt-in vehicles.

Presenting the Offer

An opt-in offer doesn't have to be in the form of a pop-up window. It can appear as part of a webpage. An abbreviated form of it can even be featured in an online ad, embedded in an e-mail signature file, or announced in discussion boards and forums. Here is an example of an online ad designed for tax preparers that incorporates an opt-in offer:

> Discover *The Best Tax Break* that can give your small business and Schedule C clients a net tax savings of $1,800 to $2,125 every year. Send for the Free Report that reveals this secret by visiting www.domain.com.

HOW TO WRITE IRRESISTIBLE AUTORESPONDER E-MAILS

Once you have captured the names of those people you enticed with the free report and confirmed their desire to subscribe to your list via a double opt-in procedure (see Chapter 4), if possible, what do you send them via e-mail? Send a series of follow-up e-mails using the autoresponder mechanism.

Quick Primer on Autoresponders

Most web hosts allow you to use e-mail addresses that automatically call up a prewritten e-mail that you upload to their server. When someone sends an e-mail to that address, your web host's server automatically sends out the prewritten e-mail that you uploaded. For example, if you send a blank e-mail to freelance@

webcopywritinguniversity.com, you will automatically receive my report titled *The Internet's Richest Source of Freelance Writing Opportunities*. That, in a nutshell, is the concept of an autoresponder.

Taking this a step further, there are web hosts, e-mail programs, shopping cart programs, and services that allow you to send a series of prewritten e-mails to your opt-in list at predetermined intervals, say, every three days. This automates the follow-up system for you.

Marketers often use the rule of seven, which has its roots in radio and television advertising. The rule states that prospects must see or hear your message seven times before they consider buying. It's not a hard-and-fast rule, just a rule of thumb. It applies not only to radio and television advertising but to online advertising as well. When you use autoresponders to send out seven or more marketing e-mails at predetermined intervals, you increase the chances of the prospect buying from you.

Crafting Autoresponder E-Mails to Your Opt-In Prospects

Step 1: Get recipients to consume what you just gave them for free. What's the use of getting them to download three free chapters, receive a free report, or download free software if you don't get them to read or use it? Most people don't read or use what they send for. If you don't get them to read the free chapters, they'll never buy the entire course. If you don't get them to read the free report that shows them how to save money, you'll never get them to sign up to join the discount buying club.

In the first autoresponse I developed to send to those who signed up to receive *How to Pay Less for Almost Everything,* I wrote:

> Somewhere in the free report you received is the "best-kept secret" for amazing savings that is truly simple and effortless.
>
> Most people miss it altogether because they skim through the report too fast—and yet it's probably the most important thing you can do in *1 minute flat* that can give you cash back on all your purchases at hundreds of major stores. Well, I won't keep you in suspense any longer. I'll point out exactly where that best-kept secret is hidden. It's in the 11th paragraph of the report.

Later in the e-mail, I wrote:

> To save you the trouble of having to find your free report, I've made it easy
> for you and given you the link below. Click on the link and check it out to
> see how simple it is for you to get similar savings on your purchases.
>   http://www.domain.com

Step 2: With every subsequent e-mail, highlight a different benefit of your
product(s) or service(s) and explore a different angle that slides smoothly into a
compelling reason why the recipient needs to buy what you're selling. This benefit or angle can be obtained directly from your website sales copy.

The succeeding autoresponses in the *How to Pay Less for Almost Everything* series extolled different virtues of the shopper's club. Autoresponse number two reminded prospects that they could receive 30 to 70 percent discounts
on the things they bought that week or month and, in addition, they would
receive free shipping. The third reminded them that they would receive rebates
on all the purchases made by friends and family whom they bring into the club.
The fourth stressed that they were losing money each day they were not a member. Autoresponse number five told the engaging story of how the shopper's club
started out in a small apartment above a garage, how its membership grew to
more than 3 million, and how the combined buying power of its members means
more savings to the prospect.

Crafting Autoresponder E-Mails to Customers

Autoresponder e-mails are not only for prospects. You can create a series specifically for purchasers of your product or service to help multiply one sale into
a stream of ongoing back-end sales at the same time it reinforces the sale and
minimizes buyer's remorse (and returns).

The autoresponse series that I wrote to purchasers of a $995 program for
starting a promotional products distributorship consisted of seven e-mails. The
first reinforces the sale by featuring the success story of the owner of a printing business who bought the program, relating how he used what he learned
in the program to earn a six-figure income after only seven months and how

he eventually closed down his printing business to concentrate on promotional products full-time. The e-mail also suggests a quick, three-step action plan for the customer to follow to get his or her promotional business or profit center up and running quickly.

The second e-mail starts with yet another success story—this time, the story of a woman who used the program to obtain her first order, amounting to $13,000. To learn her strategy, the reader is told to listen to the first tape of the two-tape course that came with the program. The remaining three autoresponse e-mails continue in a similar vein, each offering another success strategy and reinforcing the advantages of the program.

How to Format Your E-Mails for Optimum Readability

The readability of your e-mails is of utmost importance if your e-mails are to achieve their purpose of leading prospects down the intended sales path. There's nothing worse than sending an e-mail with jagged, uneven lines (a long line, followed by a short line, then another long line followed by another short line, and so on). This occurs when your e-mail is in one format and your recipient's is in another.

To avoid this, you should format your outgoing e-mail so that it is readable by all e-mail programs. Set your line lengths to 60 characters (including spaces) per line so that the lines don't automatically wrap. Don't panic. You don't have to waste time counting characters and manually adding hard returns when a line reaches 60 characters. Instead, you can use a free utility I've made available at the Web Copywriting University website. Go to http://www.webcopywritinguniversity .com/formatter/index.php, type into the Length box the number of characters per line that you want your e-mail to have, paste the text of your e-mail in the text box, and click on the Format Text button. Your e-mail will be automatically formatted for you with your desired line length.

HOW TO WRITE FREE REPORTS AND PROMOTIONAL ARTICLES

Writing free reports or promotional articles can be one of the most profitable things you do to promote the product or service you're selling on your website.

When you write a free report or promotional article, not only can you use it as your opt-in offer, but you can also offer its content to websites, newsletters, and e-zines. The more it is picked up, the more traffic it will pump to your website.

Information is the Internet's main commodity, so when you have good content to offer, you'll find many takers. A promotional article titled *Warning: Do Not Buy a Computer Until You Read This—Or You Might Get Ripped Off* offered compelling reasons for consumers to be wary when buying a computer. It listed six of the sneakiest—and even illegal—schemes employed by unscrupulous computer vendors to take advantage of unsuspecting buyers. Nowhere in the article was there a commercial slant; it consisted of only solid, informative content. The author's byline, however, provided the opportunity to plug her book about how to save $500 or more on a computer purchase.

To achieve its goals, a free report or promotional article must:

* Provide useful, bona fide content related to the product or service you're offering
* Be written in a way that positions you as an expert in your field
* Include a byline or a link that points back to your website

The important thing to remember is that the body of the report or article must contain information of value to your target audience. The sales pitch is introduced only after identifying the author (you) in the byline or resource box. Most e-zine and newsletter publishers are looking for articles of between 500 and 800 words. Some publishers are very strict about your article not being a sales pitch in disguise.

I've seen an article titled *Nobel Prize Winner Discovers the Cause of Cancer—and How to Cure It* employed as a promotional piece by a website owner who sells a book. It starts by stating that Dr. Otto Warburg won two Nobel Prizes for discovering the cause of cancer and goes on to explain his theory. Only at the end does the vendor conclude that its product (the book) contains the necessary information that enables you to use Dr. Warburg's discoveries in order to not only prevent but also cure cancer and virtually all diseases. The one-page article is an example of a promotional piece that provides information of value to its target audience without appearing commercially slanted. It's the kind of article that would be accepted for publication by e-zine and newsletter publishers looking for content relating to health, antiaging, or longevity.

The key to writing successful free reports or promotional articles is to keep them factual, unbiased, informative, and, most important, engaging. Make them revelatory, if that's possible with your subject matter. Avoid making a sales pitch, no matter how skillfully you think you can disguise it, and, above all, never identify the name of your product or service in the article. That's a telltale sign of self-promotion. Finally, don't use superlative adjectives and phrases (*amazing, incredible, world's best, taking the world by storm, spreading like wildfire, causing quite a stir*, etc.), which will expose your commercial intent.

Tips for Creating Search-Engine-Optimized Articles That Magnetize Hot Leads and Customers

Search engine optimization (SEO) is the process of increasing the number of visitors to a website by obtaining a high-ranking placement in a search engine's "natural" or "organic" search results. The higher a website ranks in the search engine results page (SERP), the greater the likelihood that the site will be visited by the people who are searching on any given keyword or phrase.

Search engine optimization entails both on-page and off-page optimization. On-page optimization refers to anything you do within your own website to improve the chances that the site will be found by a search engine. This includes meta tags, content, navigation, sitemaps, internal linking, alt tags, and heading tags. Off-page optimization refers to the activities done outside of a website to maximize its search engine ranking for specific keywords/phrases. This includes backlinks and search-engine-optimized articles.

The key to writing search-engine-optimized articles can be summarized in two steps:

1. Determine the right keywords or keyphrases that you will use to optimize your articles.
2. Create compelling content that people love and which search engines identify as relevant to people searching via those keywords and keyphrases.

Google's Keyword Tool is very helpful in choosing which keywords and key-phrases to optimize your SEO articles for. When you go to the Google Keyword Tool (http://www.googlekeywordtool.com) and type in any word or phrase in the search box, Google gives a list of keyword ideas plus data showing how often words are searched and their ad bid competition. The Global Monthly Searches (GMS) show how often people everywhere searched for a keyword. This gives you an idea of how much traffic you might expect from a keyword if you optimize your article for it—but only if your webpage where your article resides garners a high-ranking placement.

The Google Keyword Tool ranks the keyword competitiveness based on three metrics: High, Medium, and Low rating scale. A High rating means that the keyword's competitiveness in AdWords is over .67. AdWords is Google's main advertising product, which offers pay-per-click (PPC) advertising, cost-per-thousand (CPM) advertising, and site-targeted advertising for text, banner, and rich-media ads. A Medium rating indicates a competitiveness between .33 and .66; a Low rating indicates a competitiveness under .33. It stands to reason that the keywords with a High rating may not be as attainable as those that have Medium to Low ratings because so many advertisers are vying for those keywords. A good rule of thumb to follow is to choose keywords with the highest GMS but which have a Medium to Low competitiveness rating.

Most SEO articles that succeed in ranking high among the search engines fail to hit the mark because they are poorly written. In order to be successful, SEO articles need to have response-oriented copy—and that means they need to elicit a favorable action from the reader.

The same copywriting principles described earlier for editorial-style sales copy apply to writing SEO articles as well. The content must focus on what the readers are looking for, and the best clue for identifying this is to consider the keywords or keyphrases they typed into a search engine to find an article like yours. If you want your SEO article to be optimized for the keyphrase *natural diabetes cures,* for instance, the question you must ask yourself before writing the SEO article is "What information are these prospects looking for, and how can I deliver useful content that will get them to take the action I want them to take (such as subscribe to my newsletter, pick up the phone to call me, or click through to my sales page)?"

A well-written SEO article that delivers content that prospects are looking for, and that includes a strong call to action that compels them to do what you want them to do, can go a long way in generating a substantial amount of traffic to your website and create a significant amount of leads, sales, and profits. The guidelines set forth here, although far from exhaustive, include the key components that SEO articles must have in order to achieve a high likelihood of getting a high-ranking placement in search engine results pages.

1. *Headline:* The headline (or the article title) is what search engines look for. Therefore, the text you use in the headline is the most important factor for obtaining high rankings. The headline of an SEO article should ideally include three or more keywords or keyphrases that are three to six words in length (without repeating any words). They should also have minimal punctuation and be grammatically correct and readable. Many SEO article writers make the mistake of loading their headlines with keywords and keyphrases that, when combined, produce poor syntax and grammar, thereby decreasing the impact of the article or reducing the chance of getting a favorable action from the reader. The headline should have a maximum of 100 characters, including spaces, and should be in title case and bolded.

2. *Initial website link:* In order to obtain maximum click-throughs to your website, your website link should appear between the headline and the text or body copy. Example: Click for more info: www.yourwebsite.com.

3. *Content:* Establish your knowledge and expertise by giving brief but useful advice. Your article should be easy to read and should educate your readers about topics of importance to them (and it must be related to the keywords and keyphrases your article is optimized for). It should be "client-centric,"—that is, it must focus on what's in it for them—rather than being a blatant advertisement for your business. The ideal article length is 400 to 500 words.

   To get topic ideas, search for articles on search engines using your keywords. You can also peruse trade magazines or look through your website, brochures, or sales presentations. Articles that show readers "how to" or "how to avoid" are always popular. Example: Give instructions on how to buy the best computer at the lowest price, or how to avoid losing your retirement funds in the current economic crisis. Your SEO article could also use an interview-style question-and-answer format, wherein you write four questions you would want to be asked in an interview and then answer them.

4. *Keyword frequency:* Keyword frequency is the number of times your targeted keyword phrase appears in your SEO article compared to the total number of words in the article. Opinions vary among SEO experts, but the consensus is that the optimum keyword density is between 1 and 3 percent. The use of keywords in excess of that guideline (a practice called *keyword stuffing*) could be considered search spam and could cause a webpage to be penalized by search engines. To simplify the issue of keyword frequency, especially in view of the changing algorithms used by search engines, I abide by the following rules: Each of the keyword phrases included in the headline should also be included twice in the body of the article and bolded. Two of those keyword phrases should be hyperlinks that lead to your website or landing page.

5. *Call to action:* The article should always include a call to action and your contact information, such as your website URL, at the bottom of the article. Examples of calls to action:

For more information, go to . . .
Get the free report at . . .
For immediate response, contact . . .
Learn more about this fascinating technology by visiting . . .
Send an e-mail to receive the latest update . . .

Here's an example of a well-structured SEO article: http://tinyurl.com/National NewsToday.

GUIDELINES FOR WRITING NEWSLETTERS AND E-ZINES

For the following reasons, publishing your own newsletter (also called e-newsletter) or e-zine is one of the best and most economical ways to build traffic (and sales):

1. *It's free.* Anyway, it's almost free. It costs little or no money to produce and deliver an e-newsletter or e-zine no matter how many people you send it to.

2. *It's profitable.* You can easily build rapport and credibility with your subscribers and quickly be acknowledged as an expert in your field through your e-newsletter or e-zine. In turn, anything you promote or endorse will have a greater impact than any advertisement.

3. *You have a captive audience.* One thing that people consistently do online is check their e-mail. AOL Mail, in partnership with Beta Research, conducted an online E-mail Addiction Survey of 4,000 e-mail users and found that 51 percent check their e-mail four or more times a day and 20 percent check it more than ten times a day. People may not have time to visit the millions of websites that are out there, but most people do check their e-mail regularly and read selected items in their e-mail in-boxes. Your e-newsletter or e-zine would therefore be more likely to have the undivided attention of your audience than would your website.

4. *It keeps you in touch.* Your e-newsletter or e-zine enables you to stay in constant contact with your audience, and it constantly puts your business in front of your prospects. It is a great way to remind people to do business with you or to visit your website, without sounding like an ad. Since e-newsletters and e-zines are all over the web, make sure you offer one that has unique content of great interest to your target audience. More important, to attract the most subscribers your offer must have a compelling promise but at the same time be able to deliver on that promise.

The newsletter offer of *Underground Health Reporter* (UHR) e-newsletter reads as follows:

Join 250,000 subscribers and get your daily dose of startling discoveries in health and wellness. Sign up to receive the *Underground Health Reporter* e-newsletter for free. Each week you will receive little-known health break-throughs in your e-mail box—breaking news that could make a dramatic impact on your health and the health of your loved ones. When you subscribe to this free e-newsletter, you will also receive the bonus report: "Top 5 Underground Health Secrets You Never Knew Before."

The most important thing you have to do when setting out to create an e-newsletter or e-zine is to define your goals for it. The content and the overall direction for the publication will depend on what you want to achieve with the e-newsletter or e-zine. Those goals could include some or all of the following: drive traffic to your website, promote affiliate products, reinforce your brand, sell more of your products, develop community among your readers, or sell advertising.

As with all e-mail writing, don't be tempted to put the whole kitchen sink in your e-newsletter or e-zine. While providing value is something to strive for, don't be tempted to litter your publication with a multitude of subjects and topics. It may not always be easy to stick to a single message in a multipart publication, so the best thing to do is to have a cohesive theme that enables you to lead your readers down your intended sales path.

Ideally, the content you offer in your e-newsletter or e-zine must be related to the products or services that you are selling. Make sure you always provide bona fide content. Give your subscribers something worthy of their devotion, not just some disguised sales pitch, in return for giving you their undivided attention. This could be useful information, something free or discounted, or a special offer.

Tips for Creating "Monetizable" Content

An e-newsletter or e-zine with an in-house list of subscribers has the potential to become a tremendous source of income. In order to achieve this, however, the e-newsletter or e-zine must first establish a pattern of regular issues providing informative content. The content should be designed to encourage loyal readership and build trust. After all, very few people will read an online publication that was created for the sole purpose of pushing ads and peddling products. Once the newsletter has created loyal readers through its valuable content, there are several ways to monetize the content, and the two best ways are by promoting affiliate products and selling advertisements.

Promoting Affiliate Products

Promoting your own products to your subscribers is the most obvious way of monetizing your newsletter content. However, there is a limit to the sales you can make on your own products, especially if you have a lean product line. Therefore, promoting affiliate products which earn you affiliate commissions is a more viable way of generating a substantial ongoing income through a newsletter. This can be done by endorsing affiliate products that are likely to be of interest to your subscribers. For example, if you have a subscriber list consisting of families that lead natural, holistic, and eco-friendly lifestyles, you could conceivably endorse affiliate products such as organic household products, music appreciation courses for children, or blenders for making green smoothies. You might also consider promoting products that offer recurring commissions—for example, monthly membership sites that offer conscious parenting resources. Promoting such products can create long-term residual income streams.

The key to a successfully monetized newsletter is to present valuable content in every issue (content that has no commercial slant whatsoever) and combine that with product offers or endorsements, ideally pitched in an understated manner. Striking this fine balance is an art that can easily be mastered (as seen in the case study of the *Underground Health Reporter* e-newsletter in the next section). Above all, don't overwhelm your subscribers with too many product endorsements and sales pitches, or you'll run the risk of making your readers regard your newsletter as nothing but an advertising circular—and that will make them unsubscribe from your list.

When endorsing affiliate products to your list, always keep in mind that your subscribers are probably bombarded by scores of e-mail offers every day. According to InfoGraphic, the average e-mail user receives 147 e-mail messages a day. The majority of those messages are commercial e-mails—both solicited and unsolicited. Because of this volume of e-mails clamoring for attention (not to mention the busy lifestyles people lead), recipients usually "tune out" all but the most important e-mail. However, even while in the midst of e-mail clutter, they're likely to read something that helps them become more knowledgeable about a subject that interests them. Articles that offer tips or "how-to" guides on doing something better or learning some new skill are almost always welcomed.

Selling Advertisements in Your Newsletter

E-mail advertising is skyrocketing while its traditional (offline) counterpart is plummeting. Forrester Research projected that spending on e-mail marketing in the United States will grow steadily to $2 billion by 2014, which is almost an 11 percent compound annual growth rate. Because of this trend, a record number of businesses have begun to realize that their e-newsletter can also be a tool to generate third-party advertising revenue for their business. More and more on-line enterprises are realizing that, oftentimes, advertising revenues derived from e-newsletters exceed the revenues generated by their core business (see "The Anatomy of a Successful E-Newsletter" later in this chapter).

Most businesses that are in the process of growing their e-newsletter sub-scriber base monetize their e-newsletters initially by promoting affiliate products. That's because most advertisers would not be interested in buying ads in any e-newsletter unless the e-newsletter has a subscriber base of several thousand. A good rule of thumb is to start selling advertisements only after you have at least 2,500 subscribers.

To attract advertisers, you should provide detailed information about the demographics of your subscribers. The more clearly defined your e-newsletter's target audience is, the more easily you can sell ads—and at a higher price. The *Underground Health Reporter* e-newsletter's target audience is as follows:

Audience Size: 251,000
Demographic: Approximately 55 percent male, 45 percent female

The *Underground Health Reporter* e-newsletter's audience consists of an affluent, older audience (48.7 percent baby boomers 46 to 64 years old; 42.9 percent senior citizens 65 to 85+) that is very responsive to health and wellness offers.

79 percent predisposed to spending heavily on medications online
83 percent predisposed to purchasing fitness and diet products
91 percent predisposed to purchasing vitamins and supplements

Underground Health Reporter readers are very responsive and highly educated, and they have incredible purchasing power. Our subscriber list works great for nutritional supplement offers, alternative health products, newsletter and magazine subscriptions, self-improvement, online seminars/events, and much more!

If your list's demographics are appropriate for an advertiser's product offers and your price is right, there are countless advertisers who would want to try out your list for size, even if just to test your subscribers' responsiveness to their offer. Because every dollar in a marketer's budget has to stretch even further and generate a higher return on investment (ROI) than ever before, advertising in e-newsletters is fast emerging as one of the top online marketing channels. Some advertisers would even be willing to advertise purely for lead generation, not front-end sales.

E-newsletter advertising rates are based on various online advertising pricing models: flat fee, cost per thousand (CPM), or cost per acquisition (CPA). On the CPM pricing model, a dollar amount is specified per thousand, for example, $60 CPM; and this means the advertiser pays $60 for every 1,000 e-newsletter subscribers their ad is sent to. The CPM model is still considered the standard, but it's giving way to the CPA model—in other words, advertisers pay when a desired action has occurred (a purchase, a form submission, and so on) as a result of their advertisement.

No matter which pricing model you choose to implement, you must be certain to have the systems in place to help advertisers track the click-through rates (CTR) from their ads run in your e-newsletter. It's always a good idea to keep a record of your average CTR because potential advertisers will expect you to provide that number.

The Anatomy of a Successful E-Newsletter

Now that you're familiar with the basic principles of creating monetizable content, here's a case study of a fledgling e-newsletter that grew its revenues from $0 to $1.76 million in annual revenues—and emerged as one of the key publications in the online health and wellness arena—within a span of only two years.

Company: Headquartered in Los Angeles, California, Think-Outside-the-Book Publishing, LLC (TOTBP) is a boutique publishing company marketing books and information products online.

Challenge: In 2009, the company had four book titles that it was marketing online. In an effort to increase revenues, TOTBP set out to create a health and wellness e-newsletter called *Underground Health Reporter*. The timeline of events follows:

→ *December 1, 2009*—TOTBP broadcast its maiden issue of the *Underground Health Reporter* e-newsletter to the company's in-house list (size: 124,015) consisting of customers, who had bought the company's publications, and prospects. It was a weekly e-newsletter that was to be sent out every Tuesday. Every issue was monetized by selling affiliate products (no advertising).

→ *December 31, 2009*—Five UHR issues were broadcast in December, each one endorsing two affiliate products. By the end of December, the affiliate commissions earned by *UHR* totaled $67,517.84.

→ *January 31, 2010*—Four UHR issues were broadcast in January, and affiliate commissions totaled $75,989.56.

→ *February 28, 2010*—Four UHR issues were broadcast in February, and affiliate commissions totaled $55,569.39.

→ *March–July 2010*—Weekly UHR issues were broadcast, and affiliate commissions averaged $55,000 per month. *UHR*'s subscriber list swelled to 174,350, and advertisers came knocking at *UHR*'s door asking to advertise in *UHR*.

→ *August 1, 2010*—After nine months of promoting affiliate products, *UHR* switched its monetization model to selling advertising, using a CPM pricing structure. Its ad inventory every week included one sponsorship ad ($10 CPM), a feature article, which was an advertorial type of ad ($30 CPM), and a solo (dedicated) ad that was broadcast on Fridays ($65 CPM).

→ *September 1, 2010*—Although the CPM rates were higher than industry standard, all ad inventory sold out for the next six months (September 2010 through March 2011).

→ *September 2010–February 2011*—UHR's ad revenues average $73,000.

→ *March 1, 2011*—UHR begins broadcasting two e-newsletter issues a week (Mondays and Wednesdays). Ad revenues in March soared to $133,000.

→ *July 11, 2011*—Due to the popularity of the *UHR* e-newsletter and its branding within the health and wellness online circles, TOTBP launches the UndergroundHealthReporter.com portal website.

→ *July 31, 2011*—On its first full month since its launch, the UHR.com portal website earns $22,000 in revenues, strictly from joint-venture partners featured on the website. This is in addition to the *UHR* e-newsletter advertising revenues, which were averaging $125,000 a month.

→ *December 1, 2011*—On its second anniversary, the *UHR* e-newsletter and portal website's monthly earnings exceeded TOTBP's monthly revenues from its core business (book publishing) by 41 percent.

An analysis of *UHR*'s e-newsletter model may provide clues to its success. (See Figure 8.3). The content of each e-newsletter issue consists of three parts: a "Did You Know" article, the featured topic, and a sponsorship ad.

The "Did You Know" article offers interesting information and contains no commercial slant whatsoever. It gently eases readers into the content without hitting them up for a sale. This is an important cornerstone of this newsletter model. This is the segment that gives you an opportunity to show that you provide valuable information first before asking readers to pay attention to whatever product you're endorsing, promoting, or advertising.

Ideally, a 60/40 content-to-ad ratio (which means the e-newsletter contains 60 percent content and 40 percent advertising or product promotion, at most) is the ideal ratio. There is a hidden psychology hiding in the "Did You Know" section. When an e-newsletter provides information that is juicy, newsworthy, or helpful—ideally, information subscribers would probably not have encountered elsewhere—they'll be likely *to tear open the e-mail* the moment it arrives in their e-mail box because they'll be curious to see what juicy nugget is about to be revealed. This is how the *UHR* e-newsletter gained a loyal following among its subscribers. It also made subscribers more attentive and responsive to *UHR*'s product recommendations.

The *featured topic* is the second component of the *UHR* e-newsletter, and it uses a subtle and elegant approach to promoting products. It's written like an advertorial, and there's never any blatant selling. This differs tremendously from

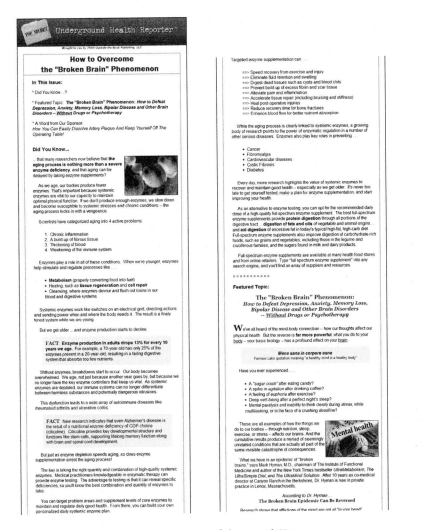

FIGURE 8.3 The anatomy of a successful e-newsletter.

the overt approach that affiliate marketers often take when they endorse affiliate products. *UHR*'s editorial style of selling may very well be the reason why it's a desirable advertising vehicle for advertisers, who are willing to pay $30 CPM for a featured topic ad (approximately $7,500 per ad). This lends credence to one of the *fundamental rules for writing web copy that sells* (see Chapter 1), which states that web users dislike overly hyped marketing language and gravitate toward factual information. They prefer to be engaged and finessed, not bombarded by blatant advertising.

The *sponsorship ad*, unlike the featured topic, is presented as a straightforward commercial message. This space, which is sold to advertisers at $10 CPM, is the secondary monetization vehicle in every *UHR* e-newsletter issue.

Ultimately, the credibility of the *UHR* e-newsletter, and the number of loyal readers it has amassed, pave the way to the creation of the *UHR* E-Alert, which features only an advertisement, often written in an editorial fashion. At $65 CPM, this *UHR* E-Alert commands the highest monthly ad revenues—exceeding the revenues of a single *UHR* e-newsletter issue by 63 percent. It is important to note that the high CPM rate that advertisers are willing to pay to run an ad in the *UHR* E-Alert is directly attributable to the responsiveness of the subscribers who have grown to trust *UHR*'s product recommendations.

GUIDELINES FOR WRITING ONLINE ADS, SIGNATURE FILES, AND BANNER COPY

Writing online classified ads, e-zine and newsletter ads, signature files, banner copy, and other advertising copy for use on the web requires strategies a little different from offline ad writing. Where an offline ad might feature a strong benefit-laden headline or give the product's or service's unique selling proposition, writing your online ad requires a different kind of discipline—the same kind required to create an editorial as opposed to an advertisement. It's so easy to use short, punchy copy reminiscent of classified ads in the offline world, such as "Lose weight while you sleep. Click here to learn more" or "Learn a foreign language in 30 days. Click here for more information."

When you have only two to five lines in which to generate a response (such as in an online classified ad, advertising banner, or e-zine ad), it's tempting to resort to the tried-and-true techniques of advertising language. But do you really want your ad to say "I'm an ad—read me?" No! On the Internet, you'll probably be ignored. The trick is to stand out from the other ads in the medium in which your ad is placed. This is accomplished not by screaming the loudest or using hype, exclamation points, capital letters, and so forth, but by featuring something newsworthy in your ad, engaging web surfers, or arousing their curiosity. For example:

> **Beverly Hills, CA**—"Topical Botox" has emerged as the new way to erase the look of wrinkles and lines from your skin—without injections. Read entire article here: http://www.domain.com.

You might think that getting someone to click on a link should be relatively easy. After all, clicking on a mouse seems like a virtually effortless task, doesn't it? It may appear so, but not when you consider that every commercial enterprise on the Internet is asking your prospects to do the same thing. The web population has learned to become selective about what they click on, particularly in view of the endless choices and the limited time at their disposal. You have to give them a compelling reason to click. Here is another example of an editorial-style ad.

> *9 Facts You Must Know Before You Buy Any Product That Promises to Grow Hair or Stop Hair Loss*
> Protect yourself from hair fallout and other horrors—and learn how to choose the right hair restoration product for your needs. Send a blank e-mail to 9facts@domain.com to receive free report.

The same applies to writing copy for banners, search engine listings, or SIG files.

Three Tips for Writing Online Ads

1. Make your ad look different, and articulate it differently from the rest of the ads in the medium where it runs so that yours will stand a chance at grabbing your audience's attention. Don't blend in with the rest.
2. Inject an element that will spark curiosity to get your audience to click.
3. Get prospects to opt in, if possible, instead of trying to sell in the ad. In the offline world, this is called the two-step approach. Only amateurs

and fools run three- to five-line classifieds and try to make a sale from that one ad. There's just not enough space in a few lines to make the sale. Use the ad as a lead generator to get people to opt in to receive a free report, a free course, or a free e-book. That way, you acquire another qualified prospect to add to your mailing list.

Here's an example of a SIG file that has a high click-through rate:

```
=====================
Did you know . . . that there's a simple
formula that has been *scientifically proven*
to prevent and CURE virtually all diseases?
Find out why this one-minute therapy is being
suppressed in the U.S. while more than
15,000 European doctors have been using it
to heal millions of patients—and how you can
use it, too. http://www.1MinuteCure.com

=====================
```

My own SIG file says simply:

```
Download your *free* eBook: "Frame-of-Mind Marketing:
How to Convert Your Online Prospects into Customers"
at http://www.webCopywritingUniversity.com/download.htm
```

The title of my e-book doubles as my sales pitch because it contains the entire benefit right there in the title. When people click on the link, they arrive at the download page, where I first collect their contact information and then allow them to start downloading. A captured name and e-mail address is more important than a site visit.

If you write an ad where readers must click on a link to go to your webpage, they might choose to ignore it, and then you'll have nothing. On the other hand, if you offer to give readers something for free, if they do not visit your website you at least have their contact information. This is gold on the Internet because you can be in constant communication with them until they finally buy your product—and, more important, buy many other products from you.

So much of your success depends on what you do after people visit your website. I estimate that up to 90 percent of your total sales will come from the skillful application of these follow-up marketing communications, combined with the e-mail strategies discussed in Chapter 4. Only a small number of visitors will become customers on their first visit to your website, but when you have mechanisms in place to capture the contact information of as many prospects as you can and start an e-mail relationship with them, that's when the real selling begins.

Writing Copy for Interactive Advertising Banners

Click-through rates for online banner ads have declined since the time banners first appeared on the Internet. Although 5 percent CTR was the norm for banners a decade ago, a 2 percent CTR these days would be considered very successful, depending on the situation. According to a report published by the Center for Interactive Advertising, the average CTR for banners had plummeted to 0.1 to 0.3 percent by 2011.

In view of these dismal click-through rates, an increasing number of advertisers are turning to interactive banners, which enjoy considerably higher click-throughs. Interactive banners are banners that respond to visitor actions such as keyboard strokes, mouse-overs, and cursor movements. Because they engage Internet surfers, they help increase user response and, hence, click-through rates.

Interactive banners range from those that have moving elements, such as the Punch-the-Monkey ads, to more complex formats, such as Hewlett-Packard's banner featuring a piano layout that allows users to create their own tunes. A wine shop created an interactive banner showing the picture of wine being poured into a glass. It poses the question "Would you like a glass of . . ." followed by three clickable buttons that give three wine options: Cabernet, Pinot Noir, Chardonnay. Whichever of the buttons is clicked, the banner displays the picture of a selection of wines, with the ad copy: "We have them all. Visit our shop."

I like to use banners that feature simulated form fields or involvement devices, such as check boxes and fill-in-the-blank mechanisms. For examples, see Figures 8.4 and 8.5.

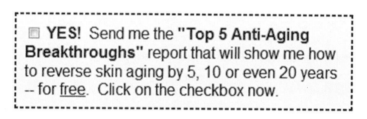

The "one-minute cure" for cancer involves which substance?

| | Go |

Type your answer in the box and click "GO" to find out the SHOCKING answer.

FIGURE 8.4 Interactive banner.

☐ **YES!** Send me the **"Top 5 Anti-Aging Breakthroughs"** report that will show me how to reverse skin aging by 5, 10 or even 20 years -- for <u>free</u>. Click on the checkbox now.

FIGURE 8.5 Interactive banner.

An example of an interactive banner that not only elicits a response from its target audience but also employs emotion uses the following copy:

Is He Cheating On You?
1) Enter His E-Mail Address
2) See Hidden Pics & Social Profiles Now!

CHAPTER 9

WEB COPYWRITING IN THE AGE OF WEB 3.0 AND BEYOND

As of the time of this writing, Web 3.0 is fast approaching—even though most people haven't fully understood the implications of Web 2.0 yet, a concept that was first recognized in 2004. Many believe that with the accelerating speed at which the web is evolving, it will not take long for the next fundamental change to reshape it into Web 3.0.

This chapter covers the broad definition of Web 3.0, which is far from exhaustive and focuses only on aspects that are related to Internet marketing and copywriting.

While a distinct definition of Web 3.0 is still up for debate, its simplistic definition is that it's "a new and improved World Wide Web" that embraces the ever-changing ways people interact with each other through the web.

Within the fundamental infrastructure of Web 3.0 exist social dynamics that a marketer can exploit in order to market much more effectively on the web. Before we can develop a strategy for marketing on Web 3.0, we first have to identify its relevant components, which include, but are not limited to, those discussed in the following sections.

BLOGS

A blog is a website that is usually maintained by an individual who regularly posts entries, consisting of personal opinions, views, descriptions of events, or other material such as pictures, audio, or video. Many blogs function as online diaries, and others provide news, updates, and commentary about a specific subject. Blogging has become such a phenomenon that Technorati, the leading blog search engine, has indexed over 133 million blogs. Approximately 77 percent of active Internet users read blogs, according to Technorati's *State of the Blogosphere 2011* report.

There's a new breed of bloggers who employ copywriting principles in order to glue readers to their blog pages and ensure that their attention stays riveted from the headline all the way to the end of the blog post. Web users want to find valuable online content; therefore, engaging content turns into advertising that sells. The same kind of copywriting skill as discussed in Chapter 8 (about monetizing newsletter content) is required in writing blogs that convert visitors into sales, and this also enables you to rank well in search engines and attract social media traffic.

SOCIAL BOOKMARKING SITES

These are sites that provide their users with a platform to save links to bookmarked webpages that they want to remember or share with other users. The bookmarks are usually public, but they can also be saved privately or shared only with specific people, groups, or networks. There are hundreds of dedicated social bookmarking sites in existence, each representing a specialized view of the World Wide Web. According to eBizMBA (http://www.ebizmba.com/articles/social-bookmarking-websites), as of May 2012 the most popular social bookmarking websites, based on the number of unique monthly visitors to each site, are Twitter (250 million), Digg (25.1 million), StumbleUpon (17.5 million), Reddit (16 million), Pinterest (15.5 million), and Delicious (5.5 million). Because social media sites like Facebook and Digg have become vehicles for sharing social bookmarks, sharing now produces an estimated 10 percent of all Internet traffic.

Just as blogs have shifted some of the power away from traditional publishers, social bookmarking sites have likewise taken some of the authority away from search engines, which used to be the only way for the Internet population to know which websites were relevant and important.

SOCIAL NETWORKING SITES

These are online communities, the most notable of which are Facebook (1.01 billion users), LinkedIn (135 million professionals spanning 150 industries), Twitter (465 million members), and Google Plus (62 million members), that bring together people who share interests and activities or who are interested in exploring the interests and activities of others. They facilitate the process of being in contact with like-minded people through a variety of methods such as messaging, chat, e-mail, file sharing, video, blogging, and discussion groups.

How to Craft Highly Targeted Facebook Ads That Deliver Leads, Sales, and Profits

Facebook, the most popular social network and the most-trafficked website in the world (according to comScore), represents significant opportunities for marketers, entrepreneurs, and business owners, both online and offline. As of October 2012, there were 1.01 billion monthly active Facebook users. During its infancy, the majority of Facebook's users belonged in the 12-to-24 age group, but in recent years the fastest-growing demographic consists of users 50 years of age and older.

The reason Facebook is an excellent advertising vehicle—no matter which age group you wish to attract—is because it is the most highly targeted marketing platform in existence. On Facebook, an advertiser could choose to run ads targeting users that satisfy various criteria, such as location (city, state, country, or radius), age, gender, marital status, education, and even the apps the users have downloaded, events they've attended, and other keyword targeting criteria.

What's truly brilliant is the ultra-targeting that advertisers can do on Facebook's advertising platform. Advertisers are able to multilayer various targeting criteria in order to narrow their target audience with laser-sharp precision, thereby enabling them to display their ads to only the prospects that are most likely to buy what they're advertising.

Suppose you own a fashion boutique in Los Angeles called QCode Threads. You could conceivably put your advertising message in front of only the Facebook users who are likely to become customers by using Facebook's multilayering capability and detailed subtargeting, as follows:

Gender: Female

Age: 21 to 35

Education: College graduate of USC and UCLA only

Connections: Fans of Lady Gaga, Alicia Keys, Black-Eyed Peas

Favorite apps: Photogene, Cook Hunting's app, Gilt

Favorite TV Shows: *Glee, How I Met Your Mother, 90210*

Radius: Lives within 10 miles of QCode Threads

Once you write an appropriate advertisement and run it on Facebook using these targeting criteria, you could potentially have a flock of high-quality shoppers (who are likely to buy) visiting QCode Threads on the same day your ad or promo is posted on Facebook.

Facebook's keyword targeting function enables you to target users based on not just demographics but also psychographics. *Psychographics* are any attributes relating to attitudes, personality, values, interests, activities, aspirations, lifestyles, opinions, and other psychological criteria. Facebook enables you to target users according to the TV shows they watch; their favorite movies, books, or music genres; sports; hobbies; occupations; and even their favorite quotes. This offers you valuable market research that allows you to extrapolate their interests, attitudes, and opinions and enables you to choose an audience that is a good match for the product or service you offer. For example, you can reasonably assume that those who like the book *Think and Grow Rich* by Napoleon Hill are business owners or entrepreneurs rather than corporate career people. You could also glean important information about people based on the kind of music they like, whether it be Michael Bublé, the Rolling Stones, or heavy metal. And, most definitely, people's favorite quotes give you a glimpse of their core values or aspirations.

So how do you write ad copy that has a likelihood of grabbing the attention of Facebook users and getting a high level of response? You simply go back to the basics (as discussed in Chapter 2), as follows:

- Know your objective.
- Know your target audience.
- Know the product or service.

First, define exactly what you want to accomplish with your Facebook ad (the objective), whether it be to make a sale, obtain a lead, brand your product, or get prospects to avail themselves of a special offer. Second, identify the attributes of your desired customer and use Facebook's ultra-targeting capability to zero in on that audience. Third, familiarize yourself with your product or service so that you can present an ad that conveys aspects that blend well with the frame of mind of the Facebook users you're targeting.

Your Facebook ad must *call out to the audience that you've ultra-targeted.* It goes without saying that if you speak to the needs and interests of your target audience, they're more likely to respond in the way you want them to. If your target audience consists of people who like Rhonda Byrne's book *The Secret,* for example, you might want to call out to them with the following ad:

> If you liked *The Secret* but haven't had much success in achieving the things you want in life, click here to discover the missing secret that will enable you to finally manifest your heart's desires.

Always remember to employ a strong call to action in your ad in order to get your target audience to click on your ad and arrive at your sales page in a responsive frame of mind. The images in your ad must be relevant as well as appealing to your target audience. The image you use may spell the difference between a successful ad campaign and a failed one.

The Anatomy of a Successful Facebook Ad Campaign

A café called Gonuts with Donuts used Facebook to build brand awareness and increase sales. Its owner, Lalin Jinasena, ran a Facebook ad inviting people to connect with his Facebook page by "liking" it. Within a few months, more than 10,000 people had connected with his Facebook page. That was followed by a huge demand for his donuts . . . and there were queues outside the café all day. As a result of successful Facebook ads, Gonuts with Donuts opened seven new stores. Gonuts with Donuts used the following ad copy to promote its "Birthday Mini Donuts" campaign:

Headline: Gonuts on your birthday

Image used: Tray of savory donuts

Body copy: Donuts are perfect for parties, as birthday gifts and office treats.

Call 495–1515. We deliver free to your party at home or office.

The ad generated 11 million impressions in only ten days.

AUTHORITY SITES

Because of their popularity for certain subjects, topics, or search terms, these sites are recognized as "authorities" by search engines. These sites usually contain very high quality and accurate content, and people often search for them. Most search engines like Google, for instance, have an algorithm that deems a website as being of a higher quality based on the number of high-quality websites linking to it (backlinks). When it comes to giving a website "authority site" status, however, Google not only makes use of backlinks to determine popularity but also observes how often people click on a specific website for those particular terms—and sometimes a careful manual review is warranted. Quality content and useful information are the key components that set authority sites apart from the rest.

When you reflect on these components that constitute the emerging social dynamics on the web, it's easy to see that the undercurrent they all share is interactivity. They also point to the online population's need to be heard, to express themselves, to contribute, and to matter. From the staggering numbers of people who participate in Facebook, Twitter, YouTube, and LinkedIn, not to mention the countless other social networks, it is plain to see that social networks have become an integral part of the fabric of Internet society. From a marketing perspective, the social media of the web present the concept of marketing as a conversation between and among people.

What does all this mean to a marketer, advertiser, or copywriter? The enhanced interactivity afforded by the web enables us to forge better relationships with our prospects and customers, and it also means that the web now has an organized feedback mechanism that lets marketers feel the pulse of their target audiences more than they ever have before.

On the whole, there has been a progressive decline in the effectiveness of the traditional sales letter (which usually begins with "Dear Friend"). We are moving toward writing more editorial-like copy that gives more content, turning the sales process into an experience and cutting down the length of copy in order to be stronger and more to the point. The web has given rise to new tools and resources that enable marketers and copywriters to relate to their prospects and customers in a whole new way. The emergence of social networks, for instance, now gives us the opportunity to start a dialogue with our prospects and customers in online social environments that feel comfortable and nonintrusive to them. We also now have continuing conversations with them in these "social" settings that enable us to anticipate their needs, serve them better, gain their trust, and demonstrate to them what it would be like to do business with us.

Never has there been a better time to be a skilled web copywriter than during this new era of the web, which requires a unique and impactful way of communicating. For example, learning how to craft powerful cyber bites (see Chapter 6) enables you to write effective blog posts about your product or service that don't come across as marketese. Telling a story (which is germane to social networking) and making sure the story has the Trifecta Neuro-Affective Principle installed in it will go a long way toward causing the bloggers and the social networking population to "feel right" about your product or service, making them decide it's a "good fit" for their particular situation, and convincing them that they need look no further than your product or service to fulfill their needs.

The deep-linking interactivity of Web 3.0 is facilitated by sharing utilities (such as ShareThis, Tweet This, and Digg This), which make it easy to distribute information to social media and allow a message, article, or story to be shared across the social web with the click of a single button or link. (See discussion later in this chapter for details about sharing utilities.)

Using the social dynamics on the web can create a cascade of interconnected benefits. One simple marketing message can snowball into an unstoppable flow of traffic and sales on Web 3.0. And that's with no cost except the time it takes to craft a cyber bite, blog post, article, story, or video.

This brings us back to the importance of web copywriting skills if you want to set yourself apart from your competitors and cause people to buy your product or service or do business with you within the web's social communities.

The important thing to remember is that all the success you can have on Web 3.0 comes down to honing the priceless skill of writing web copy. With this skill, anyone can create a breakthrough brand on the Internet and plug it into the key components of Web 3.0, such as blogs, social networking sites, or even videos on YouTube, to become famous on the web, become an authority in one's field, or become a subject matter expert in as little as 14 days. Web 3.0 requires a new kind of marketing communication—one that is cognizant of the fact that practically everyone is well connected nowadays, including your prospects and customers.

MARKETING VIA ONLINE VIDEOS

In February 2005, a fledgling company called YouTube opened for business and provided an online space where users could upload, view, and share video clips.

The collective impact that YouTube and other video-sharing websites have made on the lives of Internet users is staggering, and online video watching has reached epidemic proportions, encompassing the majority of all broadband traffic. Now its effect on the way we do marketing on the web is also becoming evident. Consider these statistics:

- YouTube has 490 million unique users worldwide per month, who rack up an estimated 92 billion page views each month (as of February 2011).

- According to the latest data from comScore Video Metrix, 182 million U.S. Internet users watched online video content in December 2011 for an average of 23.2 hours per viewer. (That's up 725 percent from 2007, when average Internet users spent 3.2 hours watching online videos.)
- The average YouTube visitor spends 15 minutes on YouTube videos per visit.
- Over 51 percent of web traffic consists of video content. Based on the current trends, Cisco predicts that between 2011 and 2014, over 90 percent of all Internet traffic will be video. This prediction is corroborated by Robert Kyncl, YouTube's head of global partnerships.
- Seventy percent of all U.S.-based Internet users watched videos on the Internet as of March 2007—and this usage is growing every month (Source: *The New York Times*).

When you consider these trends, it's easy to see why videos have become high-priority content on the web. Because of the popularity of online videos, the search engines now crawl video sites every few minutes looking for videos. That's why video links and clips often show up in Google, Yahoo!, and MSN search results even before other types of content do, sometimes in as little as minutes after a video is uploaded.

This kind of immediate search engine visibility has never been possible before, especially for a brand-new website. It usually takes a year or longer for a website with a newly registered domain name to gain any kind of search engine ranking for main keywords, typically showing up in search engine results only for keywords that are not competitive.

The online video boom represents a golden opportunity for all commercial enterprises on the web. YouTube, in particular, has been hailed as the advertising medium of the future by one of the world's biggest advertising agencies, Leo Burnett. Clearly, the viral, interactive, and community-led nature of YouTube makes it the ideal platform for advertising and marketing.

One might be tempted to assume that marketing via YouTube would work only when targeting the younger, more computer-savvy population that characterizes YouTube uploaders (average age: 26.57 years old). This is most certainly an erroneous assumption because even though the average age of video upload-ers is 26.57, the video viewers encompass practically everyone who has Internet access. That includes almost all ages and demographics except perhaps senior citizens over the age of 76 and children under the age of 12.

In the five years that iPhone has been on the market (third quarter of 2007 through second quarter of 2012), 183,078,000 iPhones have been sold. Accord-ing to *Podcasting News*, iPhone users are "30 times more likely to watch You-Tube videos" because each iPhone has the YouTube icon on its home screen, making online videos just a touch of the screen away.

Online video usage among iPhone users gives only a glimpse of the trend in online video viewing. Entrepreneurs are, therefore, able to use online video as a complement to their other online or traditional marketing campaigns, to market to practically any Internet users from age 12 to 76 in a wide variety of markets. While some products and services do lend themselves to online video marketing more than others, practically any company that has a commercial website can use online videos to drive traffic to its website, where the company can make a proper sales presentation. At the very least, the high search engine rankings alone that online videos produce (as a result of keyword loading) make online video marketing well worth the effort.

It therefore behooves all Internet entrepreneurs, copywriters, and compa-nies that do any kind of marketing on the web to learn the subculture of the video-viewing public.

SOCIAL MARKETING VIA VIDEO INCREASES SALES OF BLENDTEC BY 700%

BlendTec created enticing videos demonstrating how sturdy items (such as tennis shoes, Orabrushes, and even computer keyboards, iPhones, and iPads) are easily chopped to pieces in one of BlendTec's heavy-duty blenders. Starting with a marketing budget of only $50, BlendTec's VP of Sales and Marketing, George Wright, distributed the "Will It Blend?" video series on the social platform of YouTube and the other social media networks. The videos went viral—and as a result, sales of BlendTec blenders increased by 700%.

If you're an online marketer or entrepreneur, an advertising professional, or a marketing executive who wants to take advantage of the benefits that online videos have to offer but don't have the time, budget, expertise, or resources that you think are required to create an Internet video, I'll show you useful resources in the latter part of this chapter. These resources enable you to create an effective video in as little as a day and spend less than $100—without having to appear in front of the camera, hire actors, or even own a video camera. I'll also provide you with resources for having your video produced from start to finish for as little as a few hundred dollars.

How to Create an Online Video That Drives Massive Traffic to Your Website

Before you go about trying to create an online video (or having one created for you), and before writing a single word of copy (i.e., the script) for it, here are a few guidelines:

Limit the length. The video must necessarily be no more than three to eight minutes long. Various tests were done on videos posted on Google Video to track the length of time people were willing to watch an online video, and it was found that 3½ minutes is the optimum length. Another interesting finding is that video viewers generally pay attention to a video for 7 to 15 seconds before deciding to click away. Therefore, you have a 7- to 15-second window in which to grab their attention and get them to continue watching to the end.

This is where many of the copywriting principles described in this book, especially the Trifecta Neuro-Affective Principle, can be put to good use. The discipline that you've learned for riveting the attention of website visitors in the eight seconds they give you before clicking away will serve you well in the medium of video. While video obviously has other components, such as visuals and music, that contribute to its commercial appeal, the words that are spoken or displayed on the screen (i.e., the script or the copy) are the glue that binds them all together into a cohesive whole.

Use inexpensive, "rough around the edges" production. In order to harmonize with the culture that is present in video-sharing websites, your video must not look like a sleek, professionally produced piece. Doing so removes all doubt that it is nothing but a commercial. Companies invest huge production budgets in online video, but the ones that are successful in marketing via the video-sharing websites are the ones that cleverly disguise their videos to look like they were produced by amateur video buffs. With a little improvised acting, a script that uses natural language, deliberately sloppy camera moves, and poor production, a video can look consumer-generated and yet make a powerful commercial impact.

Remember that because we're bombarded with an average of 3,500 commercial messages per day (see Chapter 1), the last thing we want to see is yet another advertisement. No one will sit and watch your obvious commercial video any more than a TV viewer will watch just for the commercials.

Entertain, inspire, shock, or teach them—or make them laugh. The general Internet population has the mentality of not wanting to be "sold" (see Chapter 1, Morkes and Nielsen study), and the online video-watching subculture is just as averse to obvious attempts by marketers to sell them something via video. But they're not averse to being finessed into buying if you entertain, inspire, or shock them; teach them something; or make them laugh. How-to videos, funny videos, and videos that explode a myth are just a few avenues for advertising a product or service via video.

One successful YouTube video shows the story of a young man who started a burger museum in his basement to show that, because of the chemicals and preservatives put into them, burgers bought at McDonald's don't go bad. The video went viral, garnering over a million views and generating $29,950 per month in membership revenues for the website that the video directed traffic to. The video cost less than $82 to produce. But the interesting part is this: The subject matter of the video had very little to do with the website it funneled traffic to, except that the website is a resource on health, nutrition, and longevity—which leads to the next guideline . . .

Drive them to your website or sales page in the proper frame of mind. Most companies that do advertising via online video make the mistake of producing their videos as though they were extended adaptations of 60-second advertising commercials. That type of video might be appropriate for posting on a website, but if it's meant to be uploaded to video-sharing sites, it will rarely be effective. The most important job that your video needs to do is to get the viewer to your website or sales page in the proper frame of mind or, ideally, primed for the sale. It is the task of your website or sales page to do the selling.

In the video example described previously, the video doesn't do any selling. It just tells an interesting and thought-provoking story about the chemical composition of McDonald's burgers. By the end of the video, the viewers, if they happen to be health-conscious individuals, are compelled to learn more, so they visit the website, whose URL is embedded in various frames of the video.

Embed your URL strategically. One of the most important keys to promoting your website via online videos is embedding your URL (website address) throughout all frames of the video—except when the URL distracts from or competes with the content of the video. Your URL is likely to get imprinted into the brain of your viewer and be remembered long after the video has been viewed. Additionally, various video-sharing websites have their respective criteria for creating thumbnail representations of your video from the video stills that constitute it. YouTube, for instance, creates a thumbnail from the video still that is located at the exact halfway point of a video, and that thumbnail is used to represent your video in search results and other displays. Other video-sharing websites have other criteria for creating the representative thumbnail for your video. Therefore, if your URL is embedded in all the video's frames (which encompass all your video stills), all your thumbnails in all the video-sharing websites will be branded with your URL. One last advantage to embedding your URL is that even if your viewers don't reach the end of your video, where you invite them to visit your website, they would have already seen your website address.

An example of an online marketing video that adhered to the guidelines set forth here is the six-minute video produced by a boutique publishing company to promote its book, *The One-Minute Cure* (see the video at www.1MinuteCure .com/registrationtotbp.htm). The video was first uploaded on the web in September 2008, and, as of November 2012, it had been viewed 3,415,256 times and has generated $4.3 million in book sales.

How to Create High-Converting Video Sales Letters

In view of the popularity of online videos (as discussed earlier in this chapter), it was only a matter of time until videos would be used as a marketing alternative to long-form sales letters and website copy. Web users have begun to prefer consuming online content in video format rather than the traditional webpage. There is no denying that a video presentation is more engaging than reading long blocks of text. Furthermore, because an increasing number of people view their e-mails or surf the web via their mobile phones or tablet computers these days, they are less willing to read an 18-page long-form sales page and would rather view videos that fit nicely inside their browser window and require no scrolling.

Video sales letters have gained tremendous popularity among Internet marketers in recent years. A video sales letter (also called a VSL or a talking sales letter) is a video that takes the same information contained in a text-based sales page and presents it in video format.

If there's ever any doubt that VSLs are the latest favorite tool of Internet marketers, all one has to do is go through the Marketplace of ClickBank.com (the world's largest online marketplace for digital products), and you'll see how many of the top marketers have converted their old, long-copy sales letters into VSLs. And for good reason. They've been proven to significantly increase conversions when compared to their long-form sales letter counterparts. This has been observed across many industries and in my personal experience, and in many cases conversions sometimes double or even triple overnight!

Most video sales letters are not aesthetically appealing at all. Many of them don't even employ graphics, pictures, video clips, or screen enhancements but, instead, just use plain black text against a white background. The fact that these unattractive VSLs outpull long-form sales letters by a significant percentage confounds even the most experienced marketers.

Figure 9.1 is an example of a successful VSL produced by Stansberry & Associates Investment Research (http://tinyurl.com/StansberryVSL), which has been viewed more than 14 million times.

The same principles that were discussed in the earlier chapters of this book apply to the writing of scripts for a video sales letter—with only a few refinements. A VSL is simply a talking sales letter, after all. If you already have

Hello.

My name is
Porter Stansberry.

Stansberry & Associates
Investment Research

FIGURE 9.1 Successful video sales letter.

long-form sales copy written, all you need to do is condense it into a script that you (or a professional voice-over talent) can record as an accompaniment to the text to be displayed in the video. Long-form sales copy sometimes presents information in a sequence that doesn't have the same impact in video. A good guideline to follow when rearranging the sequence in which the information is presented in the video script is to use the inverted pyramid style of writing (see Chapters 1 and 4); that is, present the key, newsworthy information and conclusions first, followed by less important information and background material.

The video script doesn't have to be the same length as that of the website copy or sales letter. It can be an abbreviated version of the sales letter. A long-form sales letter that is 15 pages long may create a video that is 45 minutes long, and not everyone has that much time to watch a video, especially during a workday. In my experience, video audiences are unhappy when we send them marketing videos that are too lengthy, and this dissatisfaction reduces conversions. Therefore, I've adopted the practice of condensing an existing sales letter into a VSL that is no more than 15 to 20 minutes long but still contains the most salient points of a product's benefits, the offer, the guarantee, and testimonials.

In the event that viewers don't watch your video through to the end, it's always advisable to prepare a script for an exit pop-up that gives your prospects the opportunity to go to the webpage where your sales copy resides. Any web programmer can install a script on your video webpage that displays the exit pop-up when a viewer clicks on the Back button or tries to close the browser window. Figure 9.2 shows the standard wording of an exit pop-up for a VSL.

One variation of the VSL that has become popular as a marketing tool in recent years is the whiteboard animation video. A whiteboard animation refers to the use of time-lapse or stop-motion photography to capture an artist's hands illustrating a speaker's words via a whiteboard and a marker pen. Starting in 2009, a British nonprofit organization called the Royal Society for the Encouragement of Arts, Manufactures and Commerce (RSA) began producing whiteboard ani-

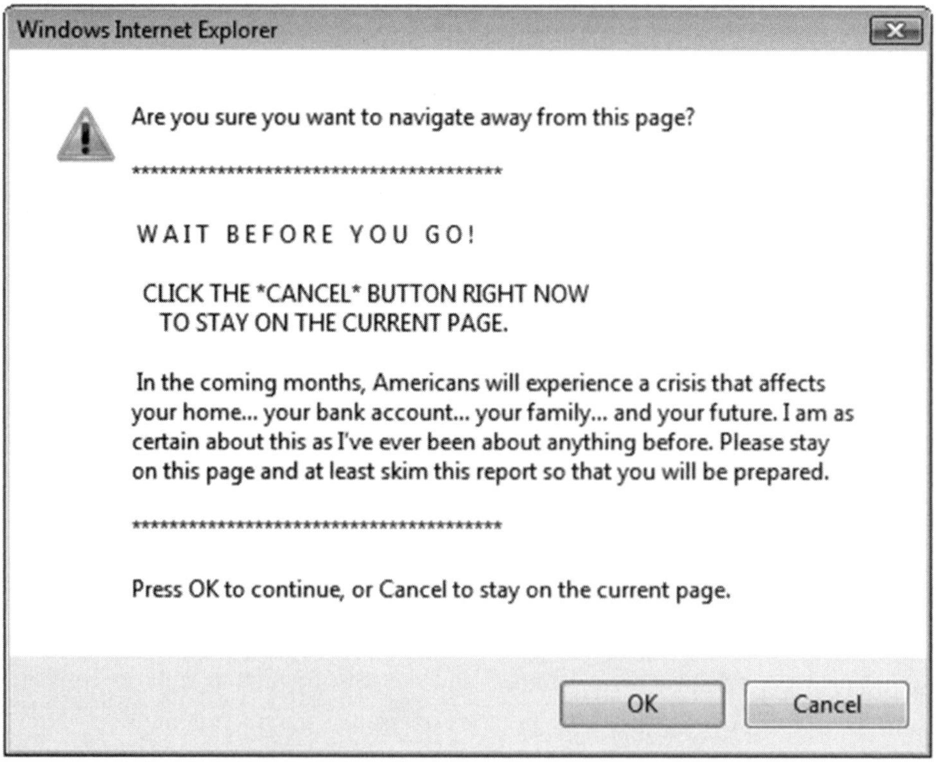

FIGURE 9.2 Exit pop-up that appears when prospects leave video webpage.

mations that carried the soundtrack of a thinker expounding on a theory or concept. Whiteboard animation videos have traditionally been used for educational purposes: to demonstrate the use of a software program, illustrate a new product's features, teach different languages, teach procedures to company employees, or present chapter summaries for educational textbooks. Lately, whiteboard animation videos have also been used to present sales letters with an animated appeal. Depending on the skill with which the whiteboard drawings are executed, viewers are engaged by what the artist's hands are creating on the whiteboard, and they eagerly anticipate what will appear on the whiteboard next.

Many businesses, both online and offline, have adopted the use of whiteboard animation in their marketing because they know that watching an illustration materialize as it is created is a hypnotic and entertaining experience for the viewer. Drawn pictures are a universal language of expression to which all humans respond. This goes a long way in presenting a persuasive selling proposition. In many business sectors, whiteboard animation videos are outpulling both long-form sales letters and VSLs by a significant margin.

One example of a successful sales letter delivered as a whiteboard animation video is Dr. Steven Sisskind's video promoting RealDose Weight Loss Formula No. 1 (see www.doubleyourfatlossnow.com).

A marketing video does not have to utilize whiteboard animation throughout. Many companies have found that when they use whiteboard animation in the first 10 or 15 minutes of their marketing video, and the rest appears in traditional video presentation format, the conversions are higher than if the entire video is presented in whiteboard animation. In fact, in certain instances, using whiteboard animation throughout an entire video sometimes results in decreased conversions. This was the experience of Barton Publishing, which used whiteboard animation in the first 15 minutes of its 25-minute marketing video promoting its Acid Reflux Solution Kit. Barton got a 40 percent increase in conversions this way. But when the company tested using whiteboard animation on the entire video, the result was an 8 percent decrease in conversions. This may be because whiteboard animation doesn't lend itself to effective call to action and could be distracting to the viewer at the point in the video that asks for the order.

The same copywriting principles discussed throughout this book apply to the writing of scripts for a whiteboard animation video. Once the script is written, you can hire a professional voice-over talent to record the script as an audio accompaniment to the whiteboard animation. Thereafter, you can hire the services of a company that specializes in creating whiteboard animations. The popularity of whiteboard animation videos has spawned an entire industry of companies specializing in the technique, such as WhiteboardAnimation.com and IdeaRocketAnimation.com.

How to Optimize Your Video for Search Engine Purposes

Thus far, I've only touched on the content of the video as it relates to getting viewers to take the action that you want them to take, which is usually to visit your website. But just as great web copy would be pointless if a website didn't have the eyeballs (traffic) to read the web copy, a video with great content that gets viewers to visit your website won't mean much if there aren't enough people to view the video in the first place.

Of course, there are a variety of ways you can promote a video, such as sending the video link to your e-mail list, if you have one, and asking your e-mail recipients to pass it on to others or post the video on their websites. However, nothing you can do to promote the video is as good as getting the video to show up on Google and the other major search engines when surfers search for keywords and phrases that your target audience uses to find a product or service like yours. Just because you've uploaded your video to YouTube doesn't necessarily mean that your video will be found on the search engines. Just as websites have search engine optimization (SEO) strategies to make them rank well in the search engines for specific keywords and phrases, so, too, do online videos. However, the SEO strategy for videos takes only a few minutes to perform, whereas SEO for websites can be time- and effort-intensive.

When uploading to a video-sharing website, you'll be asked for a few pieces of key information:

Media title: Create a compelling title of 64 characters (including spaces) or less. Load the title with your desired keywords or phrases. For example: "The Secret" Exposed—Is the Law of Attraction a Hoax?

Media author: Put the URL of your website here, such as http://www.Greatest ManifestationPrinciple.com.

Description: Put the URL of your website first (that way, your URL will be the first thing that shows in search engine results), followed by a keyword-rich description that includes what the video is about and the benefit of watching it. The ideal length is 200 characters. For example: http://www.Greatest ManifestationPrinciple.com—Why the Law of Attraction does NOT work for most people—but here's the missing principle whereby your desires CAN and MUST manifest—www.GreatestManifestationPrinciple.com.

Tags: Use *long tail* keywords whenever appropriate and do not duplicate tags. The ideal number of tags is six. For example: *Law of Attraction, the secret, manifest your desires, manifestation, manifesting, intentions.*

The search engines don't care much whether your video is professionally produced or consists merely of slides accompanied by audio—or if it's just footage of you walking your dog, for that matter—as long as it has the proper search engine optimization, as described here.

But what good is being on Page 1 of Google's search results if your listing is ignored, your prospects don't click on it, they don't watch your video, and even if they do watch your video, they don't do what you want them to do, which is visit your website? There needs to be a seamless relay, or a chain, from the moment your prospect sees your video listed in Google's search results, clicks on the link to watch your video, and then visits your website and reads your web copy. At every stage of the relay, skillful web copywriting is of the essence so as not to break the chain. I'm sure you're familiar with the saying "A chain is only as strong as its weakest link." That is certainly the case when it comes to marketing your website through online videos. That's why you need to master the principles I've covered in this book to pull off the coup that online video marketing requires.

Uploading Your Video

After your video has been created and optimized using the guidelines delineated here, you can upload your video. While you could choose to upload it only to YouTube, that wouldn't be a sufficient strategy for maximizing the chances that your video will be found by the search engines. The secret to getting a high ranking on Google and the other search engines in as little as an hour is to submit your video to as many video-sharing websites (Google Video, Yahoo! Video, Flickr .com, iFilm, etc.), blogs, social bookmarking sites, and podcast directories as possible. That way, all those sites will have links pointing to your website, and when the search engines find those inbound links they will deem your website relevant and important and rank it high in searches for your keywords and phrases.

Uploading your website to all those websites, blogs, and directories, however, is a time-consuming process that could take approximately two weeks, including the time it takes to set up accounts with each of the video-sharing sites, social bookmark communities, and podcast directories. There are software programs available that can automate certain portions of the video submission process, all with varying degrees of usefulness. One of the best resources I've found is Traffic Geyser, a subscription-based service that not only has an Auto Signup Tool that enables you to sign up for 40 accounts at the same time but uploads your site to 35 video-sharing websites, 6 blogs, and 12 social bookmarking sites simultaneously. It also converts your video into a podcast feed and submits it to podcast directories. The other is TubeMogul, which has an analytic technology that enables you to find out when, where, and how often your videos are watched; measure the impact of marketing campaigns; gather competitive intelligence; and share the data with colleagues or friends.

One of my client's videos—for which I wrote every component of the chain, from search engine listing to video script to website copy—landed on Google's Page 1 results for his top keywords (*understanding husband*) within 24 hours. In fact, his video, which was uploaded to 35 video-sharing websites, 6 blogs, 12 social bookmarking sites, and a few podcast directories, landed in two positions on Page 1 of Google. The video uploaded to GoFish.com ranked number five, and the video uploaded to YouTube.com ranked number seven on the same page! (See Figure 9.3.)

understanding husband - Google Search   Page 1 of 2

Web Images Maps News Shopping Gmail more ▾   Sign in

Google | understanding husband | **Search** | Advanced Search
                                                                  Preferences

Web   Results |1 - 10 of about **764,000**| for understanding husband. (**0.05** seconds)

Advice from a Caring and **Understanding Husband** -   Sponsored Links
Southern Maryland ... ◎
May 9, 2006 ... Advice from a Caring and **Understanding Husband** Dear   Know Your Man? ◎
Husbands: Please be aware that as your wives age, it is harder for them to Take This Quiz To Find Out.
maintain the ...   Browse Our Fun, Free Quizzes Now!
forums.somd.com/dating-marriage/73686-advice-caring-understanding-   www.LifeScript.com
husband.html - 45k - Cached - Similar pages

Divorce - **Understanding husband?** ◎
Aug 29, 2006 ... My friend is always out of town because of her job. But her **husband** told her
it deosn't bother him. She felt she was lucky to have such an.
www.iwishisaidno.com/forum/2630-understanding-husband.html - 77k -
Cached - Similar pages

Marriage and the **Husband**-Wife Relationship: A non-**understanding** ... ◎
Hi Sulakshana, Right now its not good for you and the baby to take too much pressure. Try
getting together with old friends and relatives, ...
en.allexperts.com/q/Questions-Marriage-Husband-864/non-understanding-husband.htm -
20k - Cached - Similar pages

REP-AM.COM Election NewsMichelle Obama vouches for **husband's** ... ◎
Everywhere she goes, Michelle Obama, a native of Chicago's South Side and daughter of a
city pump operator, vouches for her **husband's understanding** of ...
www.rep-am.com/news/elections/334962.txt - 43k - Cached - Similar pages

Marriage Enrichment: How to Build a Bionic Wife - marriage ... ◎
BionicWife.com - marriage enrichment, **understanding husband**, save my marriage,   ← RANK # 5
marriage counseling, bionic wife blueprint.
www.gofish.com/player.gfp?gfid=30-1209066 - 29k - Cached - Similar pages

Understanding Your **Husband's** Battle for Sexual Purity ◎
Do you understand your **husband's** battle for sexual purity?
womentodaymagazine.com/relationships/understandmenbattle.html - 18k -
Cached - Similar pages

YouTube - Marriage Enrichment and **Understanding Husband** ◎
http://www.BionicWife.comCounter-intuitive blueprint for marriage enrichment,   ← RANK # 7
understanding husband, marriage counseling, save my marriage http://www.
www.youtube.com/watch?v=w7DVOCKJDzc - 78k - Cached - Similar pages

The Key to **Understanding** The **Husband** of One Wife. :: Christian ... ◎
Apr 27, 2006 ... 1 Timothy 5:3 "Honour widows that are widows indeed" precedes and sets up
the **understanding** for 1 Timothy 5:9 "wife of one **husband**" making ...
www.christianmarriage.com/home/index.php?name=News&file=article&sid=50 - 47k -
Cached - Similar pages

Breast Cancer - A **Husband's** Guide to **Understanding** Breast Cancer ... ◎
Information on breast cancer: signs and symptoms, breast health, and breast cancer drugs
and treatments. Join a community of breast cancer support and ...
www.healthcentral.com/breast-cancer/c/5985/11957/guide-cancer/ - 41k -

http://www.google.com/search?hl=en&rlz=1T4TSHB_enUS212US212&q=understanding+...   5/4/2008

FIGURE 9.3 This video landed two positions on Page 1 of Google within 24 hours.

Resources for Creating Your Video

Clearly, online videos are the website traffic generator of choice, and the online video landscape is a level playing field, where all business enterprises of any size have an equal chance at generating massive website traffic—whether they have a large budget or a shoestring budget. By mastering the principles in this book, you can utilize your web copywriting skills to write a compelling two- to eight-minute script for your video, then employ easy-to-use video software such as iMovie, Pinnacle Studio, or Magix Movie Edit Pro to put it together without even having to shoot actual video footage if you don't want to. Your entire video could consist of stock pictures, slides, or stock video clips that you can purchase online at a very low cost. If you don't have a microphone or recording equipment, or you don't like the sound of your voice, you could hire an inexpensive voice-over professional for as little as $30 for 30 seconds. If you prefer to have someone else do the entire video for you, from script to production to uploading, you could do that as well. Following are resources I have used to create videos for my clients as well as for my own business enterprises:

Stock photos: Dreamstime.com and iStockphoto.com

Stock video clips: iStockvideo.com and Revostock.com

Online voice talent companies: ProVoiceUSA.com and VoiceTalentNow.com

Music: MusicBakery.com, BeatSuite.com, and RoyaltyFreeMusic.com

Video editor: Post job on Elance.com or type "video editor" in craigslist.com searchbox

One-stop shop for online video production: ViralVideoWizard.com (This service provides everything including writing the script, assembling all photos and video clips, producing the video, and uploading it to video-sharing sites, social bookmarking sites, blogs, and podcast directories via Traffic Geyser.)

HOW TO WRITE COPY FOR MOBILE DEVICES AND THE "PORTABLE WEB"

Cell phones and mobile devices have become a staple in everyday living throughout the world. As of the end of 2011, there were about 6 billion users of mobile devices, as estimated by the International Telecommunication Union. That's up from 5.4 billion in 2010, and it's only expected to rise even further in the coming years.

For many users, their mobile device is the central hub of their lives. It's their main means of communication with friends, family, and coworkers. It's where they store key photos and text messages, it's where they download apps that fit their lifestyles, and it's their go-to resource for finding information on the fly. The cell phone is usually the first thing most users see when they wake up and the last thing they see when they retire at night. Most users keep it by their side 24/7, and it's their primary connection to the world.

This has given rise to an interesting statistic obtained from a survey conducted by the Pew Research Center's Internet & American Life Project (April 26–May 22, 2011). The survey found that *25 percent of Americans say they're now doing most of their Internet browsing on their phones instead of a computer.*

A May 2011 Nielsen report states that 38 percent of mobile users (or approximately 2.28 billion people) own a smartphone, and 55 percent of all new phones purchased were smartphones. A striking 87 percent of smartphone owners check the Internet or e-mail on their phones, including 68 percent who do so generally every day, and 25 percent say they "mostly go online using their phone, rather than with a computer."

Because the world is going mobile, it's more important than ever for websites to be optimized for mobile devices. Mobile optimization can generate significantly more traffic for commercial websites, increase sales, boost customer engagement, and provide an edge over the competition. Yet the majority of websites are neither mobile friendly, nor are they optimized for mobile devices. According to the Directional Media Strategies 2011 Summit, only 1.25 percent of websites are mobile friendly. Another report from the 2012 Mongoose Metrics Data Series found that only 10 percent of websites are fully optimized for mobile access, which means 90 percent are not equipped to serve mobile users completely—or at all.

Kraft, one of the biggest food brands in the United States, has a slogan that underscores the undeniable importance of mobile optimization: "No Mobile Left Behind." This slogan is a cross-platform strategy message that indicates that Kraft wants its online systems to pay due importance to mobile and ensure that its webpages and online services can all be accessed via mobile.

Most businesses haven't made mobile optimization of their websites a priority because they don't realize the impact that the mobile trend could have on their business. I was one of those who initially cared very little about mobile optimization. I felt (as most website owners do) that our PC-optimized websites were sufficient, and I didn't realize that PC-optimized websites cannot work as well on mobile. When I discovered that a growing percentage of the population was surfing the Internet and checking their e-mails via their phones instead of their computers, and that mobile is expected to overtake desktop Internet usage by 2014, it was a sobering realization.

Tiffany & Company, the luxury jeweler, has a website that sells jewelry. Its digital agency in New York City, R/GA, noticed that Tiffany's website did not have a mobile-optimized version. When it implemented mobile optimization, the sales of jewelry on the mobile website more than doubled. In fact, sales increased by 125 percent.

Optimizing Your Website for Mobile: What It Means

Optimizing a website for mobile doesn't just entail making a website accessible to mobile device users but also optimizing for the "portable web," which includes smartphones as well as tablet computers like the Apple iPad and Google Nexus 7. The typical website is usually optimized for laptop or desktop computers (with large screens, full keyboards, a mouse, and a printer). Optimizing a website involves creating a version for the small screen sizes of smartphones and tablets.

Why is this important? Because if a website is designed for broadband PC users and is characterized by heavily animated screens or long-form copy, for example, it will not be as effective when viewed via the small screen of a mobile phone or even the screen of tablet computers. Furthermore, the page load time may be painfully slow, or the html format of the website may not display correctly because, on a global basis, many mobile devices still access very basic browser services on WAP (not full html) over GPRS—in other words, 2.5G networks (not 3G).

There are many programmers who specialize in designing websites that can be accessed from all platforms of electronic devices or can create a mobile version of your website. Ideally, a mobile version of your website should show only the most important information and resources and feature large components that can be easily touched or clicked. Some of the items a programmer would consider in creating a mobile version of a website include:

- Designing a responsive website interface that ensures ease of navigation
- Putting redirects in place that detect when visitors are using a mobile device and direct them to the mobile-optimized version of the site
- Determining which elements should be kept on-screen and which elements should be hidden
- Optimizing across multiple platforms (your website looks different on an iPhone than it looks on a BlackBerry)
- Avoiding the use of Java or Flash in order to ensure shorter load times (iPhones comprise about 30 percent of the smartphone marketing, and they, as well as all other Apple products, do not support Flash. Many mobile phones do not support Java either.)
- Improving mobile usability on web forms (with less zooming and scrolling required to complete the form)
- Optimizing your mobile site for search engines (Google now considers how well your site is tailored for mobile devices when determining your site's search engine ranking and your Google ads' position)
- Creating a mobile stylesheet for your website, overwriting the PC screen style sheet, changing dimensions, and modifying backgrounds
- Programming the "Give us a call" button to immediately dial your phone number

The mobile version of Tiffany & Company's website features a streamlined design, while still giving visitors the option to go to the company's full site. The mobile site simply features Tiffany's Welcome header on top, followed by the following four links:

Find A Store
Shop Tiffany Gifts
Find Your Perfect Engagement Ring
Tiffany & Co. Full Site

Before attempting to tackle the technical aspects of optimizing your site for mobile devices, the first item you must address is content. Plan your content with your target audience in mind. Mobile users are typically looking for a few key pieces of information: a summary of features and benefits of the product or service you offer (presented in a mobile-friendly format), directions to your office or store, a call to action or Order button prominently displayed or easy to locate, a click-to-call phone number, a map of your store locations, a web form that is easy to fill out, or a compelling offer (i.e., a coupon code), to name a few. What they're not looking for are long blocks of copy, nonessential information such as your staff's bios, or anything that requires them to download or print, because mobile devices lack such access.

Most people fail to take the frame of mind of the mobile user into consideration. Mobile users are on the go and are often in a hurry. They use their mobile device usually with one hand and while walking, standing, waiting in line, having coffee, waiting for a flight, in an elevator, waiting for their food to be delivered in a restaurant—and often while multitasking. They are distracted not just by things going on around them but by the endless text messages and e-mails constantly popping up on their mobile devices, as well as push notifications from their apps. They get very frustrated with delays and expect faster responses on the mobile web than on their PC. They expect an experience that is different from the one they'll get by visiting your standard website.

Guidelines on Optimizing Website Copy for Mobile

1. *Determine what key pieces of information your visitors will probably be looking for.*

   Marriott Hotels knows what mobile users who arrive at the Marriott website are looking for. So the mobile site prominently features a "Find and Reserve a Hotel" search wizard that allows visitors to type in the city where they want to find a Marriott Hotel, their check-in/checkout dates, the number of rooms they require, and the Find button.

   Domino's Pizza developed its mobile site by decluttering the site, removing confusing options, and limiting it to the items people would most likely be searching for. The site simply features a picture of hot, mouthwatering pizzas and the Domino's logo, followed by only five buttons:

   Order From Menu
   See Coupons & Promos
   Find a Store
   Track My Order
   Log in to My Account

   Tampa Bay & Company runs the VisitTampaBay.com website, which promotes economic development of Tampa Bay through tourism. The company determined what visitors to its mobile website are looking for, and those are the only buttons displayed on the site:

   Where To Stay
   What To Do
   Where To Eat

The navigation links at the bottom of the screen are simple as well: Calendar, Hot Deals, and Itinerary.

   A company that sells a product or service via a direct-response website that utilizes long-scrolling copy faces the challenge of optimizing the content of its mobile site to appeal to the frame of mind of mobile users. On mobile sites, marketers don't have the luxury of using creative storytelling, strategic lead-ins, introductory paragraphs, psychological devices (such as those discussed in Chapter 5), or the finessing nuances that characterize direct-response copy. Because mobile website visitors are not inclined to read long blocks of copy, you have to distill the PC-optimized website copy to the bare essentials for it to work on mobile devices.

The key is to pare down your sales copy to a minimum, use the Trifecta Neuro-Affective Principle, and write in cyber bites—bite-size pieces that pack a powerful selling punch—whenever possible (see Chapter 6). Include only the essential information that your target audience should see during the critical two seconds they're on your website before they have the chance to click or tap away.

2. *Use strong headlines.*

Headlines are not commonly used on mobile websites that sell items such as pizza, jewelry, hotel accommodations, or tourism (as evidenced by the previously described mobile websites of Domino's Pizza, Tiffany & Company, Marriott Hotels, and Tampa Bay & Company). However, a mobile website can only be made more effective and responsive by incorporating a strategically placed headline. The headline, in this case, can take the form of a tagline or slogan.

A mobile website for a boutique hotel in the Bay Area could conceivably use a headline such as "Simply the Best View of the San Francisco Bay" in addition to graphical elements or incorporated into the header design.

Likewise, if Domino's Pizza incorporated a headline that says "Pizza, Breadsticks, Wings and More" on its mobile website instead of just showing a picture of pizza and the Domino's logo, how much more of the target audience could the company potentially capture? Since there are so many pizza parlors clamoring for attention on the web, hungry prospective customers could change their minds and opt for Kentucky Fried Chicken (KFC) before they click on Domino's "Order From Menu" button. But the suggested headline "Pizza, Breadsticks, Wings and More," which presents a cross section of Domino's offerings, might reinforce the prospects' initial desire to order. "Hey, I can have pizza and chicken wings, too."

Notwithstanding small screens, there isn't a mobile website that couldn't be made more effective with the addition of a strong, well-crafted headline. Remember that not all website visitors who arrive at your mobile site are familiar with your company (unless your product is a brand name). Some website visitors arrive as a result of having found your website among search engine results. Therefore, their arrival at your website is the first time they've ever encountered your company or product. A headline that states your unique selling proposition (see Chapter 3) would go a long way in positioning you in the eyes of your prospective customer. Your USP distinguishes your business or product from all the others and gives your prospective customers the reason they must buy from you instead of your competitor.

At times, the headline is used in a mobile website in order to match the branding elements from your standard website. Even though your mobile site is an abbreviated version of your standard site, it's important to use the same branding elements on both websites. That's because your mobile site is a brand touchpoint and, like any other online assets, should reflect your brand essence. Visitors of your mobile site who are already familiar with your product or company feel a sense of comfort when they encounter the same headline or branding elements that they've seen on your standard website. It makes them feel like they're visiting an old friend, and this fosters customer loyalty.

An established company that successfully uses its branding and USP on its mobile site is TOMS shoes. The standard TOMS site displays the full USP right beside the company logo on the website header: "With every pair you purchase, TOMS will give a pair of new shoes to a child in need. **One for One**™" Because "One for One" is now a registered trademark of TOMS and the concept has become synonymous with TOMS, the company opted to use this abbreviated version of its USP on the mobile site, right next to the company logo.

A website that sells an antiaging supplement called Rejuvenation uses the following headline on its mobile website:

Rejuvenation: "Age Backwards" While You Sleep

The principles for constructing a riveting headline for a PC-optimized website (see Chapter 3) apply to the writing of headlines for a mobile site—with a few exceptions. Headlines for mobile sites must necessarily be shorter (no more than ten words), employ simple descriptions, reveal the important facts up front (rather than using teaser copy), use the second person (and the word *you*) whenever possible, and provide concrete rather than abstract concepts.

3. *Use the inverted pyramid style of writing.*

   Journalists employ the inverted pyramid style of writing (see Chapters 1 and 4), which entails presenting the key, newsworthy information and conclusions first, followed by less important information and background material. This front-loading method is an effective way of writing copy for mobile devices because, most of the time, website visitors are going to read only headlines or the first two lines of sales copy. This style of writing allows you to get your main point across immediately so that users can decide whether they want to read on.

   It's also important to note that some mobile devices truncate headlines. Therefore, front-loading increases the chance that your copy will make sense even if the headline is cut in half.

4. *Use a balanced amount of copy on each page.*

   Pay attention to how visitors of your mobile website browse the content, and optimize your copy with that in mind. Minimize the number of times visitors have to click links or buttons to get to the content they're looking for. With each click you require visitors to make, you increase the chances of losing their interest altogether.

   On the other hand, you must also avoid cramming too much content on a single page, because mobile users find it tedious to scroll through long blocks of text.

5. *Employ video and audio on your mobile site.*

   According to a 2010 mobile video report from The Nielsen Company, nearly 25 million U.S. mobile subscribers watch video on their mobile devices, and this number is rising more than 40 percent every year. These mobile video users watched an average of 4 hours and 20 minutes of mobile video per month.

The growing popularity of mobile video is due partly to the proliferation of media-friendly mobile devices, including smartphones. Over time, it also has become easier to view and share mobile video through mobile apps or the mobile web.

Employing video to deliver a sales message, therefore, blends well with the mobile culture. If you have a video sales letter (see "How to Create High-Converting Video Sales Letters" in Chapter 9), you might consider featuring it on the mobile version of your website instead of your standard, text-intensive, long-scrolling sales letter.

Audio, too, is a format that blends well with the mobile culture. This is evidenced in the fact that 60.7 percent of the general population listens to music on their mobile phones every day, while another 34.6 percent do so every now and then. Furthermore, one in five users turns on a radio app to listen to FM radio via mobile phone daily, while another 56.6 percent use it from time to time (source: GSMArena.com). When you add these statistics to those tabulating the number of people who listen to audiobooks and podcasts, it's easy to see that audio is a mainstay among mobile device users.

It stands to reason that sales messages delivered via audio represent another viable marketing platform.

6. *Allow people to visit the full site.*

Once your website is optimized for mobile devices and you've successfully pared down your content, there is still a high likelihood that some of your mobile site visitors (especially those who use tablet computers) want information you've chosen not to display.

As such, it is always advisable to include links on multiple pages that allow users to view the full version of the site. In the case of Tiffany & Company, previously described, the mobile website has a link to the standard website: Tiffany & Co. Full Site. Many major mobile websites give their users the same option, including *USA Today*, Home Depot, and Target.

HOW TO WRITE COPY FOR INFOGRAPHICS TO GENERATE FREE WEBSITE TRAFFIC

One content platform that is expected to achieve massive penetration in social media in the coming years is information graphics. Information graphics, more popularly called *infographics,* have become increasingly more prevalent on the web, and their power is apparent especially in social media, where infographics tend to spread like wildfire.

From late 2009 to the beginning of 2012, interest in infographics has increased by over 800 percent, according to Google "Insights for Search" analytics. Statistics from Digg.com, the leading social news website, show that since 2007 the number of infographics on its website have increased by 250 times. This is positive proof that infographics are emerging as the hot trend for content distribution.

Although infographics have been around in their earliest form since the days of the caveman, in the current information age, advertisers and graphic designers across a wide spectrum of industries are using infographics as a vehicle to present a variety of information. And with good reason. Studies have shown that *the brain processes visual information 60,000 times faster than text,* and text accompanied by graphics is understood by the brain more easily than plain text. According to a report from Purdue University, approximately *65 percent of the population are visual learners,* which means they usually prefer graphics, illustrations, and charts, and they're also able to recall details in picture form.

What are infographics—and why have they become a marketing vehicle of choice on the web?

Infographics are graphic visual representations of information, data, or knowledge. Their historical purpose was to take complex ideas or concepts—from the world of math, computer science, biology, or statistics—and clarify and distill them into a graphic form that could be easily understood by most people. This use continues through the present day, but the next generation of infographics is a visually compelling communication medium that, when executed well, can be a powerful content marketing vehicle that could potentially go viral.

The Role of Copy in Creating Infographics

Although it was established in the introduction of this book that writing content for the web is distinctly different from writing web copy, whenever infographics are used for content marketing, web copywriting principles do apply.

In many ways, writing content for infographics is synonymous with the copywriting model that I've presented in this book, wherein a sales proposition is wrapped in the cushions of a content piece. In the writing of editorial-style web copy, nothing appears like an ad, but, rather, it appears like content, and the same is true in the writing of content for infographics.

Keep in mind that Facebook users are not in a buying mode, but they *are* looking for information. Therefore, providing valuable information for free is paramount. The "selling" accomplished by a well-crafted infographic comes in the form of branding, positioning the content provider as an authority or an expert, building trust and relationships with social media fans, and, ultimately, generating traffic to your website.

Copywriting skill also comes into play in the writing of killer headlines for infographics. Headlines could be miniaturized versions of your blog post titles. Whenever possible, include little-known, eye-opening, shocking, or even weird facts that rivet the attention of your target audience. Offer information and tips that can help or benefit them, and give them something to talk about or share with others. If the topic is chia seeds, for example, you might want to use a headline such as "Why This 'Miracle Seed' Is the World's Healthiest Raw Food," followed by a list of the health benefits of chia seeds.

The key to a successful infographic is how well it *engages* your target audience. You can measure engagement by the amount of "likes," shares, and comments. You could have a million fans, but if they are not engaged with your content, your social media strategy will not be effective. It's infinitely better to have a few truly engaged fans who comment, share, and "like" your posts than thousands of fans who are indifferent and don't respond to your content. This is where implementation of the psychological and involvement devices may prove useful (see Chapters 5 and 7).

Case Study: UndergroundHealthReporter.com Portal Website

Jamie Martorano and Katerina Kavouklis, who manage the health and wellness portal website of UndergroundHealthReporter.com, learned the traffic-generating power of infographics firsthand. They generated tremendous additional traffic to the portal website, increased the number of subscribers to the *Underground Health Reporter* e-newsletter, and gained thousands of "likes" on Facebook.

They approached the task of creating infographics as they did any other piece of website content—they examined what topics people were searching for and what they wanted to know about those topics. They studied what was already working on their Facebook pages—that is, which of the images and content pieces they had posted were getting the most "likes," shares, and comments. They also observed what other companies were doing successfully on Facebook. Thereafter, they selected images and created content to meet their target audience's needs, assembling health-related quotes and little-known (but well-researched) health facts. Each infographic designed by Katerina incorporated the UndergroundHealthReporter.com watermark at the bottom and used an impactful photo and a clear, cohesive message that rose above the clutter on Facebook status updates and the text-heavy messages in social media. They invited their Facebook fans and friends to check out their infographics and share them with their friends.

Katerina posted the very first UndergroundHealthReporter.com infographic on Facebook on July 8, 2012. Prior to that, she had 25 health-related photos that she had posted on their Facebook wall that received only 0 to 5 "likes" per photo. In contrast, the first infographic received 105 "likes."

Spurred by the promising results of that first infographic, Jamie and Katerina proceeded to create a series of additional infographics that they posted on Facebook. Their infographics have received hundreds of "likes" apiece and were shared hundreds or thousands of times. These were some of their most popular infographics:

Headline: Magnesium—The Essential Forgotten Mineral (See Figure 9.4)

854 likes/2,085 shares

MAGNESIUM
THE ESSENTIAL FORGOTTEN MINERAL

Magnesium is a mineral needed by EVERY CELL of your body.

Foods Highest In Magnesium

- Crude Rice Brain 922mg
- Swiss Chard 860mg
- Purslane 850mg
- Spinach 756mg
- Dark Cocoa Powder 499mg
- Almonds 395mg
- Coffee 327mg

Did you know..refined grains remove 80-97 percent of magnesium?

The Spark of Life

It creates energy in each and every cell by activating ATP the storage molecule and the fuel that drives each cell of your body.

Our bodies need the correct amount of magnesium in our diets for us to sleep properly. If it's too high or too low, we can suffer from sleep disturbance.

Can Magnesium Deficiency Cause Cancer?

Researchers found that 46% of the patients admitted to an intensive care unit in a tertiary cancer center presented as deficient in magnesium.

In Egypt, the cancer rate was only about 10% of that in Europe and America. Among the rural population, it was practically non-existent. These cancer-free populations have an extremely high magnesium intake of 2.5 to 3g which is 10 times more than in most Western countries.

www.undergroundhealthreporter.com

FIGURE 9.4 Infographic: Magnesium—The Essential Forgotten Mineral.

Headline: The Power of Your Amazing Brain (See Figure 9.5)

406 likes/1,082 shares

FIGURE 9.5 Infographic: The Power of Your Amazing Brain.

Headline: True Healthcare Reform Starts in Your Kitchen, Not in
Washington (See Figure 9.6)
369 likes/1,881 shares

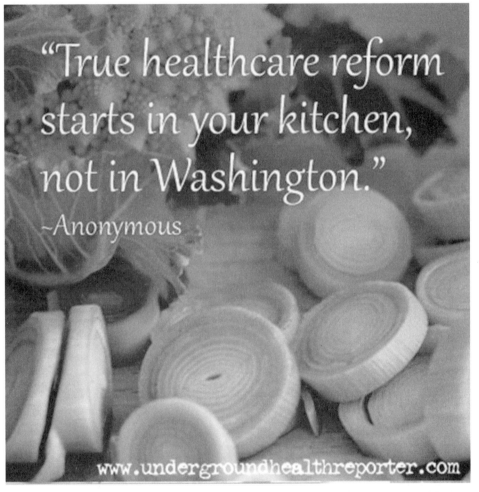

FIGURE 9.6 Infographic: True Healthcare Reform Starts in Your Kitchen, Not in Washington.

Headline: Five Best Memory-Boosting Foods (See Figure 9.7)

253 likes/790 shares

FIVE BEST MEMORY BOOSTING FOODS

#5 Avocados

This healthy monounsaturated fat increases blood flow to the brain. That means more oxygen getting to those parts of your brain that help you to think and to remember details.

#4 Apples

Apples could have dementia–fighting qualities. Vitamin C is a known factor in the reduction of Alzheimer's.

#3 Dark Chocolate

Dark chocolate reduces inflammation and may help prevent oxidation in the brain, which is the precursor to many neurological diseases.

#2 Green Tea

EGCG protects the brain. It lowers the amount of protein that builds up as plaque linked to memory loss and nerve damage.

#1 Blueberries

Nutrients packed in these berries help reverse age–related problems in the area of brain function, improve learning, motor skills, and vision.

www.undergroundhealthreporter.com

FIGURE 9.7 Infographic: Five Best Memory-Boosting Foods.

Headline: Why You Should Eat an Avocado a Day (See Figure 9.8)

232 likes/506 shares

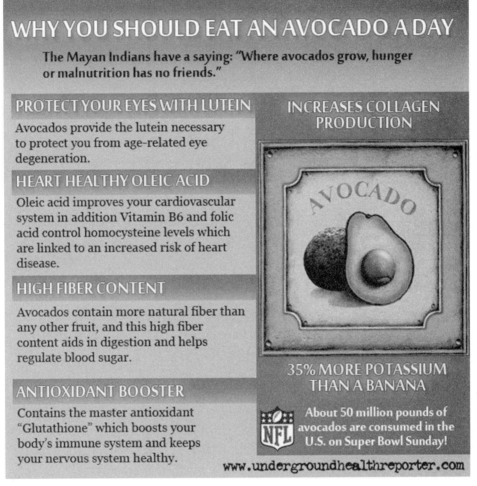

FIGURE 9.8 Infographic: Why You Should Eat an Avocado a Day.

Results: Since posting daily infographics, the number of Facebook fans has doubled each month. Before implementing the infographics, there were 1,400 fans. By the end of July (the first month of posting infographics), the number of fans doubled to over 2,800. By the beginning of September, the number of fans reached 6,000. In addition, since the implementation of info-graphics, the health portal website doubled its traffic of new unique visitors and converted 5 percent of them into subscribers of the *Underground Health Reporter* e-newsletter.

Whenever an infographic is shared by Facebook fans, even those who are not *Underground Health Reporter* fans see the images in their friends' Face-book feeds. This is one reason why the social reach of infographics expands tremendously. Since the website's URL (watermark) appears at the bottom of each infographic, fans know where to go to find more valuable information. This goes a long way toward positioning *Underground Health Reporter* as an authority for providing valuable, well-researched health and wellness content.

Additional Tips for Using Infographics for Online Marketing

1. The three steps involved in creating infographics are design, market-ing, and copywriting. The design needs to be attractive—something that would stop the viewer long enough to take a look. The photo(s) need to be clean and have enough room for text, so the overall graphic won't look cluttered. You can create the infographic yourself if you have graphic skills or use an agency or service provider (from oDesk or Elance.com) to create a custom infographic. A custom design may deliver the best results as opposed to a template design. Refer to the re-sources section in Chapter 11 of this book for websites that showcase a variety of well-designed infographics, as well as infographic tools and resources.

   Within the copy, create actionable steps and takeaways for the viewer. In the Facebook update status, you can create a call to action to increase engagement: Read this post, Share with your friends, Click "like" if you agree.

2. When featuring facts, figures, and statistics in your infographic, use only those that are actually verified by scientific studies or reliable research. Don't be tempted to "lift" information that you might find on the first page of Google's search results because, oftentimes, those "statistics" and findings are derived from blog posts, peoples' personal opinions, or erroneous information that has been rehashed. Endeavor to find at least two verified scientific studies or research references to support the information you plan to feature in your infographics. Here's why: The farther your reach extends, the more likely you will attract trolls, who make it their mission to say you're giving inaccurate or false information.

3. In addition to promoting your infographics to your own Facebook fans, expand your promotions to include visual social media sites such as Instagram and Pinterest, social news websites such as Digg.com, and other social sites like Twitter, Google+, LinkedIn, and social bookmarking sites. There are also infographic directories and infographic aggregators that will willingly post your infographic on their websites. Some of them have a high page rank and will generate quality backlinks that can potentially turn into significant monthly traffic. (See the "Directory of Resources" in Chapter 11 of this book for a list of sites for infographic distribution.)

The Benefits of Using Infographics in Your Content Marketing Strategy

- It's low-cost marketing. There's a minimal cost involved in the creation of infographics, and disseminating them represents zero-cost organic marketing for traffic generation and list building.
- Creating infographics that are embedded with your logo or website URL watermark is a powerful way to enhance brand awareness and drive traffic to your website as people "share" and "click."
- The research required to create infographics displays your knowledge and positions you as an authority or expert on a given topic.
- Due to the visually compelling nature of infographics, they are likely to be shared on social networks, and the likelihood of an infographic becoming viral is much higher than for ordinary text content.

- Infographics are embeddable. This means that when you provide an embed code to those who wish to put your infographic on a WordPress blog or website, this creates an automatic link from their site to yours.
- When people embed your infographic on their blogs or websites, those infographics create inbound links to your site. As a result, Google and the other search engines will index your website higher due to their "Page Rank" algorithms. This increases the importance that search engines place on your site.

CHAPTER 10

LAST BUT NOT LEAST

Tying It All Together

Nothing in the world can take the place of persistence. Talent will not. Nothing is more common than unsuccessful men with talent. Genius will not; unrewarded genius is almost a proverb. Education will not; the world is full of educated derelicts. Persistence and determination alone are omnipotent. The slogan "Press on" has solved and always will solve the problems of the human race.

—CALVIN COOLIDGE

Success in any endeavor, particularly in selling, is part ambition, part observation, and part determination. Writing web copy that sells is no different. As with any discipline, some people who practice the principles discussed in this book will fail to meet their sales objectives. Barring unrealistic expectations, I wish to offer solutions that will prevent that from happening. This chapter examines tracking and testing, troubleshoots web copy that is not generating sales, and presents a four-step process to web copywriting success.

TRACK IT, FIX IT: WHAT TO DO WHEN WEB COPY IS NOT WORKING

When I was creating offline copywriting, I learned one lesson I'll never forget. Do you remember those infomercials advertising contour pillows? In the original infomercials, the advertisers highlighted what they thought were the pillow's top two benefits: that they help you sleep better and that they make you more comfortable while you sleep.

When the pillows didn't sell too well, the advertisers phoned 100 actual buyers and asked them why they had purchased the pillows. Over half bought because of neck pain, the other half because of sleeplessness or because their spouse snored—benefits not even mentioned in the infomercial.

Based on these findings, they rewrote the pillow offer. Since 52 percent bought because of severe neck pain, the alleviation of neck pain became the lead benefit. Sales multiplied by more than ten times. Comfort Sleeper, the company that manufactures the pillows for Walmart, and the largest retail foam manufacturer in the United States, reported that sales in the stores went up 1,000 percent. The packaging for the entire industry changed to emphasize these benefits, and, as a result, a dormant product became a hot item overnight.

The advertiser also phoned people who didn't purchase (those who called the order line but decided not to order) or who returned the pillows. Those who did not purchase were confused by certain things said in the infomercial, and they had objections or questions that weren't answered to their satisfaction. Those who returned them said the pillows made their neck hurt more.

Consequently, the ad company further refined the infomercial to remove the confusion and answer objections. Comfort Sleeper also put a note inside the package sent to pillow customers that forewarned them that their neck might hurt during the first few days of using the pillow because the neck was still adjusting to the contour but that they could look forward to comfort after that (which was the truth). As a result, sales soared again, and this time returns were greatly reduced.

It all boils down to knowing your audience. Sometimes copywriters think they know their audience well, but, in actuality, they don't. In the case of the contour pillows, the ads overlooked key problems, pains, and predicaments (the three Ps) of their customers (neck pain, sleeplessness, and snoring spouses). Not until the phone survey provided feedback did the ad copy get it right.

Similarly, copywriters can guess what the target audience's hot buttons are, but if we don't know why people are buying the product or service, we won't know how to rewrite the copy if it isn't pulling in sales.

If you are the web copywriter hired to write the copy for a flat fee, you may not care much about this, except that you might not get repeat business. If, however, you're a web copywriter who is getting a percentage of the sales or an Internet marketer who writes web copy for your own products and services, this matters a great deal.

Surveying customers is so much simpler on the Internet. You no longer have to phone 100 people. All you need do is send a well-designed e-mail to those who bought the product and ask the following questions:

- "What are the reasons you bought this product or service, or what motivated you to buy?"
- "Can you list the top benefits of the product or service that convinced you to act?" Alternatively, you may prefer to list the main benefits and say, "Here are a few of the benefits of our product or service. Please rank them in order of importance."

When the copy I wrote for a diet pill website didn't pull as well as I expected, I used these questions in a minisurvey that I created for free at www.freeonline surveys.com, which then added a link in my e-mails to purchasers of the pills. All the customers had to do was click on the link and a pop-up appeared, which enabled them to answer and submit their answers in a matter of seconds. Therefore, I was able to do my research easily (and at zero cost) and make the necessary changes to the copy based on the survey findings.

For those who don't buy but have provided their contact information and for those who return the product they bought, try asking the following questions:

- "Why didn't you buy?"
- "What, if anything, was confusing about the offer?"
- "Why did you return the product?"

When you survey your customers, you often discover that the top benefit is something you buried somewhere in the middle of your web copy. Based on this information, you can restructure it accordingly. One of my clients, who sells a program that teaches people how to start their own promotional products (advertising specialties) business, used this headline on his website:

How to Get Your Share of the $18 Billion Promotional Products Industry

When it didn't pull, we surveyed those who bought the program and learned that the main reason they bought was because they wanted to find the factories that manufacture the promotional products. We rewrote the headline to read:

Start a lucrative promotional products profit center or
distributorship easily with . . .
The Ultimate Resource for Finding Promotional
Product Factory Sources

The new headline boosted response by 23 percent, without changing a single word of the body copy. We would not have had those incremental sales had we not bothered to query the customers. The bottom line is that you must be willing to do what it takes to accomplish your objectives.

Another way to find out what people's opinions are about your product or service is by doing a search on Google or other search engines to see what is being said about it in relevant forums, newsgroups, or blogs. A client of mine who markets a health book that discusses the merits of a natural oxygenating substance "eavesdropped" on the conversation threads in popular health forums and blogs. She found out that people had the mistaken notion that the book was about Miracle Mineral Solution (MMS), sodium dichloroacetate (DCA) or ozonated water, which it wasn't. She also found out that people had many unanswered questions that made them skeptical and kept them from buying her book. I suggested the addition of a prominently positioned Frequently Asked Questions (FAQs) section on her website to address all the objections people had voiced in the forums and blogs. This effectively quadrupled her sales even while her website traffic remained constant.

FOUR STEPS TO WEB COPYWRITING SUCCESS

I learned a foolproof secret to success in any undertaking, and I've applied it to web copywriting, as follows:

Step 1: Understand exactly what you want your web copy to accomplish. In other words, define your objective, but this time be more specific. If you can, quantify the results you want to get. It could be to convert 10 percent or more of your web visitors into customers, or to sell ten books per day, or to generate $1,000 in sales per day. Write down exactly what you want to accomplish.

Step 2: Take action to fulfill your objective. This includes writing the best possible web copy and marketing communications and getting traffic to your website (using linking strategies, search engine optimization, a revenue-sharing (affiliate) program, pay-per-click search engine advertising, online video, or any other traffic-generating methods).

Step 3: Observe what's working and what isn't working. Track and test your results continually. Do more of what's working, and eliminate what's not working (including, but not limited to, key elements of your web copy).

Step 4: Keep adjusting your actions. Do this until you accomplish your desired objective.

When you do these four things, you'll never be without options. You'll never sit there and say, "Why does it work for others and not for me?" Probably the most important step is Step 3, "Observe what's working and what isn't working." That is how I developed my own unique model of web copywriting, and I did it through tracking and testing.

On the Internet, you have to be tracking results and testing continually. I'm fortunate to have come from a web copywriting environment in which we tested everything. We tested e-mail subject lines; we tested whether personalizing the subject line was better than not personalizing the subject line. We tested lead-ins, dissonance elements, and various formats of newsletters. We tested web copy headlines, web designs, sites with pictures, and those with no pictures. We even tested different prices, offers, guarantees, closes, and bullet points. You name it—we tested it.

However, as I mentioned earlier, things change so rapidly on the Internet that I cannot confidently say that what worked six months ago still works as effectively today. Search engines change their algorithms constantly, spam filters and pop-up blockers are becoming ever vigilant, and acceptable business practices on the Internet are being altered by regulations and sanctions. That's why nothing beats the practice of constant testing and tracking to obtain your own marketing intelligence for your particular audience.

The kinds of things you discover when you track and test are astounding, and they affect the profitability of the website not just for the here and now but also for the long term. Testing and tracking are so fundamental in direct-response marketing that they are a given; yet most people on the web don't test anything. They write the web copy once, they launch the product or service, and when it doesn't pull, they wonder why. They don't realize that tracking and testing can significantly boost the sales of a website.

The concepts of tracking and testing would require another book to explain thoroughly, but here are some fundamental concepts that will help you get started.

Track Your Results

We've discussed a number of marketing methods, including writing a free report or promotional article and disseminating it in newsletters and e-zines, ads in e-zines, online classified ads, pay-per-click advertising, a great SIG file that your affiliates use every time they send out e-mail, and so on. Let's assume that this month you did all of these things and you received a decent number of orders. What do you do next month? Repeat all of the same things again, right? Wrong!

You find out which things worked and which didn't so that you can repeat more of what worked and none of what didn't. If, for instance, you determine that your promotional article that ran in an e-newsletter last month accounted for 93 percent of your sales and the online classified ads did not produce a single sale, then you would contact more e-newsletter publishers to run your promotional article and you'd cancel your online classified ads.

The thing to remember is that it isn't you who decides what works, no matter how many years of experience you have in marketing, nor is it you who determines the best-performing headline, offer, guarantee, or price. Nothing works until the tests prove it works.

Marketing great Ted Nicholas, who reportedly spent over $500,000 testing and tracking copy elements, asserts that simply by changing the headline you can increase the pulling power of a direct-response ad by 1,700 percent, even when the rest of the ad is identical! The only way to learn this is through testing.

Let's say you are running an ad that's pulling a 2 percent click-to-sale conversion rate. You figure that since 2 percent is a decent response rate, you're earning a net profit of $1,000, and your advertising cost is $500, you can't complain. "Why, that's a 100 percent return on my investment," you say to yourself. But what if you discover, through testing, that another one of your ads pulls a 4 percent response rate, you're earning a net profit of $2,000, and, since your advertising is a fixed cost of $500, that means you increased the return on your investment from $500 to $1,500, or from 100 percent to 300 percent!

Online, many programs and scripts are available that enable you to test and track results. There are also ad tracking programs that are built into e-commerce shopping cart services like 1ShoppingCart.com. These programs allow you to track the clicks and sales generated by two or more different versions of copy without hassles. In a nutshell, here's how these programs work: A unique tracking URL is assigned to each campaign you run, which allows you to count actions such as clicks, sales, and sign-ups to your newsletter or opt-in offer. It allows you to view detailed information and analysis for each campaign: for example, how your Google AdWords pay-per-click campaign is doing, how your ad in the Yahoo! classifieds is doing, how that free report that you're giving away via autoresponder is doing, and so on.

In addition to these basic tracking functions, a tracking service allows you to evaluate all your visitors' click trails so that you can

- Know exactly what trail buyers take and, as a result, streamline your site to get all visitors to follow that proven linear path

- See what paths nonbuyers take and eliminate the bottlenecks and road-blocks at your site
- See what visitors who subscribe to your newsletter or opt into your lead generation system really do on your site
- See which traffic sources create the most sales—or no sales—so you know where to focus your efforts

For those of you who have e-newsletters or who run e-mail marketing campaigns, there are also good direct e-mail marketing services that enable you to easily track and test the results of your e-mail marketing. For example, you can find out who opened your e-mail message, who clicked on which link, what they looked at on your website, how long they stayed on your site, whether they bought something, which item(s) they bought, how much they spent, and who they are, based on demographic and registration data.

Here are three e-mail services that track and test results:

www.constantcontact.com
www.iContact.com
www.bronto.com

Two Degrees of Separation

I'm certain you're familiar with the concept of six degrees of separation, which refers to the idea that if a person is one step (or degree) away from every person he or she knows and two steps away from every person who is known by any of the people he or she knows, then every person is an average of six steps away from any other person on the planet. On the Internet, especially since the advent of Web 3.0 social media, there's an average of two degrees of separation between you and any person on earth—or maybe less. Think about it. If you wanted to establish a connection with any person you can think of, and you're a member of Facebook (1.01 billion) or LinkedIn (47.6 million)—or all of the social media networks—chances are, at least one of those members already knows the person with whom you want to connect. And there's a high probability that the person with whom you want to connect is already on Facebook or LinkedIn, which means you're one step away from that person!

But again, that kind of easy accessibility means nothing unless you know how to communicate on the web in a way that will get you heard amid those billions of online conversations that are going on at any given time. Only skillful web copywriting will distinguish you from the ocean of sameness and enable you to capture the attention and devotion of those you want to connect with—be they prospects, customers, or possible friends, lovers, or business partners. This brings to mind again the words of author Sidney J. Harris: "The two words 'information' and 'communication' are often used interchangeably, but they signify quite different things. Information is giving out; communication is getting through." I assure you that the principles I've covered in this book will enable you to get through.

Ultimately, the current dynamics of Web 3.0 will cause online entrepreneurs and business enterprises to become better and more honest marketers and motivate companies to develop quality products and services. That's because the online buying population is relying more and more on blogs and social media to get feedback regarding products or services they're considering buying. A simple search on Google for a product's name, for instance, will most likely pull up blog entries—good or bad—about that product. Search engines often crawl blogs, especially if their content is regularly updated. When consumers view blog comments and other entries posted on social networking sites, they are able to obtain a more balanced assessment of your product or service than merely relying on the information you give them at your website, which is obviously skewed in your favor. Good comments travel fast on the web nowadays, but bad ones travel even faster, able to circle the globe in a matter of minutes. Therefore, if a company's product, service, or way of doing business is substandard or downright unscrupulous, that company won't be able to stay in business for long because its online reputation, thanks to Web 3.0, will be jeopardized, if not completely destroyed by social networks.

I estimate that the majority of Internet users go to search engines to see what other people have said about a product or service they're considering buying before they actually make their buying decision. That's true whether they're buying a software program, an air purifier, a skin care product, a travel package, a weight loss program, a course, a book, or a widget. In fact, even when buying products or patronizing service businesses in the brick-and-mortar world, people generally rely on reviews of people online before making their buying decisions—whether they're buying a car, thinking of patronizing a local restaurant, choosing videos, or considering that new gadget or gizmo they saw on an infomercial. For a great many people, the Internet has become one gigantic consumer reporting machine, and with the workings of Web 3.0, even more so.

Web 3.0 will also reward those marketers who take the time to learn how to navigate its new terrain and who learn how to communicate effectively within its unique social dynamics. It will also prosper those who make it a priority to serve the best interests of people rather than being the modern counterpart of snake oil salesmen who gave salespeople and marketers a bad name. And one day we'll all learn that marketing is not about viewing people as website visitors, eyeballs, prospects, customers, or means to our own selfish ends—but as human beings who crave emotional connection . . . just as we ourselves do.

CHAPTER 11

THE LUCRATIVE BUSINESS OF WEB COPYWRITING

The preceding chapters of this book have shown you one of the most important skills on the web, and that is writing compelling web copy. Once you master this skill, you can parlay it into a lucrative web copywriting career, should you choose to do so.

The copywriting principles, building blocks, and psychological and involvement devices presented in this book should help get you started and steer you in the right direction. However, should you wish to seek advanced education on the art of web copywriting, you can choose to enroll in the Web Copywriting University (www.WebCopywritingUniversity.com) or seek accreditation as a Certified Master of Web Copywriting. You can also refer to the "Directory of Resources" section later in this chapter to obtain additional copywriting resources.

Back in 2002, when I became a freelance web copywriter, I had no idea how to find clients. Using the strategies I present in this chapter, within 60 days I was able to get more clients than I could handle, and within two years I became one of the highest-paid female web copywriters in the world. It is my hope that you will meet with the same good fortune in your copywriting journey.

HOW TO FIND WEB COPYWRITING CLIENTS

There's an abundance of potential web copywriting clients that you can find online. The ideal ones are those with websites that sell excellent but poorly marketed products. Here are just a few companies and individuals that are good prospects:

→ Companies that sell perennially popular products or services such as weight loss systems, hair loss remedies, and credit repair

→ Authors who are looking for ways to market their books

→ Health and wellness companies that sell nutritional supplements, skin care products, or health gadgets

→ Companies that have effective brick-and-mortar marketing but have lackluster online marketing (such as those that sell products via TV infomercials or products sold through multilevel marketing)

→ High-tech companies or independent software developers that sell outstanding programs that no one knows about

→ Internet marketers that have courses or products to sell (but poor copywriting skills)

→ Professional companies or individuals that offer a specialty product or service, such as the following:

A financial company that sells subscriptions to an investment newsletter

A stock-trading expert who sells a stock-picking service

A chiropractor who specializes in curing acid reflux

An elder-law attorney who offers a self-help kit for families caring for a loved one with Alzheimer's disease

An individual who helps laypeople qualify for Medicaid to cover the expenses of a nursing home

These represent only a small cross section of the diverse array of enterprises that need good copywriting services. You can begin your search for prospective web copywriting clients simply by typing a keyword or phrase into a search engine for the type of product you'd like to write copy for. For example, if you're interested in writing copy to sell investment newsletters, type the keyphrase "investment newsletters" in the search box of Google, Bing, or another search engine. The search results will display a variety of investment newsletters, and you can view the sales copy of each investment newsletter to see if it's a candidate for a copy overhaul. If so, you can send the newsletter the template prospecting e-mail in the next section of this chapter.

An even better way to prequalify your prospective web copywriting clients is to identify only those businesses whose websites already get considerable traffic. This is the beauty of the web copywriting profession. You don't have to settle for the clients that happen to come your way—you actually get to choose your clients. And if you're going to choose your clients anyway, you might as well pursue those that have high traffic, the ones that are already making money, the ones that are already spending money on advertising. Why? Because those companies are likely to understand the value of good web copy, able to afford professional web copywriting services, and probably accustomed to hiring copywriters.

How do you go about finding these prospects? One way is by using Alexa and Quantcast. Go to Alexa.com, a website that helps you find and evaluate businesses worldwide with its free web analytics. Let's suppose you found an investment letter called ValueLine from your Google search. You can type in ValueLine's website address in Alexa's search box, and it will give you Site Details, such as the following:

Alexa Traffic Rank: 149,664
Traffic Rank in U.S.: 39,853
Sites Linking In: 880

Thereafter, go to Quantcast.com, which enables you to cross-reference a website's profile and see the site's audience reports for free. If you type ValueLine's website address in Quantcast's search box, you'll find that the website gets 59,599 monthly U.S. visitors. It's ranked number 25,502 among websites, based on the number of people in the United States who visit the site within a month.

Based on the analytics from Alexa and Quantcast, ValueLine.com appears to be a great web copywriting prospect because of the website traffic it gets and its traffic rank.

Another way to find prospective clients is to click on the "Top Sites" tab at the top of the Alexa.com home page. This displays the top 500 sites on the web (based on Alexa's traffic ranking). Click on the By Category tab to choose a specific category of high-traffic websites. If you click on Health, for example, subcategories ranging from Addictions to Women's Health appear. In this way, you can zero in on just the websites you'd like to write copy for. Likewise, on QuantCast.com, you can click on the Top Sites link to obtain similar information.

Yet another way to find an unlimited number of prospective copywriting clients is at ClickBank.com, a marketplace where thousands of publishers of digital products (such as e-books, downloadable audiobooks, videos, and courses) offer their products to ClickBank's network of over 100,000 affiliates. At Clickbank.com, click on the Marketplace link and you'll arrive at a webpage where you can choose from categories of products that are available for sale. If you click on the Self-Help category, for example, you'll arrive at a webpage where you can sort out all the Self-Help products by order of popularity. Click on the dropdown menu under Sort Results By and select Popularity. The first page of the results will display the most popular products in the Self-Help category. It's reasonable to assume that the sales copy for these first-page products is effectively converting prospects into customers. The way to find out how well any given product's sales copy is written is by clicking on the product name (e.g., Panic Away—End Anxiety and Panic Attacks). This takes you to the product's sales page. It's also reasonable to assume that since the product is selling well, the sales copy is probably performing well, and that means the product owner (or website owner) may not be motivated to have the sales copy rewritten.

The trick is to scroll down to the less popular products—that is, those that appear on page 3 or beyond in the popularity search. Why? Because there's a high likelihood that those business owners or website owners feel the 3 Ps (pain, problem, and predicament) most. They probably think their copy needs improvement, but they don't know whom to contact to get it done. They're looking for help in generating more leads, sales, and profits.

HOW TO CONTACT PROSPECTIVE CLIENTS

Once you've identified the online businesses that you'd like to pursue as web copywriting clients, and you've obtained the names of the key contact people and their e-mail addresses, it's important to approach them in a manner that will make them take notice.

In Chapter 3, I presented the Formula for Mathematically Measuring the Selling Quotient (SQ) of web copy. Most business owners and website owners would be interested in knowing their website's SQ. People are always interested in getting their "score"—especially when you explain that the SQ is the predictor of a website's sales performance based on its web copy.

You can plug the formula into your prospective web copywriting client's existing web copy and determine exactly what kind of a selling job the website is doing. Remember: To avoid having to manually add up your worksheet score, you can go to www.WebCopywritingUniversity.com/formula.htm. That webpage enables you to simply plug in the numbers, and the CGI script automatically calculates the total for you.

Once you've calculated your prospect's SQ, all you have to do is send the following prospecting e-mail. Note: This is the only piece of e-mail that I ever sent out to obtain web copywriting business. When you see how it rivets your prospect's attention and how helpful your constructive comments can be, you'll understand why it works so well.

SUBJECT: Your website's score . . .

Hi [Business Owner/Website Owner's Name],

My name is [*put your name here*]. I am an experienced web copywriter who specializes in converting web traffic into sales and converting your prospects into customers—and I can prove it at virtually no out-of-pocket cost to you.

I just came across your website at [*put prospect's URL here*]. I am impressed by your outstanding [*put name of prospect's product or service here*] and its potential for generating an incredible amount of sales.

Therefore, I took the liberty of running your website through the Selling Quotient Formula and found out that it scored [*put score here*]% out of a possible score of 100%.

This means that your website is getting only [*put percentage here*]% of the potential sales it could *easily* be making. When you apply a few web copywriting techniques that are scientifically proven to increase sales by 340% or more, your website could be maximizing its sales potential.

I realize that you may have put in a lot of time and money to create your website, and it is not my intention to point out its shortcomings. I simply want you to know that since I know what works and what doesn't work online, it's easy for you to change and improve your website so that it can sell more of your [*put name of product or service here*].

Just off the top of my head, here are 5 things that could be improved easily and immediately:

1. Your website doesn't have a benefit-laden headline that stops people dead in their tracks and compels them to read on. DID YOU KNOW that adding a headline (or changing one word or phrase in your website's headline can account for up to a 1,700% increase in sales—even if you didn't touch one word of the body copy?

2. No emotional/psychological triggers or involvement devices are employed to ensure maximum sales. DID YOU KNOW that applying just 1 or 2 of these triggers or devices can compel your prospect to buy willingly without any resistance?

3. You have no unique selling proposition. DID YOU KNOW that if you don't differentiate your product or service from those of your competitors, you have little or no chance of making a sale?

4. You have no highly visible mechanism for capturing web visitors' contact information. DID YOU KNOW that if you don't employ an irresistible opt-in offer to get your web visitors to give you their e-mail address, you're missing up to 90% of your potential sales?

5. You have no effective order form. DID YOU KNOW that the right wording on an order form can increase your sales by as much as 32%?

These are just 5 of the [*put number here*] items I've identified in your
website that need to be corrected right away if you expect your website
to sell effectively. I hope this brief evaluation is useful in helping you improve your website.

If you'd like a more in-depth evaluation with specific advice, or if you'd
like me to rewrite your website copy, I'd be more than happy to help you
get it to 100% Selling Quotient.

With all the time, expense, and energy that goes into creating your website, you can't afford *not* to have it be as persuasive as possible—and I
strongly believe I can give you valuable, response-enhancing recommendations.

Please reply to this e-mail if you'd like me to work with you to optimize
your website in order to sell your [*name of product or service here*] more
effectively.

All the best,
[*Your Name Here*]

WHAT TO CHARGE—AND HOW TO ENSURE THAT YOUR CLIENTS PAY YOU

When your prospect has expressed his or her willingness to hire you and has
agreed to your price, send an engagement letter that summarizes the scope of
the work. This letter details the copywriting tasks you're going to do, the price
for each of the tasks (including the total), the terms, and the anticipated date
of completion. You can find a sample of an engagement letter that you can use
as a model for writing yours here: http://www.webcopywritinguniversity.com/
EngagementLetter.htm.

Experienced direct-response copywriters who work on a freelance basis
charge between $125 and $235 per hour—or $3,000 to $12,000 to write a sales

letter or sales page. By contrast, the full-time yearly salaries of junior and senior copywriters in the Los Angeles area are as follows:

Junior copywriter—$37,420 to $61,607 (Median: $46,724/year, $22.46 per hour)

Senior copywriter—$59,599 to $96,280 (Median: $75,560/year, $36.32 per hour)

The median salaries for copywriters in smaller urban areas are approximately 11 to 12 percent less than those in major cities like Los Angeles.

Clearly, experienced direct-response copywriters who work on a freelance basis command much higher rates (about five or six times more) than salaried copywriters. You can use these rates as a springboard for establishing the rates you're going to charge for your copywriting services. You have the option to charge by the hour, on a project basis, or based on a percentage of the sales generated by your copy—or a combination of two or more of these.

If you're a new web copywriter who's looking to hone your skills while building your portfolio of business, it is advisable to charge low copywriting fees initially—between $2,000 and $3,000 for a sales page, which may be all that a small business owner can afford to pay. You could also offer to charge a small up-front fee, with a written agreement that if your copy generates a certain level of conversions or sales, the client will pay an additional flat fee of $2,000 or more.

Intellectual Property Licensing

There are also opportunities for you to write web copy on a performance-based compensation platform. That means you do not receive any compensation up front, but if the copy you write generates sales, you'll earn a substantial percentage of the sales generated by your copy. This type of arrangement is entered into by copywriters who feel confident that they can rewrite a prospective client's sales copy and reasonably expect their copy to make a significant difference in the client's sales and profits.

When you enter into this type of agreement, you'll be writing the copy *on spec* (or "on speculation") in the hope that your copy will prove to result in higher conversions, higher sales, and higher profits than the client's existing copy. In this scenario, since you're writing the copy at no cost to the client, the copy is deemed intellectual property that belongs to you. It is also your responsibility to prove, through market testing, that your copy converts or generates more sales than the client's existing copy.

I've entered into many of these types of performance-based intellectual property licensing agreements, and they've always proven to be profitable. Whenever I license to a client any copy I've written, I stipulate in the agreement a royalty of between 5 and 10 percent of gross revenues less marketing costs. Each one of this type of intellectual property licensing deal earns a six-figure royalty on an annual basis, so they represent an ongoing passive income stream for me. Many A-list copywriters prefer to enter into intellectual property licensing deals rather than projects that pay on a flat-fee or per-project basis.

A template for an intellectual property licensing agreement can be found at http://www.webcopywritinguniversity.com/agreement.htm.

Entering into a joint venture with a prospective copywriting client is another variation of the performance-based copywriting model. This usually happens when a client who has an outstanding product, but no budget to pay for copywriting fees, meets a copywriter who's willing to write the copy without getting paid up front. The copywriter earns nothing until the copy he or she writes generates revenues. In this type of arrangement, there's always a risk that the copywriter could spend a substantial amount of time writing the copy and the client never implements it. Therefore, a client must agree to implement the copy within a set period (usually 30 calendar days) and spend an agreed-upon amount of money to advertise the website in order to measure the copy's performance.

DIRECTORY OF RESOURCES

Books and Courses

Copywriting

Bly, Robert W. *The Copywriter's Handbook, Third Edition: A Step-by-Step Guide to Writing Copy That Sells.* New York: Holt Paperbacks, 2006.

Lewis, Herschell Gordon. *Direct Mail Copy That Sells.* Englewood Cliffs, NJ: Prentice Hall, 1984.

Nicholas, Ted. *How I Sold $400 Million Worth of Products: The Ultimate Swipe File.* Indian Rocks Beach, FL: Nicholas Direct, Inc., 2011.

Nicholas, Ted. *The Million Dollar Copywriting Bootcamp: A Home Study Course.* Indian Rocks Beach, FL: Nicholas Direct, Inc.

Sugarman, Joe. *Advertising Secrets of the Written Word: The Ultimate Resource on How to Write Powerful Advertising Copy from One of America's Top Copywriters and Mail Order Entrepreneurs.* Las Vegas, NV: DelStar, 1998.

Marketing, Advertising, Sales, and the Art of Persuasion

Caples, John. *Tested Advertising Methods.* Upper Saddle River, NJ: Prentice Hall, 1998.

Cialdini, Robert B. *Influence: The Psychology of Persuasion.* Revised ed. New York: Collins Business, 1998.

Girard, Joe. *How to Sell Anything to Anybody.* New York: Simon & Schuster, 1978.

Godin, Seth. *Permission Marketing: Turning Strangers into Friends and Friends into Customers.* New York: Simon & Schuster, 1999.

Hopkins, Claude C. *My Life in Advertising.* New York: Harper & Brothers, 1936.

Hopkins, Claude C. *Scientific Advertising.* Reprint. New York: Cosimo Classics, 2010.

Levinson, Jay Conrad. *Guerrilla Marketing: Easy and Inexpensive Strategies for Making Big Profits from Your Small Business.* 4th ed. Boston: Houghton Mifflin, 2007.

Levinson, Jay Conrad, Mitch Meyerson, and Mary Eule Scarborough. *Guerrilla Marketing on the Internet: The Definitive Guide from the Father of Guerrilla Marketing.* Irvine, CA: Entrepreneur Press, 2008.

Ogilvy, David. *Confessions of an Advertising Man.* New York: Atheneum, 1988.

Ogilvy, David. *Ogilvy on Advertising.* New York: Knopf, 1985.

Reeves, Rosser. *Reality in Advertising.* New York: Knopf, 1961.

Ries, Al, and Jack Trout. *Positioning: The Battle for Your Mind.* 3rd ed. New York: McGraw-Hill, 2000.

Schwartz, Eugene. *Breakthrough Advertising.* Des Moines, IA: Bottom Line Books, 2004.

Schwartz, Eugene. *The Brilliance Breakthrough: How to Talk and Write So That People Will Never Forget You.* Instant Learning, 1994.

Scott, David Meerman. *The New Rules of Marketing and PR: How to Use News Releases, Blogs, Podcasting, Viral Marketing and Online Media to Reach Buyers Directly.* Hoboken, NJ: Wiley, 2007.

Sugarman, Joe. *Triggers: 30 Sales Tools You Can Use to Control the Mind of Your Prospect to Motivate, Influence and Persuade.* Las Vegas, NV: DelStar, 1999.

Resources for Creating Online Marketing Videos

Stock photos: Dreamstime.com and iStockphoto.com

Stock video clips: iStockvideo.com and Revostock.com

Online voice talent companies: ProVoiceUSA.com and VoiceTalentNow.com

Music clips: MusicBakery.com, BeatSuite.com, and RoyaltyFreeMusic.com

One-stop shop for online video production: ViralVideoWizard.com
This service provides everything including writing the script, assembling all photos and video clips, producing the video, and uploading it to 35 video-sharing sites, 12 social bookmarking sites, 6 blogs, and podcast directories.

Video editor: Post job on Elance.com or type "video editor" in craigslist.com searchbox

Resources for Creating Infographics

World's largest community of infographics and data visualization: Visually
Blog showcasing a huge variety of the best-designed infographics: www.coolinfographics.com

Other Sites for Infographic Distribution
http://brandlessblog.com
http://dailyinfographic.com
http://iheartinfographics.tumblr.com
http://infographicjournal.com
http://infographiclist.com
http://www.infographicpost.com
http://infographicsbin.tumblr.com
http://infographicsonline.com
http://infographipedia.com
http://infographr.tumblr.com
http://submitinfographics.com
http://theinfographics.blogspot.co.uk
http://videoinfographic.com
http://visualoop.tumblr.com
http://www.amazinginfographics.com
http://www.bestinfographics.co.uk
http://www.cloudinfographics.com
http://www.dailystatistic.com
http://www.info-graphic.co.uk
http://www.infographicas.com
http://www.infographicheaven.com
http://www.infographiclove.com
http://www.infographicsarchive.com
http://www.infographicsinspiration.com
http://www.infographicsshowcase.com
http://www.loveinfographics.com
http://www.omginfographics.com
http://www.pureinfographics.com

Infographic Tools and Resources (Categorized)
www.tinyurl.com/InfographicTools

INDEX